CLASSICAL RHETORIC
AND CONTEMPORARY LAW

RHETORIC, LAW, AND THE HUMANITIES

CLASSICAL RHETORIC AND CONTEMPORARY LAW

A Critical Reader

EDITED BY FRANCIS J. MOOTZ III, KIRSTEN K. DAVIS, BRIAN N. LARSON, AND KRISTEN K. TISCIONE

THE UNIVERSITY OF ALABAMA PRESS
Tuscaloosa

The University of Alabama Press
Tuscaloosa, Alabama 35487-0380
uapress.ua.edu

Typeface: Garamond Pro

Cover design: Lori Lynch

Cataloging-in-Publication data is available from the Library of Congress.
ISBN: 978-0-8173-2189-5 (cloth)
ISBN: 978-0-8173-6139-6 (paper)
E-ISBN: 978-0-8173-9492-9

For Lety, my conversation partner.
—FJM III

For Chris, who always believes I can do it.
—KKD

For Bob, who continues to embrace the possible.
—BNL

For my rhetoric friends and Nick, my life support.
—KKT

Contents

Acknowledgments

I am deeply grateful to Brian Larson for organizing a classical rhetoric discussion group that provided the inspiration for this volume. Brian, Kirsten Davis, and Kris Tiscione have ensured that creating this book was not only intellectually stimulating but also fun. I benefited greatly from their knowledge and enthusiasm. I fear that we have not yet adequately responded to Vico's lament, but I want to acknowledge the hardy band of scholars who seek to promote the importance of rhetorical knowledge in contemporary society. Their work inspires me and gives me hope that we might continue to build a democratic society grounded in agreement rather than power.

—Francis J. Mootz III

When I began my rhetoric journey in 1988, I had no idea that a project like this awaited me. I thank my coeditors who enthusiastically included me in this work and have become my friends. I appreciate the willingness of the many experts who contributed their ideas to this volume; learning from them has been an honor. I thank Stetson University College of Law for supporting my work as a law and rhetoric scholar and teacher. And I am more grateful than words can express for my teacher, rhetoric scholar Dr. Daniel C. Brouwer, who passed away as we worked on this book. Dan cared deeply about our rhetorical sensibilities and commitments, and I hope he would be proud of my work here.

—Kirsten K. Davis

I feel warm affection for folks willing to step outside their comfort zones to learn and discuss difficult material; the members of the classical rhetoric and contemporary law reading group did that and became along the way the best teachers, classmates, and students I've ever had. It's hard to imagine working on a collaboration with better colleagues, and I thank Jay Mootz, Kirsten Davis, and Kristen Tiscione for this opportunity. Thanks, too, are due the Texas A&M

Arts and Humanities Fellowship, funding from which has made my participation in this project and its antecedents possible.

—Brian N. Larson

As a law practitioner, professor, and scholar, I find that to engage with the law without knowledge of rhetorical theory or an interest in the epistemic power of language is like a day without sunshine. My scholarly journey into the light began with an attempt to understand the legal profession's rhetorical roots, grasp the complex and uneasy relationship between law and rhetoric, and restore in some small part to legal education that which has been lost to contemporary advocacy. Both the insights and the challenges of this classical tradition are as relevant today as they were in ancient Greece and Rome. Thank you to my coeditors for their shared interest, friendship, and support.

—Kristen K. Tiscione

CLASSICAL RHETORIC
AND CONTEMPORARY LAW

Part I

INTRODUCTIONS

1

Contemporary Law through the Classical Lens

Kirsten K. Davis and Francis J. Mootz III

Earl Warren joined the Supreme Court after having served for fifteen years as attorney general and governor of California. He was attentive to his transition from long-time politician to serving as a judge. Upon arriving at the court, Warren asked Justice Black how he might best learn to write judicial opinions. Justice Black, famous for his simple and direct prose,[1] suggested that Warren read Aristotle's *Rhetoric*.[2] Warren took the advice, and the rest, as they say, is history.

This vignette symbolizes our book's thesis. Aristotle's *Rhetoric* epitomizes the ancient rhetoric of the West, often called "classical rhetoric," and the Warren Court vibrantly expresses contemporary law. That Warren would look to Aristotle for the means of effective persuasion provides the clearest example of the classical rhetorical tradition's salutary effects on contemporary legal practice and theory. The classical rhetorical tradition eschews logical formalism and syllogistic reasoning where, as in legal reasoning, there is no single right answer. Instead, it serves to guide lawyers and judges in situations where judgments must be grounded in practical wisdom addressing probabilities rather than in formal, deductive certainties. It should be no surprise that Aristotle's *Rhetoric* played a role in the Warren Court's dramatic remaking of contemporary constitutional law.

PURPOSE OF THE VOLUME

This book emerged from a reading and discussion group organized by coeditor Brian Larson for scholars interested in classical rhetoric and contemporary legal practice. For over a year, the group read classical rhetorical texts and discussed their relevance to the law. Based on these conversations, coeditor Jay Mootz proposed a critical reader that paired edited primary texts in the classical rhetorical tradition with contemporary legal texts. The four coeditors then developed the book's template and invited scholars of rhetoric and legal theory to write chapters.

The book serves several purposes. First, it is the only book of which we are aware that uses primary texts in both rhetoric and law to explore the relationship between these disciplines. This enables scholars and students in law and in rhetoric to easily explore legal rhetoric without first having to master the literature of the other field. Each chapter contains a "pairing" of a legal text and a rhetorical text to provide a uniquely interactive and sophisticated entrée into inter- and multidisciplinary investigation. Second, the book is accessible to advanced undergraduate and graduate students, providing a compact introduction to the fertile relationship between the traditions to a wide audience. Both audiences will benefit from the critical assessment section of each chapter, which explores enduring questions for scholars in a manner that students can approach in a seminar. Finally, the book uses discussion questions to facilitate the reader's interaction with the primary texts. Readers can ponder and discuss the issues raised by the pairings and tease out their own understandings.

DISRUPTING OUR UNDERSTANDING OF CONTEMPORARY LAW BY READING *THROUGH* CLASSICAL TEXTS

This volume is premised on the relevance of classical rhetorical texts to our understanding of contemporary law. This classical framework advances traditional notions of logic and practical reasoning, sometimes identified as "Western" ways of thinking, as the ground for argumentation. These ideas about rhetoric originate in Greek and Roman societies that promoted democratic citizen participation; but it is also true that these societies (like others of that time period) were culturally insular, slave-holding, demarcated by caste systems, and patriarchal. As Cheryl Glenn writes, "Aristotle's rhetor and audience were powerful, citizen-class, land-owning men who discussed and voted on issues in the agora, where they participated in the life *they* believed in. According to tradition, Athenian democratic life wasn't complicated by Others, by men of other nations and castes or by women."[3] Because these classical communities differ so significantly from our contemporary understandings of liberty, equality, and democracy, some contemporary thinkers argue that the intellectual achievements of these communities are suspect and express concerns about the appropriateness of classical Western rhetorical texts as a way of understanding rhetoric.[4]

Our view is that the Western rhetorical texts excerpted in this volume represent an important perspective on rhetoric, the bounds and substance of rhetorical theory, and the methods of rhetorical analysis. The perspectives provided to readers by these excerpts are important and useful because they can disrupt readers' assumptions and provoke critical questions about the contemporary legal texts with which they are paired. In other words, we learn something new about contemporary law by reading *through* the ancient texts.

The temporal distance between classical texts and our contemporary ones may work to disrupt our contemporary understandings, which we often think are superior to those of the past.[5] As the German philosopher Hans-Georg Gadamer emphasized, it is precisely the temporal distance of the classical texts from the present time, the very fact that they are embedded in a "foreign" context, that enables readers to read contemporary texts *through* the lens of the classical texts that form the often unacknowledged tradition within which we participate. Not all ancient texts are useful and relevant; indeed, it is only when texts prove their value by provoking productive questioning of our contemporary understandings that they become "classics."[6] In other words, the critical experience of using the texts of the ancient Western rhetorical tradition to disrupt readers' experiences of contemporary texts is what reveals their value.[7]

Jay Mootz's chapter in this volume, pairing an oration by Vico more than three hundred years old with a contemporary, run-of-the-mill case involving statutory interpretation, is an example of the disruption that classic rhetorical texts can pose for contemporary law. Vico does not express a hidden solution to the legal problem confronting Judge Gorsuch, nor does Vico provide us with a timeless method for analyzing law. Rather, for those of us confronted with a disappointing opinion, Vico's oration offers a frame within which to see how and why Judge Gorsuch fails to meet our expectations of judging well. Vico's lament about the failure to cultivate ingenuity in students at the turn of the eighteenth century resonates today in stark terms. Certainly there are many social, cultural, and political aspects of Vico's time that have no appeal for us today, but Vico's persistent critique of an overly intellectualized ("Cartesian") approach to wisdom illuminates the limits of Judge Gorsuch's reasoning.

Beth Britt's chapter is another example of how seeing *through* the classical texts disrupts how we might understand the meaning of contemporary law. Britt uses the ancient *Dissoi Logoi*, the claim that there are arguments on both sides of any nondeductive question, to consider the claims made in the context of a child custody case that involved allegations of domestic violence. She encourages readers to think about the arguments made in the opposing appellate briefs from a viewpoint that accepts the *Dissoi Logoi*, to think about what the *Dissoi Logoi* teaches us about framing modern legal arguments, and to consider how legal arguments that are built upon what the *Dissoi Logoi* teaches are always a form of partial knowledge.

This volume invites readers to critique contemporary legal texts *through* the lens of classical rhetorical texts, but readers of this book should also hold the classical texts accountable to their own critical reassessment. A tradition has authority, but it must continue to earn its authority through the constant appropriation by members of the community. For example, at some point, Aristotle's

Rhetoric may prove not to be a source of insight and understanding. Someday, it may fail to provoke us to ask productive questions about our contemporary practices. If so, the book will slowly fade into obscurity as something merely of antiquarian interest, if it is noted at all.[8] As this project demonstrates, though, we still have much to learn from classical rhetoric as we endeavor to understand and critique contemporary law.

ORGANIZATION AND THEMES OF THE VOLUME

Each chapter begins with a rhetoric text that introduces an ancient Western rhetorical theory or concept. This text is paired with an excerpt from a legal text that serves as the rhetorical artifact for critical analysis and exploration. The chapter provides a critical assessment along with discussion questions to explore the relationships between the rhetorical and legal texts along with other connections, criticisms, and meanings tied to the chapter's theme.

The order of the chapters is both conceptual and chronological. Larson and Tiscione's introduction to the ancient Western rhetorical tradition provides context for the rhetoric excerpts contained in the remainder of the chapters. This overview is organized chronologically to help readers develop a sense of the historical development of rhetoric. The chapter also provides an overview of how this tradition has connected and disconnected from law over time.

Part 2 provides the book's conceptual frame. In chapters 3 and 4, Mootz and Frank position the work of Giambattista Vico, a rhetorical theorist writing at the beginning of the eighteenth century CE, and Chaïm Perelman and Lucie Olbrects-Tyteca, scholars working in the mid-twentieth century CE, as "bookends" of an era during which classical rhetorical theory fell out of favor. Vico's unsuccessful effort to counter the hegemony of Enlightenment epistemology, which not only separated law and rhetoric as modes of thought but also assigned rhetoric to a subordinate role in the pursuit of knowledge and truth, describes the wisdom of the classical tradition that has been cast aside. Frank then shows how Perelman and Olbrects-Tyteca successfully resurrected classical rhetoric in the modern era, renewing the link between rhetoric and law.

Mootz pairs Vico's well-known oration, "On the Study Methods of Our Time," with an opinion by Supreme Court Justice Neil Gorsuch, written while Gorsuch served as a federal appellate judge, that focused on statutory interpretation. Mootz shows that in contrast to Vico's rhetorical approach to knowledge, then-Judge Gorsuch takes what one might argue is a reductive view of statutory meaning. Vico's and Gorsuch's approaches could not be more different; readers are challenged to consider the competing interpretive strategies and how modes of interpretation are (or should be) taught in law school.

In his chapter, Frank uses the rebirth of the rhetorical tradition in the last century to assess how judges make moral advances in the law. Frank pairs Perelman and Olbrechts-Tyteca's *The New Rhetoric* with the United States Supreme Court's opinion in *Lawrence v. Texas*. In *Lawrence*, the court held that a Texas statute criminalizing sexual intercourse between persons of the same sex was unconstitutional. Key to this decision was the majority's willingness to overturn a recent case that had held just the opposite. Frank invites readers to understand this change by considering five concepts from *The New Rhetoric* that are in tension with the Cartesian philosophy privileging formal reasoning and rationality. Frank reveals how Justice Kennedy used rhetorical reasoning to overturn established precedent and reconfigure the meaning of equality and liberty as constitutional concepts. It is this humanistic tradition of rhetoric, Frank suggests, and not Cartesian rationality, that allows law to respond to the needs of justice.

In part 3 of the book, ten chapters connect ancient Western rhetorical texts and contemporary legal ones to reveal the enduring relationship between Western rhetorical traditions and contemporary law. Covering a wide range of classical authors, modern legal artifacts, and important themes, the chapters chronologically sample rhetorical theorists and theory to inform modern legal texts, moving from the Sophists, through Aristotle and Plato and their Greek contemporaries, to the Roman rhetoricians Cicero and Quintilian, and finally, to the early medieval rhetorician St. Augustine.

Chapters 5 and 6 invite readers to think about the meaning of truth within the law and how lawyers make knowledge claims. In chapter 5 Michael Gagarin questions how circumstantial evidence works in modern law by comparing the "probability arguments" contained in the Greek Sophist Antiphon's *First Tetralogy*—a fictional murder trial written in the fifth century BCE—with arguments and jury instructions about circumstantial evidence from the O. J. Simpson case, a murder trial that took place in the United States in 1995. Gagarin's pairing attends to the rhetorical limitations and possibilities of circumstantial evidence and the relationship between probability arguments and the pursuit of legal "truth."

Elizabeth Britt also uses sophistic rhetorical theory to consider what constitutes "truth" (or the proof of it) in legal contexts in chapter 6. Britt pairs the sophistic *Dissoi Logoi* with a Massachusetts state court opinion resolving questions about the "truth" of domestic violence in the context of a child custody case. Britt's critical analysis examines the partiality of legal knowledge claims and looks for the values that underlie those competing claims in modern judicial opinions. Notably, she uses the concepts in *Dissoi Logoi* to evaluate the ways in which the court opinion accounts for the social problem of domestic violence.

Nick Sciullo and Craig Meyer's chapter 7 compares a classical speech and a contemporary legal opinion that are both rhetorical responses to questions of "outsiders." Sciullo and Meyer pair Isocrates's *Panegyricus*, a speech in which

Isocrates expresses his distrust of foreigners in Greek society, with the United States Supreme Court's majority opinion in *Trump v. Hawaii*, a case in which the Supreme Court upheld President Trump's restrictions on immigration targeted at citizens of countries with predominantly Muslim populations. By calling attention to the ways Isocrates devalues outsiders, Sciullo and Meyer encourage readers to examine critically the rhetorical moves by Chief Justice Roberts in *Trump*.

Returning to the theme of "legal truth," chapter 8 explores Plato's theories on rhetoric as applied in the well-known *Citizens United* case, which held that corporations have a First Amendment right to spend general funds to engage in political speech. Kristen Tiscione points readers to Plato's criticism of rhetoric as a false art of justice in the *Gorgias* and then asks readers to observe Justice Kennedy struggle with this ancient theme of "rhetoric v. reality" in a context where the court ultimately upholds the primacy of "a marketplace of ideas." Ultimately, Tiscione urges readers to think carefully about what "truth" means in the legal context, and whether truth and justice are the same thing.

Chapters 9, 10, and 11 connect Aristotle's rhetorical theory with contemporary legal texts. First, Gene Garver applies Aristotle's rhetorical theory to the landmark dissenting opinion of Oliver Wendell Holmes in *Abrams v. U.S.*, to show how Holmes, a century ago, established contemporary First Amendment doctrine *rhetorically* as well as legally. Garver encourages readers to find Aristotle's rhetorical strategies at work in Holmes's reasoning that locates "truth" in the marketplace of ideas, places power in public speakers, and arguably transforms the nature of judicial decision-making.

Katie Langford focuses chapter 10 on Aristotle's concept of topoi. Langford assesses *United States v. Lopez*, a case in which the United States Supreme Court struck down the federal Gun-Free School Zones Act as unconstitutional under the commerce clause. Langford invites readers to consider how topoi are in tension between the majority, concurring, and dissenting opinions in the *Lopez* case and to explore whether, and how, Aristotle's topoi operate in appellate legal arguments.

Vasileios Adamidis and Laura Webb also consider how Aristotle's topoi operate in legal arguments, but they look at arguments that rely on the theme of "tradition." Chapter 11 pairs Demosthenes's speech *On the Crown* with an amicus brief submitted to the United States Supreme Court in the *Obergefell* case. In *Obergefell*, the Supreme Court struck down as unconstitutional state limitations on marriage between partners of the same sex. Acting as a friend of the court, the Commonwealth of Virginia relied on the theme of tradition to help convince the court that marriage equality was consistent with America's traditions. Adamidis and Webb's analysis helps readers consider how the themes of tradition in *On the Crown* and in the Virginia amicus brief relate to one another, even though two millennia separate the arguments.

The next two chapters focus on Roman rhetorical theory. In chapter 12, Brian Larson and Sue Provenzano pair Cicero's discussion of *stases* in *On Invention* with *Chickasaw Nation v. United States*, an opinion in which the Supreme Court interpreted the meaning of the Indian Gaming Regulatory Act. In their critical analysis of the case, Larson and Provenzano show how Cicero's stases of "ambiguity" and "letter and intent" appear in the several opinions.

In chapter 13 Kirsten Davis turns to the question of how legal texts rhetorically constitute and problematize the identity of lawyers. Davis pairs Quintilian's description in the *Institutes of Oratory* of the characteristics of the "ideal orator," with the Supreme Court case of *Gentile v. Nevada*, in which the court wrestled with the question of what it means for a lawyer to ethically advocate "in public" on behalf of a client. Davis invites readers to consider how Justices Kennedy and Rehnquist constitute the identity of the "ideal lawyer, speaking in public." Davis challenges us to think carefully about the identity, purpose, and performances of "ideal" lawyers.

Finally, in chapter 14, Mark Hannah focuses on the last "classical" rhetorical theorist, St. Augustine, who was writing just after the fall of the Roman Empire and at the time the Christian Church was becoming the source of both religious doctrine and the law. Hannah pairs an excerpt from Augustine's *The City of God* with the transcript of the oral argument in the *Masterpiece Cakeshop* case, where the Supreme Court held that the Colorado Civil Rights Commission violated the religious freedom of a wedding cake baker because the commission was hostile towards the baker's religious beliefs. Hannah shows how the oral argument colloquy in *Masterpiece Cakeshop* reveals the continuing tensions between law and religion and how both lawyers and judges engage in rhetorical practices to help resolve these tensions.

Readers may work their way through the text chronologically, or they may choose to read the chapters thematically. For example, readers might explore the chapters through the following thematic units: legal "truth" and knowledge (chapters 5, 6, and 8); "legal methods" (chapters, 5, 6, and 12); "rhetorical strategies in appellate argument and judicial decision-making" (chapters 9, 10, 11, and 12); "legal rhetorics" (chapters 7, 9, 11 and 13); or culturally important Supreme Court cases on immigration, free speech, gun control, campaign finance, marriage equality, and freedom of religion (chapters 7 through 11, 13, and 14).

CONCLUSION

To our knowledge, this is the first book to explicitly apply classical rhetorical theory to law by pairing classical rhetorical artifacts with contemporary legal texts and offer readers a framework for discussion of that pairing. The volume aspires to empower all readers, whether in graduate school or law school, to interrogate and reimagine law through the lens of rhetorical theory. Moreover, it supports law faculty in reintroducing rhetoric into legal education as a counter to the Langdellian pedagogical method of Socratic questioning, and it offers classical rhetorical theory as a tool for creative and critical legal thinkers. This volume continues the tradition of using questions to facilitate learning but poses guided discussion questions rather than Socratic ones to explore the depths of connection between law and rhetoric. This technique offers a unique opportunity for students to engage in critical reflection on how the argumentative moves of contemporary law continue to utilize the classical rhetorical teachings.

2

Classical Rhetoric

Then and Now

Brian N. Larson and Kristen K. Tiscione

INTRODUCTION

Histories of Western rhetoric tend to begin in ancient Greece. In this context, "rhetoric" refers to the theory and practice of persuasion in the public sphere: law courts, legislative assemblies, ceremonial events, and other political venues.[1] Rhetoric was taught to young men in the ancient world to prepare them for civic life, which included participating in the resolution of legal disputes and public debate, acting as jurors, and engaging in military service. The majority of the rhetorical theorists represented in this volume date back to this so-called classical period in Greco-Roman culture, which for our purposes spans from the fifth century BCE until after the end of the Roman Empire around one thousand years later. Although these ancient theorists did not claim to invent persuasion itself, they were some of the first in the Western world to develop a rigorous theory to inform the practice of persuasion and educational institutions devoted to teaching it primarily for use in these contexts.

Rhetoric's influence on education—from grammar to graduate school—and legal training in particular evolved but continued uninterrupted in Europe, then in Britain and the United States, from the classical period until the late nineteenth century. By then, US law schools had made an abrupt curricular shift from studying law as an art form to approaching law as a science, the subject of which was judicial decisions. In the twentieth century, the study of rhetoric outside law schools was divided among English, communication, and speech departments. As a result, US law students today have little familiarity with the rhetorical tradition that developed in part to train students for the practice of law.

The goal of this chapter is not to provide a comprehensive history of rhetoric;

rather, it is to introduce the historical context and significance of the theorists featured in the volume. We focus our attention on the practice of "forensic" or "judicial" rhetoric—advocacy in legal disputes—because that is the focus of the contemporary texts that the authors in this volume excerpt. We also end our history at the beginning of the twentieth century, when a rupture between training in rhetoric and law occurred in the United States that has only gradually begun to heal.

RHETORIC AND THE GREEK SOPHISTS (FIFTH CENTURY BCE)

Oratory in Greece predates rhetoric. It appears in Homer's epic poems, *The Iliad* and *The Odyssey* (eighth century BCE). Their key characters engage in all forms of discourse, including monologue, dialogue, questions and answers (later known as dialectic), and even legal argument.[2] The collective need to study, develop, and teach rhetorical methods for the resolution of disputes by nonviolent means, however, did not appear to arise until some three hundred years later.

As democracy grew in Greece, so did the demand for training in rhetoric, particularly in the law courts. Several philosopher-teachers, collectively known as *Sophists* (see chapters 5 through 7), traveled among the city-states teaching rhetoric and other subjects to sons of wealthy families and others who could afford them. The Sophists' teaching methods are not fully known, but they likely required students to observe and read their speeches and then memorize and deliver them. Famous Sophists in Athens included Antiphon, Protagoras, Gorgias, Prodicus, Hippias, and Isocrates, though not all of them would have accepted the "Sophist" label, in part because Sophists were accused of manipulating truth. Represented in this volume are Antiphon (480–11 BCE) (see chapter 5), a logographer who wrote speeches for others to deliver in court, and the unknown author of *Dissoi Logoi* (Double Arguments) (see chapter 6), which illustrates arguments on the same issue from opposing points of view. Gorgias of Leontini (ca. 483–376 BCE) is likely the most famous of the early Sophists, known for his oratorical skill as well as his highly artificial, yet poetic prose.

Also represented here is Isocrates (436–338 BCE) (see chapter 7), a student of Gorgias and perhaps Socrates. The most influential teacher of oratory for almost fifty years, Isocrates began as a logographer and later wrote political speeches. In 393 BCE he founded the first permanent institution of higher learning in Athens, predating Plato's Academy by almost six years. His goal was to train young men of moral character to be the future leaders of Greek society.

Although "sophist" may translate roughly into "expert" or "teacher," the figures we know as Sophists were criticized harshly by some philosophers of their day. The Sophists challenged basic beliefs and assumptions of Greek society, including the existence of the gods, and suggested that "[humans, not divine beings] are the measure of all things."[3] Teaching students how to argue both sides of an issue, to use a populist approach, and to argue from probabilities instead of truth meant that, from the point of view of the Sophists, truth and justice do not preexist but are determined on a case-by-case basis. Plato (428–348 BCE) (see chapter 8) highlights his discomfort with these practices in *Gorgias*, where Socrates disagrees with Gorgias's definition of rhetoric as an art form, claiming instead that it is a form of cleverness—a trick or ruse. Nevertheless, we know the Sophists mostly through the writings of their opponents, and even the historical Socrates was caricatured as a Sophist in Greek drama of his time.[4]

Before proceeding, we note that the class of persons allowed to speak on matters of public concern in ancient Athens and Rome was, as far as we know, quite narrow. Only male citizens of Athens could bring legal claims in its courts and speak before its legislative assembly. Excluded were women, noncitizens, enslaved persons, and metics—resident aliens present in Athens to work.[5] Twentieth- and twenty-first-century scholars have thus questioned the continued relevance of classical rhetoric in Western culture, explored the extent to which it silenced and continues to silence female and minority voices (both racial and cultural), and called for a more inclusive public discourse (see chapter 1).

In antiquity, women orators existed primarily as characters in male-authored literary works. Yet scholars have begun to explore the ways that women might in fact have contributed to rhetoric and oratory. Of importance here are two women mentioned by Plato: Aspasia and Diotima of Mantinea. Aspasia was born in the Greek city of Miletus (now Turkey) and gained favor with the Athenian general and statesman Pericles (fifth century BCE). In his dialogue *Menexenus*, Plato's Socrates hints that Aspasia wrote Pericles's famous funeral oration.[6] The Roman orator and rhetorician Cicero depicts Aspasia teaching reasoning by induction to Xenophon—the Athenian general, author, and student of Socrates—and his wife.[7] Diotima of Mantinea is a central figure in Plato's *Symposium* who challenges Socrates's conception of love.[8] A small number of women were orators in Rome, notably Hortensia, the daughter of Hortensius (114–50 BCE), a famous orator and rival of Cicero. In 42 BCE Hortensia successfully argued before the ruling triumvirate (Caesar Octavian, who became the first emperor of Rome; Marcus Lepidus; and Marc Antony) to repeal a tax levied on wealthy women.[9]

ATHENS (FOURTH CENTURY BCE)

Athenian Judicial Rhetoric

In the first two-thirds of the fourth century BCE, trials were conducted before juries of male Athenian citizens at least thirty years old. At the beginning of each year, six thousand citizens were selected by lot to serve as a pool of jurors.[10] Each day the Athenian court sat, a subset of the six thousand would show up, and some were selected to serve that day. Jurors were paid a small fee, perhaps one-fifth to one-third what a worker might receive for a day's labor. Jury sizes ranged from 201 for smaller, private disputes to as many as 2,500 for public actions.

After brief preliminary proceedings, cases went directly to trial, which consisted of reading testimony, hearing the parties' speeches, and concluding with a vote by secret ballot.[11] The trial day could last as long as nine and a half hours, and a magistrate, also selected by lot, presided over it. None of the participants was a professional: the jurors and magistrates were citizens, there was no public prosecutor, and the litigant was required to speak for himself, though he could pay a logographer to write his speeches.

Trials often involved significant political issues, beyond private disputes, but very few of these trial speeches still exist. Those considered to have argued eloquently on their own behalf include Demosthenes (384–22 BCE) (see chapter 11) and Aeschines (390–22 BCE). Among the logographers, the most famous were probably Isocrates (see chapter 7) and Lysias (458–380 BCE).

Aristotle

In this context, Aristotle (384–22 BCE) (see chapters 9 and 10), who was a student of Plato, disagreed with Plato about the value of rhetoric, which Aristotle defined as the counterpart of dialectic. He was the first Westerner to divide subjects of learning into separate disciplines and define them. He was probably the first in the world to set out a theoretical system of logic[12] and rhetoric, which he conceived of as useful to all disciplines.

In his works on logic (*Categories, On Interpretation, Prior and Posterior Analytics*), Aristotle described a system of reasoning about knowable and known truths and did not speak of rhetoric. But in *Topics* (treating dialectic) and *Rhetoric*, Aristotle shed the certainty associated with deductive reasoning and echoed the Sophists' embrace of plausible and probable truth. Aristotle explained that certainty of knowledge is not possible in matters of the public good—if such matters were certain, there would be no point in debating them—yet rhetoric can lead us to the best course of action.

Aristotle defined rhetoric as the "ability in each [particular] case, to see the available means of persuasion. This is the function of no other art."[13] Aristotle divided rhetoric into three categories. Deliberative (political) speech concerns the good of the people and future conduct. Forensic (judicial) speech concerns justice and the nature of past conduct. Finally, epideictic (ceremonial) speech concerns cultural values and how to instill or preserve them in the present. Each category signaled a difference in the purpose of the rhetoric, the nature of the audience, and the rhetor's approach. Aristotle also defined the three artistic appeals of the rhetor:

logos (argument or reason), pathos (emotion), and ethos (the speaker's credibility, as constructed within the speech).[14] "Inartistic" appeals consisted of extrinsic or preexisting evidence, such as eyewitness testimony, oaths, and documents.

Aristotle envisioned the rhetor's process (later known as the canons) as the same regardless of the category of speech: invention, arrangement, style, memory, and delivery. Invention is the "discovery" of arguments, the act of consulting the general and special topics for available lines of argument. General topics are those common to all argument, such as matters of degree and the possible versus the impossible. Special topics are those specific to a particular subject; the special topics of judicial speech involve motive, states of mind, and wrongdoing. Arrangement is the ordering of arguments. Aristotle articulated a pattern for the arrangement of judicial speech common in his day: an introduction, statement of the facts, argument, and conclusion.[15] Style refers to the language used; Aristotle said it should be clear and appropriate to the purpose and audience of the speech.[16] He did not explore memory or delivery in detail, stating that delivery in rhetoric had yet to be developed but was akin to acting. He may have treated these canons more fully in a rhetoric handbook, available to later authors like Cicero, but lost to us.

THE HELLENISTIC PERIOD (CA. 323–27 BCE)

With the death of Alexander in 323 BCE and Aristotle in 322 BCE, the classical period ended in Greece, but Greek culture expanded throughout Greek city-states in Asia Minor and North Africa. Scholars continued to study rhetoric, with more interest in style, including the use of figures and tropes and the canons of memory and delivery. Aristotle's pupil Theophrastos wrote treatises—lost to us—on style, delivery, and other subjects.

Another important treatise on style, the first known to address the rhetoric of letter writing, survived and is attributed to Demetrios, an Athenian from the late fourth or early third century BCE, though the attribution is disputed, and the text is probably later. Hermagoras (second century BCE) wrote a treatise on rhetoric—also lost to us—that dealt primarily with invention and developed in detail the theory of *status* or *staseis*, the nature of the issues in a legal dispute. (See chapter 12.) Greek philosophers also wrote about rhetoric, including the Stoics Kleanthos and Khrysippos (fourth to early third centuries BCE), who advocated for a concise and pointed style, and the Epicurean Philodemos (first century BCE), who claimed that true men of politics did not need rhetoric.

THE ROMAN REPUBLIC (CA. 509–27 BCE)

The Roman Republic (established in the late sixth century BCE) was part oligarchy and part democracy, consisting of elected officials, an advisory senate, and citizen assemblies. The Senate consisted of men from noble and wealthy families.

They met in closed session and debated matters of foreign policy, religion, and finance. The citizen assemblies consisted of private citizens, responsible for electing magistrates and passing laws. Knowledge of the art of public speaking—*ars dicendi* in Latin—was considered necessary to speak effectively in each venue. The phrase comes from the Latin word *dicere*, to speak, which suggested speech with the authority to establish or proclaim, and authority was derived more from one's public reputation than from the development of one's ethos within a given speech.[17] By the second century BCE, young Roman men were studying rhetoric in Greece, and Greek teachers had come to Rome to teach rhetoric. As Rome conquered the entire Mediterranean region, it adapted Greek rhetoric to Roman contexts.

Cicero

Cicero (106–43 BCE) (see chapter 12) is considered the greatest Roman orator and rhetorician of the republic. He was a successful lawyer and politician and dominated rhetoric during his lifetime. Roughly sixty of his courtroom and political speeches survive today. He began his career in law, gaining notoriety through trying landmark cases. As late as the nineteenth century, American lawyers and legislators were still overtly emulating his style.

Cicero started a handbook on rhetoric, *De Inventione* (ca. 87 BCE), when he was still a teenager. He intended to write about all five canons but completed only the canon on invention, spending considerable time on the *staseis* handed down from Hermagoras.[18] At the outset, Cicero defended rhetoric against Plato's criticisms, arguing that "wisdom without eloquence does too little for the good of states, but . . . eloquence without wisdom is generally highly disadvantageous and is never helpful."[19] Contemporaneous with Cicero's *De Inventione* is an anonymous work, the *Rhetorica ad Herennium*, which delivered a more complete treatment of the canons, covering not just invention but also arrangement (to a lesser extent), style, memory, and delivery.[20] For hundreds of years, this work was attributed to Cicero, probably because he shared many of the views of its author(s).

Roman Judicial Rhetoric

Roman judicial rhetoric evolved over time with the Roman legal system.[21] Any citizen could bring a charge against another citizen in a court of law through a *patronus*, such as Cicero, acting as his advocate. In the late second century BCE, written pleadings (claims) were introduced, and the parties agreed to a "formula," a document setting forth the legal issues, any defenses, potential remedies, and their choice of judge. In imperial Rome the *cognitio* system replaced this formulary system. Instead of lay judges, magistrates presided over trials, and they had more discretion in rendering decisions. Under previous approaches, successful claimants had to enforce their own verdicts, but under *cognitio*, the court could enforce them.

Different courts heard civil and criminal claims, and there were courts both in equity and at law. Criminal cases were tried before a magistrate and a jury, selected by lot. Trials consisted primarily of witness testimony, courtroom speeches, and voting by the jury. The courts held session all over Rome, particularly in the Forum and nearby meeting halls. Trials were open to the public and created quite a spectacle, due in part to the nature of the proceedings and the skilled oratory of the patrons.

IMPERIAL ROME (CA. 27 BCE–410 CE)

After the rise of imperial rule in Rome, deliberative rhetoric in the Senate fell to the wayside, and the courts became the main arena for rhetoric. Although the need to train citizen orators decreased dramatically, rhetoric remained an integral part of Roman education. Students of rhetoric began with grammar at the age of six or seven and ended their studies ten to twelve years later. Throughout their training, they performed exercises called *progymnasmata* in Greek, and *declamatio*, *suasoria*, and *controversia* in Latin.

Rhetorical education in Rome reached a high point with the work of Quintilian (ca. 35–96 CE) (see chapter 13). He founded the first public school in Rome. At the age of fifty, he wrote *Institutio Oratoria*, a twelve-volume work on the study of rhetoric throughout one's life. Quintilian wrote more than any other Roman about courtroom technique. In book 12, he expanded on Cato the Elder's concept of the perfect orator as a "good man skilled in speaking."[22] Cato the Elder (239–149 BCE) was a Roman soldier, senator, and historian. According to Quintilian, only a good man—free from vice, a lover of wisdom, a sincere believer in his cause, and a servant of the people—could appeal to ethos. The fact that an orator had to be able to argue both sides of the same question did not detract from his goodness.

Beginning in the first century CE, a group of orators traveled extensively throughout Greece and Rome giving speeches designed to entertain audiences and demonstrate their rhetorical prowess. This movement, known as the Second Sophistic (ca. 50–400 CE), did not emphasize the substance of speeches (which could be dangerous, given imperial whims) and instead focused on style and delivery. Also common at this time and later was the practice of *panegyric*, or speeches of praise, often directed at the emperor.[23]

FROM EARLY CHRISTIANITY THROUGH THE MIDDLE AGES (CA. 150–400 CE)

Despite the empire's effort to suppress it, Christianity grew steadily. In 313 CE Emperor Constantine issued the Edict of Milan, proclaiming a tolerance for Christianity. As Christians sought to defend and spread their faith, a Christian rhetoric emerged. The early Christians were opposed to classical rhetoric because of its pagan roots, but at least eight of the Latin Fathers of the Church had been teachers of rhetoric—including Tertullian, Cyprian, Arnobius, Lactantius, and Augustine—or had trained in it, including Ambrose, Hilary, and Jerome. Each wrestled with using rhetorical principles in his writing. Augustine of Hippo (354–430 CE) (see chapter 14), who converted to Christianity in 386, came to believe that rhetoric could be used to persuade people to lead holy lives. Like Plato, Augustine sought truth, but he did not believe truth could be discovered through dialectic: truth resided in the Bible. In 396 Augustine began a four-volume treatise on preaching, *De Doctrina Christiana*, which was heavily influenced by Cicero. Augustine argued that rhetoric was acceptable in preaching because it was "not produced by human labour, but poured from the divine mind with both wisdom and eloquence."[24]

In 410 the Visigoths (Germanic tribes) attacked Rome, and various northern cultures continued to invade Italy for the next forty-five years. Although a working knowledge of Greek was lost in western Europe, much of Roman and Greek culture survived in the eastern Empire until 1453, when the Turkish Ottomans conquered Constantinople (Eastern Christianity's capital in what is now Turkey). Until that time, rhetoric continued to be useful in government and church-related matters. Ceremonial oratory was the predominant form of rhetoric, used to strengthen loyalty to the government and the Christian Church.

In the Middle Ages (roughly the sixth through the fifteenth centuries CE), rhetoric in Europe adapted to its surroundings. There was a focus on religious matters and Christianity, but the tools of rhetoric were also turned to other political, business, and personal problems. Three distinctly medieval genres developed during the eleventh and twelfth centuries: the *ars dictaminis*, *ars poetriae*, and *ars praedicandi*. The first of these, the *ars dictaminis* or art of letter writing, deserves some attention here because of its role in legal matters. The other two, relating to poetry and preaching, we will leave to the side.

The center of development of the *ars dictaminis* was northern Italy, and it arose there at the same time as early universities, particularly that in Bologna. The art of letter writing included all types of letters, but importantly, many legal documents of the time were in the form of letters, including charters from rulers granting legal rights, etc.; thus, the art encompassed everything from love letters to royal grants. The five parts of a letter, which became canonical during the thirteenth through fifteenth centuries, were closely modeled on Cicero's six-part oration. Aristotle's works, in contrast, even the *Rhetoric*, were attended to more in the fields of dialectic and moral philosophy.[25] A development related to the *ars dictaminis* was the *ars notaria*, the methods and forms for legal documents such as contracts. The latter, too, found its origins in the commercial and legal centers of northern Italy and in teaching at the University of Bologna.

Through much of the Middle Ages, rhetoric was not a prominent subject in the universities, and the works of the Greek theorists mentioned above played little role in the teaching of rhetoric.[26] Instead, Cicero and the *Rhetorica ad Herennium* were at the center of rhetorical education and commentary. Aristotle's works, meanwhile, particularly his *Topics* and *Sophistical Refutations*, were at the forefront in teaching the *disputatio* or method of scholarly debate.

THE RENAISSANCE (REBIRTH) OF RHETORIC (CA. 1400–1600 CE)

In the early fifteenth century, an explosion of creativity in the arts and sciences occurred in Europe. The Renaissance signaled a return to the subjects of antiquity. Both Greek and Latin rhetorical texts, particularly those of Aristotle, Cicero, and Quintilian, were rediscovered, as well as Greek oratory itself, including speeches of the Attic orators, such as Isocrates and Demosthenes. The invention of the printing press in 1436 made it possible to reproduce and distribute all these works throughout Europe.

The study and practice of rhetoric was again valued. This renewed interest was due, in large part, to teachers and scholars of the humanities—grammar, rhetoric, history, poetry, and philosophy, to name a few. The humanists, including Lorenzo Valla, Desederius Erasmus, and Thomas Wilson, translated classical texts into their own languages, commented on rhetorical theories, and taught rhetoric. Wilson's *Arte of Rhetorique* (1553), for example, was the first English treatise of classical rhetoric. Drawing heavily on Cicero, Quintilian, and the *Ad Herennium*, Wilson sought also to impart Christian values, incorporating examples from Greek literature as well as the Bible.

Rhetoric's revival met with resistance from Peter Ramus (1515–72 CE), a French humanist and logician, who taught philosophy and rhetoric. Ramus was not interested in revitalizing secular rhetoric for civic use. He was interested in teaching students to write in a plain and direct manner, rejecting Cicero's ornate style. Troubled by the doctrinal overlap between philosophy and rhetoric, Ramus argued that invention and arrangement belong to philosophy (the acquisition of knowledge), whereas style and delivery belong to rhetoric (the expression of knowledge). Ramus's views strongly influenced curricular reforms in the Western world, including what would become the American colonies.

THE AGE OF SCIENCE AND THE DAWN OF RATIONALISM (CA. 1600–1700 CE)

Inspired by the scientific advances of their day, philosophers began to explore epistemology, the process of acquiring knowledge, attempting to distinguish the certain from the probable. Potential sources of knowledge included the teachings of the Christian Church, deduction, reason, and sensory perceptions of the world. For the most part, the early empiricists, such as Francis Bacon (1561–1626 CE), who was also attorney general and chancellor under James I, rejected deduction (a part of Aristotelian logic) as a method for discovering knowledge, arguing that deduction could demonstrate only the relationship between things already known. Bacon ultimately concluded that knowledge is acquired by induction, a systematic method of careful observation that leads from particular sensory observations to general conclusions.

The rationalists, such as Rene Descartes (1596–1650 CE), a French philosopher and mathematician, stood in sharp contrast to the empiricists. Like Bacon, Descartes rejected deduction as the means of acquiring knowledge but concluded that a process grounded in reason led to certain knowledge. The growing interest in empirical science and formal logic caused critics to question rhetoric's intellectual validity. Philosophers such as Thomas Hobbes (1588–1679 CE) and John Locke (1632–1704 CE) criticized rhetoric for many of the same reasons Plato did. For example, in his *Essay Concerning Human Understanding* (1690), Locke argued that rhetoric is a "powerful instrument of error and deceit."[27] Like Bacon, Locke believed the mind has two major faculties: the understanding and the will. He defined understanding as the result of sensory perceptions that lead to ideas that the mind sorts by association. He thus rejected deduction as a source of knowledge. Because understanding alone is not sufficient to persuade, he believed emotion was necessary to motivate the will.

Giambattista Vico (see chapter 3), an Italian rhetoric professor at the University of Naples, disagreed with these dismissals of rhetoric. In *On the Study Methods of Our Time*, Vico defended rhetoric as a method for resolving questions of uncertainty. Echoing the Sophist Protagoras, he argued that the idea of reducing knowledge to a mathematical certainty is a fiction. Vico argued that logic should be taught after rhetoric (a reversal of the traditional order) so as not to stifle students' imagination, and that students should be exposed to all the arts and sciences. Vico later argued that rhetoric is the key to the study and understanding of past cultures, including their ideas, customs, and modes of communication.

NEOCLASSICISM AND THE AGE OF ENLIGHTENMENT (CA. 1700–1800 CE)

By the early eighteenth century, interest in classical rhetoric had taken many forms in the United Kingdom, Europe, and the United States. Particular areas of interest included neoclassicism, the belles lettres movement, and further developments in the psychological and epistemological school.[28] In England and

Ireland, neoclassicists such as Jonathan Swift, Alexander Pope, John Lawson, and John Ward worried that the fascination with science would negatively affect literary principles grounded in the classics. In the mid-1800s, both Lawson and Ward published lectures on oratory based on classical rhetoric.

The belles lettres movement combined classical rhetoric with an interest in clarity, taste, and sublimity. Influenced by Longinus's *On the Sublime* (first century CE), scholars like Joseph Addison, John Baillie, Edmund Burke, Charles Rollin, and Adam Smith analyzed whether good taste is innate or learned and what makes a work of art beautiful or sublime.[29] The belletristic movement expanded the focus of rhetoric to include all forms of literature (e.g., poetry, drama, oratory, history, and philosophy) and literary criticism. In *The Method of Teaching and Studying the Belle Lettres*, for example, Rollin analyzed eloquence in the courtroom as well as in Christian oratory. The most influential of the belletristic scholars was Hugh Blair (1718–1800), a Scottish minister and professor of rhetoric at the University of Edinburgh. His *Lectures on Rhetoric and Belles Lettres* (1783), published in sixty-two complete editions, was popular in England, Europe, and the United States well into the nineteenth century. Blair modified the three forms of classical speech by combining deliberative and epideictic speech (as speech of the "public assembly") and adding "pulpit oratory."

During this period, scholars continued to explore the nature and origin of knowledge, which they believed formed the basis for rhetorical invention. Like Locke, David Hume (1711–76 CE), a leader in what is known as the Scottish Enlightenment, believed that knowledge is acquired through experience and observation, but Hume doubted the reliability of human perception, particularly with regard to religion. These doubts translated into a direct attack on the reliability of inductive reasoning in *An Enquiry on Human Understanding*.

Influenced by Bacon, Locke, and Hume, George Campbell (1719–96 CE), another Scot, used his observations of human nature to study argument, poetry, and preaching. In 1776 he published *The Philosophy of Rhetoric*, which combined theories of classical and eighteenth-century philosophers, rhetoricians, and scientists. For Campbell, logical appeals were based on what he called moral evidence—experience, analogy, testimony, and probabilities. He criticized the "chicanery" of contemporary legal discourse and advised speakers to use clear and lively language that was reputable, national, and of present use.

Like Campbell, Richard Whately (1787–1863 CE) was an ordained minister and interested in rhetoric's ability to defend Christianity. In *Elements of Rhetoric* (1828), Whately argued that rhetoric involves the invention of arguments. Whereas philosophers and scientists start with premises (i.e., observations) from which to infer knowledge, rhetoricians search for reasons or premises to prove a preexisting conclusion, such as a client's innocence. Whately is best known for his work on the nature and reliability of testimony, presumptions, and burdens of proof. In contrast to the weight or preponderance of evidence, a presumption is the existence of fact unless and until it is disproved. The burden of proof thus rests on the party seeking to disprove it. As an example, an accused person is presumed innocent at trial, and the prosecution has the burden of proving guilt. Once a presumption is refuted, the burden of proof shifts back to the party whose position the presumption initially favored. These concepts hold true today in the law.

DECLINE OF RHETORICAL STUDY AND RISE OF THE MODERN AMERICAN LAW SCHOOL (CA. 1800s CE)

Beginning in the eighteenth century, rhetorical theory and instruction in the United States were heavily influenced by the British and European Enlightenment. Until roughly the Civil War, rhetoric was taught chiefly at small colleges, where young men learned Greek and Latin by translating classical works and practiced public speaking. This classical approach to undergraduate education helped prepare them for careers in public service, law, and the ministry. In 1806 John Quincy Adams, the sixth president of the United States, was appointed the first Boylston Professor of Rhetoric at Harvard University. In that role, Adams delivered thirty-six lectures on rhetoric (published in 1810), convinced that the young republic depended in part on emulating ancient oratory, particularly that of Cicero.

At roughly the same time as the Continental Congress's adoption of the Declaration of Independence, law schools were forming in the United States. In 1775 Tapping Reeve, a practicing lawyer in Litchfield, Connecticut, opened the Litchfield Law School. William and Mary College in Virginia hired its first law professor soon thereafter. These early schools took diverse approaches to teaching law. For example while Litchfield focused on teaching legal principles and their application to any situation, William and Mary offered a broader range of studies in law, politics, history, and science. In 1817 Harvard formally adopted a professional model for legal education and offered the first graduate degree for the practice of law.

After the Civil War, a surge of interest in science shifted the approach in higher education, resulting in the creation of separate departments, majors in specific subject matters, and electives. The perceived value of rhetoric as an area of study or training declined. By the early 1870s legal educators became convinced that law should be taught more as a science than an art. Charles Eliot, then president of Harvard University, and Christopher Langdell, then dean of Harvard Law School, adopted the case method of teaching law. Langdell believed an inductive method could lead to the discovery of truth. The object of this method was to read selected judicial opinions on a given legal topic to discover its true principles. In conjunction with the so-called Socratic method, law professors sought to evince these principles in class discussion and, in turn, to develop students' analytical skills. Practitioner teachers were replaced with full-time faculty scholars and legal treatises with judicial opinions.

By the mid-1890s several law schools, including Columbia, Northwestern, Cornell, and Stanford, had been established and switched to the case method. The case method turned out to be better, however, for teaching students to think like lawyers than for discovering universal principles of law, in part because it ignored statutes and regulations. Moreover, it foreclosed a broader legal education in government, politics, ethics, or the social sciences and failed to account for a judge's persuasive role in drafting opinions. Still, training in rhetorical theory overlapped with the legal theory that typified legal education at least until the end of the nineteenth century. For example, William C. Robinson, a trained minister and practicing lawyer in New Haven, Connecticut, published *Forensic Oratory: A Manual for Advocates* (1893), which examined oratory in general, dividing it into invention, expression, arrangement, and delivery, and courtroom oratory in particular. In 1869 he joined the Yale law faculty. Robinson relied heavily on Cicero and Quintilian, exploring the nature of legal issues and examining in detail the qualification, preparation, and examination of witnesses.

By then, the shift away from rhetoric in legal education was irreversible: the editors of the *Law Student's Helper*, a periodical that began in 1893 targeted at those seeking to enter and excel in the legal profession, responded to a reader's question, observing, "We do not know of any school of oratory that teaches law, or any school of law that teaches oratory."[30] This shift away from understanding the theory of rhetoric (or "oratory") as part of a theory of law continued until law schools (re)discovered skills training in the 1970s and '80s in the form of law clinics. Only later in the twentieth century did law schools introduce research and writing courses and, later still, externships reminiscent of the apprenticeship model that had been abandoned for the case method. It is this extended disconnection between law and its ancient rhetorical roots that this book seeks in part to address.

ADDITIONAL READINGS

Allen, Danielle. *Why Plato Wrote*. Blackwell Bristol Lectures on Greece, Rome and the Classical Tradition. Chichester, West Sussex, UK: Wiley-Blackwell, 2010.

Aristotle. *On Rhetoric: A Theory of Civic Discourse*. Translated by George A. Kennedy. 2nd ed. Oxford: Oxford University Press, 2007.

Bacon, Francis. "The First Book of Francis Bacon of the Proficience and Advancement of Learning, Divine and Human." In *Selected Writings of Francis Bacon*, edited by Hugh G. Dick, 157–220. New York: Modern Library, 1955.
Bizzell, Patricia, Bruce Herzberg, and Robin Reames, eds. *The Rhetorical Tradition: Readings from Classical Times to the Present*. 3rd ed. Boston: Bedford, 2020.
Camargo, Martin. *Ars Dictaminis, Ars Dictandi*. Turnhout, Belgium: Brepols, 1991.
Camper, Martin. *Arguing over Texts: The Rhetoric of Interpretation*. Oxford: Oxford University Press, 2018.
Cicero. *Brutus; Orator*. Translated by G. L. Hendrickson and H. M. Hubbell. Rev. ed. Cambridge, MA: Harvard University Press, 1962.
Cicero, Marcus Tullius. *On the Ideal Orator [De Oratore]*. Translated by James M. May and Jakob Wisse. New York: Oxford University Press, 2001.
Descartes, Rene. *Discourse on the Method*. Floyd, VA: SMK Books, 2018.
Dillon, John, and Tania Gergel, trans. *The Greek Sophists*. London: Penguin, 2003.
Frost, Michael H. *Introduction to Classical Legal Rhetoric: A Lost Heritage*. Abingdon, UK: Routledge, 2005.
Glenn, Cheryl. *Rhetoric Retold: Regendering the Tradition from Antiquity through the Renaissance*. Carbondale: Southern Illinois University Press, 1997.
Habinek, Thomas. *Ancient Rhetoric and Oratory*. Blackwell Introductions to the Classical World. Oxford: Blackwell, 2005.
Hansen, H. V., Fred J. Kauffeld, James B. Freeman, and Lilian Bermejo-Luque, eds. *Presumptions and Burdens of Proof: An Anthology of Argumentation and the Law*. Rhetoric, Law, and the Humanities. Tuscaloosa: University of Alabama Press, 2019.
Kennedy, George A. *Classical Rhetoric and Its Christian and Secular Tradition from Ancient to Modern Times*. 2nd ed. Chapel Hill: University of North Carolina Press, 1999.
———. "Introduction." In *Aristotle, On Rhetoric: A Theory of Civic Discourse*, translated by George A. Kennedy, 2nd ed. Oxford: Oxford University Press, 2007.
Lunsford, Andrea A., ed. *Reclaiming Rhetorica: Women in the Rhetorical Tradition*. Pittsburgh: University of Pittsburgh Press, 1995.
McManis, Charles R. "The History of First Century American Legal Education: A Revisionist Perspective." 59 *Washington University Law Quarterly* (1981): 597–659.
Murphy, James J. *Rhetoric in the Middle Ages*. Berkeley: University of California Press, 1974.
Murphy, J. J., R. A. Katula, and M. Hoppmann. *A Synoptic History of Classical Rhetoric*. 4th ed. New York: Routledge, 2013.
Perelman, Chaïm, and Harold J. Berman. *Justice, Law, and Argument*. Synthese Library 142. Dordrecht, Netherlands: D. Reidel, 1980.
Perelman, Chaïm, and Lucie Olbrechts-Tyteca. *The New Rhetoric: A Treatise on Argumentation*. Notre Dame, IN: University of Notre Dame Press, 1969.
Pernot, Laurent. *Rhetoric in Antiquity*. Translated by W. E. Higgins. Washington, DC: Catholic University of America Press, 2005.
Stevens, Robert. *Law School: Legal Education in America from the 1850s to the 1980s*. Chapel Hill: University of North Carolina Press, 1987.

Vickers, Brian. *In Defence of Rhetoric*. New York: Oxford University Press, 1989.
Vico, Giambattista. *The New Science*. Edited and translated by Jason Taylor and Robert Miner. New Haven, CT: Yale University Press, 2020.
Whately, R. *Elements of Rhetoric: Comprising an Analysis of the Laws of Moral Evidence and of Persuasion, with Rules for Argumentative Composition and Elocution*. Edited by D. Ehninger. Landmarks in Rhetoric and Public Address. Carbondale: Southern Illinois University Press, 2010.

Part II

BACK TO THE FUTURE

The Eclipse and Revival of Rhetoric

3

Giambattista Vico

Lamenting the Decline of Classical Rhetoric

Francis J. Mootz III

INTRODUCTION

Donald J. Trump's presidential campaign in 2016 focused on restoring the judiciary by appointing judges who simply apply the text of the law to the case before them, rather than introducing values into their decisions. When Justice Antonin Scalia died shortly before the election, Senate Majority Leader Mitch McConnell refused to consider the nomination to the Supreme Court of Judge Merrick Garland by President Obama. This sharp deviation from traditional practice signaled the extreme importance that the political parties placed on appointments to the court.

Judge Neil Gorsuch was one of twenty-one judges on a list prepared by candidate Trump, illustrating the kind of judge he pledged to nominate for a position on the Supreme Court. Shortly after the 2016 election, President Trump nominated Judge Gorsuch to replace Justice Scalia. At the time, Judge Gorsuch faced intense criticism from Democratic senators who rejected his "textual" and "plain meaning" approaches to interpreting written law. These exchanges brought into sharp relief very different conceptions of judging. There appeared to be little bulwark against the assumption that a judge who referred to anything other than the apparent plain meaning of the text of the law was acting improperly. As is well-known, at the Senate hearings, Judge Gorsuch was questioned about his dissent in a case involving a trucker stranded in frigid temperatures. His response that he was simply following the law raised eyebrows. This case provides an excellent focus for an inquiry into the proper role of judging as articulated by Giambattista Vico at the turn of the eighteenth century.

Giambattista Vico (1668–1744) was a professor of rhetoric at the University of Naples from 1699 until 1741. He was trained in law and sought a position on the law faculty but was never able to secure the appointment. He was not widely known during his lifetime, but now he is acknowledged to be the leading voice against the overreaching claims of the Cartesian method and the Enlightenment faith in reason. Descartes rejected the significance of culture and rhetoric because they interfere with certainty that can be achieved only through clear statements of the truth. In contrast, Vico championed the power of the imagination and argued for an anthropological view that each culture had its own way of thinking and resolving problems.

In his position as professor of rhetoric, Vico was charged with delivering the inaugural oration at the beginning of the academic year. His seventh oration, later published as *On the Study Methods of Our Time*, contains his vigorous defense of the rhetorical tradition against the totalizing claims made by Cartesian philosophers. He acknowledges the undeniable power of the "modern" approach but urges the students not to forget the necessity of the ancient tradition of rhetoric to address questions of uncertainty. He readily admits that Cartesian geometry produces more certainty than previous efforts but argues that the same methodology cannot be applied to ethical and political questions. These problems require students who have been trained to be imaginative and to invent arguments using the culturally prescribed topics.

Vico's magnum opus, the *New Science*, promised to uncover the distinctive ways each culture thinks and reasons. From the modern perspective, ancient myths appear to be bad "science," but Vico argued that thinking is defined by the common sense of the era. His "scientific" approach, then, was to reconstruct the patterns of thought from previous cultures imaginatively, by tracing the effects of divine wisdom. His approach to law was firmly grounded in the natural law tradition but also strongly influenced by the ancient rhetorical tradition.

We begin with Vico's lament that the ancient rhetorical tradition was being eclipsed by modern rationalism as a way to focus on what is lost by not attending to the connections between rhetoric and the maintenance of political and legal traditions. By beginning with what we have lost, we hope to focus on recovering the ancient heritage.

This excerpt from *On the Study Methods of Our Time* is a continuing provocation to our practices of legal rhetoric. Does Vico's lament still register today when considering the rhetorical approach to legal argumentation and judicial decision-making? The case that follows is a contemporary example of statutory interpretation, and Judge Gorsuch's dissent is a model of how judges seek to hew to the "plain meaning" of the statute and to rise above reliance on what they regard as mere rhetoric and judicial policymaking. With Judge Gorsuch now sitting on the Supreme Court, does this suggest that interpretive practices will deviate even further from the goal of rhetorical knowledge defended by Vico?

GIAMBATTISTA VICO, *ON THE STUDY METHODS OF OUR TIME* (1708–9)

Editors' Note: The excerpt by Vico is reprinted with permission from Giambattista Vico, *On the Study Methods of Our Time*, trans. Elio Gianturco (New York: Cornell University Press 1990), pages 4–41.

Mootz Note: Vico begins by posing his question: Has modern rationalism surpassed the ancients with regard to ways of knowing?

We, the men of the modern age, have discovered many things of which the Ancients were entirely ignorant; Ancients on the other hand, knew much still unknown to us. We enjoy many techniques which enable us to make progress in some branch of intellectual or practical activity; they likewise had talents for progress in other fields. They devoted all their activity to certain arts which we almost totally neglect; we pursue some others which they apparently scorned. Many disciplines conveniently unified by the Ancients have been partitioned by us; a certain number which they inconveniently kept separate, we treat as unified. Finally, not a few sectors of culture have changed both appearance and name.

The foregoing provides the theme of the present discourse: Which study method is finer and better, ours or the Ancients? In developing this topic I shall illustrate by examples the advantages and drawbacks of the respective methods. . . .

My goal . . . is to indicate in what respect our study methods are superior to those of the Ancients; to discover in what ways they are inferior, and how we may remedy this inferiority. . . .

Mootz Note: Vico urges his audience to let younger students explore topics with their imagination before seeking the certainty of scientific inquiry (which he calls "philosophical criticism").

Let us begin with the *instruments* with which modern sciences operate.

Philosophical criticism is the subject which we compel our youths to take up first. Now, such speculative criticism, the main purpose of which is to cleanse its fundamental truths not only of all falsity, but also of the mere suspicion of error, places upon the same plane of falsity not only false thinking, but also those secondary verities and ideas which are based on probability alone, and commands us to clear our minds of them. Such an approach is distinctly harmful, since training in common sense is essential to the education of adolescents, so that that faculty should be developed as early as possible; else they break into odd or arrogant behavior when adulthood is reached. It is a positive fact that, just as knowledge originates in truth and error in falsity, so common sense arises from perceptions based on verisimilitude. Probabilities stand, so to speak, midway between truth and falsity, since things which most of the time are true, are only very seldom false.

Consequently, since young people are to be educated in common sense, we should be careful to avoid that the growth of common sense be stifled in them by a habit of advanced speculative criticism. I may add that common sense, besides being the criterion of practical judgment, is also the guiding standard of eloquence. It frequently occurs, in fact, that orators in a law court have greater difficulty with a case which is based on truth, but does not seem so, than with a case that is false but plausible. There is a danger that instruction in advanced philosophical criticism may lead to an abnormal growth of abstract intellectualism, and render young people unfit for the practice of eloquence.

Our modern advocates of advanced criticism rank the unadulterated essence of "pure," primary truth before, outside, above the gross semblances of physical bodies. But this study of primal philosophical truths takes place at the time when young minds are too immature, too unsure, to derive benefit from it.

Just as old age is powerful in reason, so is adolescence in imagination. Since imagination has always been esteemed a most favorable omen of future development, it should in no way be dulled. Furthermore, the teacher should give the greatest care to the cultivation of the pupil's memory, which, though not exactly the same as imagination, is almost identical with it. In adolescence, memory outstrips in vigor all other faculties, and should be intensely trained. Youth's natural inclination to the arts in which imagination or memory (or a combination of both) is prevalent (such as painting, poetry, oratory, jurisprudence) should be no means be blunted. Nor should advanced philosophical criticism, the common instrument today of all arts and sciences, be an impediment to any of them. The Ancients knew how to avoid this drawback. In almost all their schools for youths, the role of logic was fulfilled by geometry. Following the example of medical practitioners, who concentrate their efforts on seconding the bent of Nature, the Ancients required their youths to learn the science of geometry which cannot be grasped without a vivid capacity to form images. Thus, without doing violence to nature, but gradually and gentle and in step with the menial capacities of their age, the Ancients nurtured the reasoning powers of their young men.

In our days, instead, philosophical criticism alone is honored. The art of "topics" far from being given first place in the curriculum is utterly disregarded.

Again I say, this is harmful, since the invention of arguments is by nature prior to the judgment of their validity, so that, in teaching, that invention should be given priority over philosophical criticism. In our days, we keep away from the art of inventing arguments, and think that this skill is of no use. We hear people affirming that, if individuals are critically endowed, it is sufficient to teach them a certain subject, and they will have the capacity to discover whether there is any truth in that subject. It is claimed that, without any previous training in the *ars topica*, any person will be able to discern the probabilities which surround any ordinary topic, and to evaluate them by the same standard employed in the sifting of truth. But who can be sure that he has taken into consideration every feature of the subject on hand? The most eulogizing epithet that can be given to a speech is that it is "comprehensive": praise is due to the speaker who has left, nothing untouched, and has omitted nothing from the argument, nothing which may be missed by his listeners.

Nature and life are full of incertitude; the foremost, indeed, the only aim of our "arts" is to assure us that we have acted rightly. Criticism is the art of true speech; "*ars topica*," of eloquence. Traditional "topics" is the art of finding "the *medium*," i.e., the middle term: in the conventional language of scholasticism, "medium" indicates what the Latins call *argumentum*. Those who know all the loci, i.e., the lines of argument to be used, are able (by an operation not unlike reading the printed characters on a page) to grasp extemporaneously the elements of persuasion inherent in any question or case. Individuals who have not achieved this ability hardly deserve the name of orators. In pressing, urgent affairs, which do not admit of delay or postponement, as most frequently occurs in our law courts—especially when it is a question of criminal cases, which offer to the eloquent orator the greatest opportunity for the display of his powers—it is the orator's business to give immediate assistance to the accused, who is usually granted only a few hours in which to plead his defense. Our experts in philosophical criticism, instead, whenever they are confronted with some dubious point, want to say: "Give me some time to think it over!" . . .

Mootz Note: Vico suggests how we might gain the benefits of both approaches to knowledge.

Each procedure, then, has its defects. The specialists in topics fall in with falsehood; the philosophical critics disdain any traffic with probability.

To avoid both defects, I think, young men should be taught the totality of sciences and arts, and their intellectual powers should be developed to the full; thus they will become a familiar with the art of argument, drawn from the *ars topica*. At the very outset, their common sense should be strengthened so that they can grow in prudence and eloquence. Let their imagination and memory be fortified so that they may be effective in those arts in which fantasy and the mnemonic faculty are predominant. At a later stage let them learn criticism, so that they can apply the fullness of their personal judgment to what they have been taught. And let them develop skill in debating on either side of any proposed argument.

Were this done, young students, I think, would become exact in science, clever in practical matters, fluent in eloquence, imaginative in understanding poetry or painting, and strong in memorizing what they have learned in their legal studies. . . .

But the greatest drawback of our educational methods is that we pay an excessive amount of attention to the natural sciences and not enough to ethics. Our chief fault is that we disregard that part of ethics which treats of human character, of its dispositions, its passions, and of the manner of adjusting these factors to public life and eloquence. . . .

Since, in our time, the only target of our intellectual endeavors is truth, we devote all our efforts to the investigation of physical phenomena, because their nature seems unambiguous; but we fail to inquire into human nature which, because of the freedom of man's will, is difficult to determine. A serious drawback arises from the uncontrasted preponderance of our interest in the natural sciences.

Our young men, because of their training, which is focused on these studies, are unable to engage in the life of the community, to conduct themselves with sufficient wisdom and prudence; nor can they infuse into their speech a familiarity with human psychology or permeate their utterances with passion. . . .

The difference, therefore, between abstract knowledge and prudence is this; in science, the outstanding intellect is that which succeeds in reducing a large multitude of physical effects to a single cause; in the domain of prudence, excellence is accorded to those who ferret out the greatest possible number of causes which may have produced a single event, and who are able to conjecture which of all these causes is the true one. Abstract knowledge—science—is concerned with the highest verity; common sense, instead, with the lowliest. . . .

Therefore, it is an error to apply to the prudent conduct of life the abstract criterion of reasoning that obtains in the domain of science. A correct judgment deems that men—who are, for the most part, but fools—are ruled, not by forethought, but by whim or chance. . . .

Mootz Note: Vico defends his recourse to the classical rhetorical tradition against claims that it would engender false opinions and ambiguity and that the radical democracy of the polis is past.

Here some learned pundit might object that, in the conduct of life, I would have our young students become courtiers, and not philosophers; pay little attention to the truth and follow not reality but appearances; and case down morality and put on a deceitful "front" of virtue.

I have no such intention. Instead, I should like to have them act as philosophers, even at court; to care for truth that both is and has the appearance of truth, and to follow that which is morally good and which everybody approves.

As for eloquence, the same men assert that the modern study methods, far from being detrimental, are most useful to it. "How much preferable it is," they say, "to induce persuasion by solid arguments based on truth, to produce such an effect on the mind that, once that truth coalesces with reason, it can never again be separated from it, rather than to coerce the listener's soul by meretriciously eloquent allurements, by blazes of oratorical fire which, as soon as they are extinguished, cause him to revert to his original disposition!"

The answer is that eloquence does not address itself to the rational part of our nature, but almost entirely to our passions. The rational part of us may be taken captive by a net woven of purely intellectual reasonings, but the passional side of our nature can never be swayed and overcome unless this is done by more sensuous and materialistic means. The role of eloquence is to persuade; an orator is persuasive when he calls forth in his hearers the mood he desires. Wise men induce this condition in themselves by an act of volition. This volition, in perfect obedience, follows the dictates of their intellect; consequently, it is enough for the speaker to point their duty to such wise men, and they do it. But the multitude, the *vulgus*, are overpowered and carried along by their appetite, which is tumultuous and turbulent; their soul is tainted, having contracted a contagion from the body, so that it follows the nature of the body, and is not moved except by bodily things. Therefore, the soul must be enticed by corporeal images and impelled to love; for once it loves it is easily taught to believe; once it believes and loves, the fire of passion must be infused into it so as to break its inertia and force it to *will*. Unless the speaker can compass these three things, he has not achieved the effect of persuasion; he has been powerless to convince.

Two things only are capable of turning to good use the agitations of the soul, those evils of the inward man which spring from a single source: desire. One is philosophy, which acts to mitigate passions in the soul of the sage, so that those passions are transformed into virtues; the other is eloquence, which kindles these passions in the common sort, so that they perform the duties of virtue.

It may be objected that the form of government under which we live at present no longer allows eloquence to exercise its control over free peoples. To which I answer that we ought to be thankful to our monarchs for governing us not by fist but by laws. However, even under the republican form of government, orators have gained distinction by their fluent, broad, impassioned style of delivery in the law courts, the assemblies, and the religious convocations, to the greatest advantage of the state, and to the signal enrichment of our language. . . .

In conclusion: whosoever intends to devote his efforts, not to physics or mechanics, but to a political career, whether as a civil servant or as a member of the legal profession or of the judiciary, a political speaker or a pulpit orator, should not waste too much time, in his adolescence, on those subjects which are taught by abstract geometry. Let him, instead, cultivate his mind with an ingenious method; let him study topics, and defend both sides of a controversy, be it on nature, man, or politics, in a freer and brighter style of expression. Let him not spurn reasons that wear a semblance of probability and verisimilitude. Let our efforts not be directed towards achieving superiority over the Ancients merely in the field of science, while they surpass us in wisdom; let us not be merely more exact and more true than the Ancients, while allowing them to be more eloquent than we are; let us equal the Ancients in the fields of wisdom and eloquence as we excel them in the domain of science.

TRANSAM TRUCKING, INC. V. ADMINISTRATIVE REVIEW BOARD, 833 F.3d 1206 (10th CIR. 2016)

Mootz Note: This case assumed great significance during the confirmation hearings for Justice Neil Gorsuch to replace Justice Scalia on the US Supreme Court. Critics charged that Gorsuch approaches the law simplistically and merely logically, rather than implementing the statutory purpose. Justice Gorsuch defended his approach as hewing to the narrow role for judges to follow the plain meaning of a statute. Judge Murphy's majority opinion in this case sets the stage for Judge Gorsuch's dissenting opinion. Consider how Vico's oration provides a means of criticizing the approach to judicial decision-making by Judge Gorsuch. In this excerpt, internal footnotes and some internal citations are omitted.

MURPHY, Circuit Judge.

I. Introduction

Alphonse Maddin was employed as a truck driver by Petitioner TransAm Trucking ("TransAm"). In January 2009, Maddin was transporting cargo through Illinois when the brakes on his trailer froze because of subzero temperatures. After reporting the problem to TransAm and waiting several hours for a repair truck to arrive, Maddin unhitched his truck from the trailer and drove away, leaving the trailer unattended. He was terminated for abandoning the trailer.

Both an administrative law judge ("ALJ") and Respondent, the Department of Labor ("DOL") Administrative Review Board ("ARB"), concluded Maddin was terminated in violation of the whistleblower provisions of the Surface Transportation Assistance Act ("STAA"). He was ordered reinstated with back pay. TransAm filed a Petition for Review of the ARB's Final Decision and Order with this court. Exercising jurisdiction pursuant to 49 U.S.C. § 31105(d), we deny the petition for review.

Mootz Note: This procedure is typical of an administrative law case. The governing statute (STAA) provides that an administrative agency will adjudicate claims under the statute, but the decision of the administrative law judge (ALJ) to reinstate the worker can be appealed to the court of appeals.

II. Factual Background

Maddin was employed by TransAm as a truck driver. In January 2009, he was driving a tractor-trailer for TransAm on I-88 in Illinois. At approximately 11:00 p.m., Maddin pulled to the side of the highway because he was unable to find the TransAm-mandated fuel station and his gas gauge was below empty. When he attempted to pull back onto the road ten minutes later, he discovered the brakes on the trailer had locked up because of the frigid temperatures.

Maddin reported the frozen brakes to TransAm at 11:17 p.m. and was advised by TransAm's Road Assist service that a repairperson would be sent to his location. While waiting for the repair truck, Maddin discovered that his auxiliary power unit ("APU" or "bunk heater") was not working and there was no heat in the cab of the truck.

Maddin eventually fell asleep in the truck but was awakened at approximately 1:18 a.m. when he received a telephone call from his cousin, Gregory Nelson. According to Nelson, Maddin's speech was slurred and he sounded confused. When Maddin sat up, he realized his torso was numb and he could not feel his feet. He called Road Assist again and told the dispatcher his bunk heater was not working. He also told the dispatcher about his physical condition and asked when the repairperson would arrive. The dispatcher told Maddin to "hang in there."

About thirty minutes after his second call to Road Assist, Maddin became concerned about continuing to wait in the freezing temperatures without heat. He unhitched the trailer from the truck, pulled the truck about three feet away, and called his supervisor, Larry Cluck. Maddin told Cluck he couldn't feel his feet and was having trouble breathing because of the cold. Cluck repeatedly told Maddin to turn on the APU even though Maddin told Cluck several times it was not working

When Maddin told Cluck he was leaving to seek help, Cluck told Maddin not to leave the trailer, instructing him to either drag the trailer with its frozen brakes or remain with the trailer until the repairperson arrived. Maddin did not follow either instruction but, instead, drove off in the truck leaving the trailer unattended. The repair truck arrived less than fifteen minutes after Maddin left. Maddin drove the truck back to the trailer and met with the repairperson.

After the repairs to the brakes were completed, Maddin called Cluck for instructions on where to purchase fuel. During this conversation, Cluck threatened to write Maddin up for either a late load or for missing his fuel stop earlier. During a subsequent conversation, Cluck informed Maddin he was being written up for abandoning the trailer. Less than a week later, Maddin was fired for violating company policy by abandoning his load while under dispatch.

After his termination, Maddin filed a complaint with OSHA, an agency within the DOL, asserting TransAm violated the whistle-blower provisions of the STAA when it discharged him. After the complaint was dismissed by OSHA, Maddin requested a hearing before a DOL ALJ. 49 U.S.C. § 31105(b)(2)(B). The ALJ issued a written interim decision and order on October 26, 2012, ruling that Maddin was terminated in violation of the STAA. Specifically, the ALJ concluded Maddin engaged in protected activity when he reported the frozen brake issue to TransAm and again when he refused to obey Mr. Cluck's instruction to drive the truck while dragging the trailer. The ALJ further concluded Maddin's protected activity was a contributing factor in TransAm's decision to fire him because Maddin's refusal to operate the truck while dragging the trailer was "inextricably intertwined" with TransAm's decision to terminate him for abandoning the trailer at the side of the highway. The ALJ provided Maddin with an opportunity to present evidence of economic damages.

Mootz Note: OSHA, the Occupational Safety and Health Administration, has general authority regarding safe workplaces. When OSHA did not accept his claim, Maddin filed for reinstatement to his job under the more specific statute, STAA, that protects workers who are disciplined for refusing to act in a dangerous manner.

The ALJ issued a final decision and order on January 7, 2013, awarding backpay to Maddin in an amount calculated from the date of his discharge to the date of his reinstatement. Included in the award were per diem travel allowances which the ALJ concluded were part of Maddin's compensation. Maddin's interim earnings were not deducted based on the ALJ's finding that those earnings were more than offset by interim expenses that Maddin would not have incurred but for his termination. The ALJ also ordered TransAm to take steps to remove all negative reports made to any entity about Maddin or his termination.

TransAm appealed the ALJ's decision to the ARB. The ARB affirmed the

ALJ's interim and final decisions, concluding that substantial evidence supported all the applicable findings. The Board also affirmed the amount of backpay.

III. Discussion

. . . [The relevant provision of the statute] is codified at 49 U.S.C. § 31105(a)(1)(B)(ii) and makes it unlawful for an employer to discharge an employee who "refuses to operate a vehicle because . . . the employee has a reasonable apprehension of serious injury to the employee or the public because of the vehicle's hazardous safety or security condition." For an employee's apprehension of serious injury to be reasonable, the employee must show that a reasonable individual in the employee's circumstances "would conclude that the hazardous safety or security condition establishes a real danger of accident, injury, or serious impairment to health." *Id.* § 31105(a)(2). An employee seeking protection under this provision must also show that he "sought from the employer, and [was] unable to obtain, correction of the hazardous safety or security condition." *Id.* TransAm does not dispute that Maddin had a reasonable apprehension of serious injury if he either stayed with the trailer or dragged the trailer down the highway. Neither does TransAm dispute that the trailer's frozen brakes were unsafe and Maddin, who had been waiting more than three hours in freezing temperatures in an unheated truck, was unable to obtain correction of the unsafe condition.

The ARB agreed with the ALJ's finding that Maddin engaged in protected activity under this provision when he unhooked the trailer and "refused to operate the truck under the conditions set by Mr. [C]luck." TransAm argues that because Maddin drove the truck after being instructed to "stay put," he actually operated his vehicle and the ARB erred by concluding his conduct fell within the "refusal to operate" provision of the STAA. . . .

TransAm's argument equates the term "operate," as used in the statute, with driving. However, TransAm has not directed this court to any authority for the proposition that Congress intended the refusal-to-operate provision of the STAA to be interpreted so narrowly, and has not explained how such a narrow interpretation furthers the purposes of the STAA. The ARB interpreted the term "operate" to encompass not only driving, but other uses of a vehicle when it is within the control of the employee. [*Footnote in the court's opinion:* "The language used by the ARB—particularly its statement that 'a refusal to operate may encompass actually operating a vehicle'—is somewhat confusing, but its meaning is clear when read in context."] Thus, under the ARB's interpretation, the refusal-to-operate provision could cover a situation in which an employee refuses to use his vehicle in the manner directed by his employer even if that refusal results in the employee driving the vehicle. Thus, by way of example, an employee who partially unloads an overweight trailer in direct contravention of his employer's instruction to continue pulling the overweight trailer on the public roadways, has refused to operate the vehicle for purposes of the STAA even if the employee completes the trip after unloading the trailer. *See Beveridge v. Waste Stream Envtl., Inc.*, ARB No. 97–137, 1997 WL 806522, at *1 (ARB Dec. 23, 1997). Similarly, an employee who moves a disabled trailer from the middle of a busy roadway to the shoulder of the road after being told by his employer to remain in the roadway, has refused to operate his vehicle for purposes of the STAA whistle-blower protection under the interpretation of § 31105(a)(1)(B)(ii) adopted by the ARB.

The STAA was enacted, [in part], to "promote the safe operation of commercial motor vehicles," "to minimize dangers to the health of operators of commercial motor vehicles," and "to ensure increased compliance with traffic laws and with . . . commercial motor vehicle safety and health regulations and standards." 49 U.S.C. § 31131(a). The STAA's whistle-blower provisions were enacted to "encourage employee reporting of noncompliance with safety regulations governing commercial motor vehicles." *Brock v. Roadway Express, Inc.*, 481 U.S. 252, 258, 107 S.Ct. 1740, 95 L.Ed.2d 239 (1987). The ARB's interpretation of § 31105(a)(1)(B)(ii) furthers the purpose of the STAA by prohibiting an employer from discharging an insubordinate employee whose insubordination was motivated by the employee's reasonable apprehension of serious injury to himself or members of the public. . . .

Having concluded the ARB's interpretation of § 31105(a)(1)(B)(ii) is a permissible construction of the statute, we also conclude the ARB's finding that Maddin engaged in STAA-protected activity when he unhitched the trailer and drove off in the truck is supported by substantial evidence. Here, Mr. Cluck instructed Maddin to either drive his truck while dragging the trailer or stay with the trailer on the side of the roadway until the repairperson arrived. Maddin refused to obey either instruction given by Mr. Cluck and, instead, unhooked the truck from the trailer and drove off, leaving the trailer unattended—the very thing Mr. Cluck ordered him not to do.

Mootz Note: The appellate court must show deference to the administrative determinations by the ALJ under a doctrine known as the *Chevron* Doctrine. The court must accept a "permissible" interpretation of the statute, even if it is not the interpretation that the court would have adopted.

As to Maddin's refusal to drag the trailer, TransAm argues that dragging the trailer was a "ridiculous alternative option" and, thus, Maddin could not refuse to operate his vehicle under the conditions set by his employer because it was impossible to do so. TransAm's argument is unpersuasive. First, both the ALJ and the ARB accepted Maddin's uncontroverted testimony that Mr. Cluck ordered him to drag the trailer with the frozen brakes. Further, TransAm has not directed this court to any evidence in the record demonstrating that dragging the trailer was impossible. It is true that Maddin testified he could not release the brakes because they were frozen. But Maddin did not testify that he seriously attempted, but was unable, to drag the trailer.

Because the refusal-to-operate provision can be interpreted to cover multiple uses of a vehicle while it is in the control of an employee, the ARB did not err in concluding that Maddin's act of unhitching the trailer and driving off in the truck was a refusal to operate the tractor-trailer for purposes of § 31105(a)(1)(B)(ii). Maddin was instructed by Mr. Cluck to operate his rig by remaining with the trailer until the repairperson arrived. He disobeyed that instruction and drove off in the truck, leaving the trailer behind. Thus, as the ARB concluded, although Maddin actually drove the truck after unhitching it, he refused to operate his tractor-trailer in the manner instructed by his employer. This conclusion is supported by substantial evidence. . . .

TransAm's petition for review is denied.

GORSUCH, Circuit Judge, dissenting.

A trucker was stranded on the side of the road, late at night, in cold weather, and his trailer brakes were stuck. He called his company for help and someone there gave him two options. He could drag the trailer carrying the company's goods to its destination (an illegal and maybe sarcastically offered option). Or he could sit and wait for help to arrive (a legal if unpleasant option). The trucker chose None of the Above, deciding instead to unhook the trailer and drive his truck to a gas station. In response, his employer, TransAm, fired him for disobeying orders and abandoning its trailer and goods.

It might be fair to ask whether TransAm's decision was a wise or kind one. But it's not our job to answer questions like that. Our only task is to decide whether the decision was an illegal one. The Department of Labor says that TransAm violated federal law, in particular 49 U.S.C. § 31105(a)(1)(B). But that statute only forbids employers from firing employees who "refuse[ ] to operate a vehicle" out of safety concerns. And, of course, nothing like that happened here. The trucker in this case wasn't fired for *refusing* to operate his vehicle. Indeed, his employer gave him the very option the statute says it must: once he voiced safety concerns, TransAm expressly—and by everyone's admission—permitted him to sit and remain where he was and wait for help. The trucker was fired only after he declined the statutorily protected option (refuse to operate) and chose instead to *operate* his vehicle in a manner he thought wise but his employer did not. And there's simply no law anyone has pointed us to giving employees the right to operate their vehicles in ways their employers forbid. Maybe the Department would like such a law, maybe someday Congress will adorn our federal statute books with such a law. But it isn't there yet. And it isn't our job to write one—or to allow the Department to write one in Congress's place.

My colleagues suggest that the Department should be permitted to read the statutory phrase "refuse[ ] to operate" to encompass its exact opposite and protect employees who *operate* their vehicles in defiance of their employers' orders. They justify this unusual result on the ground that the statutory phrase is ambiguous and so we owe the Department deference. . . . [I]t seems to me that the statute is perfectly plain—and plainly doesn't capture the conduct here—just as TransAm suggests. The term "refuse" means "[t]o decline positively, to express or show a determination not to do something." 8 THE OXFORD ENGLISH DICTIONARY 495 (2d ed. 1989). Meanwhile, "operate" means "[t]o cause or actuate the working of; to work (a machine, etc.)." 10 *id.* at 848. Putting this together, employees who voice safety concerns about their vehicles may *decline to cause those vehicles to work* without fear of reprisal. And that protection, while significant, just does not give employees license to *cause* those vehicles to work in ways they happen to wish but an employer forbids. Indeed, my colleagues' position would seem to require the addition of more than a few new words to the statute. In their view, an employee should be protected not just when he "refuses to operate a vehicle" but also when he "refuses to operate a vehicle *in the particular manner the employer directs and instead operates it in a manner he thinks safe.*" Yet those words just aren't there; the law before us protects only employees who refuse to operate vehicles, *period.* Imagine a boss telling an employee he may either "operate" an office computer as directed or "refuse to operate" that computer. What serious employee would take *that* as license to use an office computer not for work but to compose the great American novel? Good luck.

To be sure, my colleagues invoke the statute's purposes—employee "health" and "safety"—and suggest the result they reach is consistent with them. After all, they note, the employee here who chose to defy his employer's instructions and drive his truck as he thought best didn't do so to write a novel or with some other esoteric end in mind, but because he bore safety concerns. Just the sort of employee safety concerns, my colleagues indicate, Congress intended to protect. Maj. Op. at 1211.

Even supposing all this is true, though, when the statute is plain it simply isn't our business to appeal to legislative intentions. *Gemsco, Inc. v. Walling*, 324 U.S. 244, 260, 65 S.Ct. 605, 89 L.Ed. 921 (1945) ("The plain words and meaning of a statute cannot be overcome by legislative history which, through strained processes of deduction from events of wholly ambiguous significance, may furnish dubious bases for inference in every direction."). And it is a well-documented mistake, too, to assume that a statute pursues its putative (or even announced) purposes to their absolute and seemingly logical ends. Especially to ends as ephemeral and generic as "health and safety." After all, what under the sun, at least at some level of generality, *doesn't* relate to "health and safety"? The fact is that statutes are products of compromise, the sort of compromise necessary to overcome the hurdles of bicameralism and presentment. And it is our obligation to enforce the terms of that compromise as expressed in the law itself, not to use the law as a sort of springboard to combat all perceived evils lurking in the neighborhood. Maybe Congress found it easier to agree that an employee has a right to sit still in response to his employer's order to operate an unsafe vehicle rather than try to agree on a code detailing when and how an employee can operate a vehicle in a way he thinks safe and appropriate but his employer does not. Maybe Congress would not have been able to agree to the latter sort of code at all. Or maybe it just found the problem too time consuming and other matters more pressing. Or maybe it just didn't think about the problem at all. Whatever the case, it is our job and work enough for the day to apply the law Congress did pass, not to imagine and enforce one it might have but didn't.

I respectfully dissent.

CRITICAL ASSESSMENT

Vico's oration sheds light on important features of contemporary legal education and practice. We can view these topics through the lens of Judge Gorsuch's dissenting opinion by posing the following questions: how does Vico believe that lawyers and judges should be trained, and how would such properly trained lawyers decide difficult cases? Judge Gorsuch's opinion is an example of the type of narrow, unimaginative approach that Vico warned would be cultivated by a slavish adherence to the Cartesian method, but even the narrow approach adopted by Judge Gorsuch illustrates the inevitability of rhetorical constructions in legal reasoning. Even those who would defend Judge Gorsuch's result should agree on the need to revitalize the ancient arts that Vico celebrates, if only to make their case more persuasively.

Vico calls on his audience to preserve the rhetorical wisdom developed by the ancients in the face of the ascendant Cartesian claim that the only true knowledge is certain knowledge. He does not reject the Cartesian method of study that dominates the modern age but warns that if we restrict intellectual inquiry only to matters that can be definitively established as true, we will lose our rhetorical facility to develop arguments that persuade based solely on probabilities. This loss is profound, because ethics, politics, and law operate in this rhetorical realm that does not produce definitive knowledge.

Rhetorical knowledge is grounded in common sense and embodied in practical judgments (prudence) that can be defended with eloquence. Lawyers do not have the luxury of waiting for all the relevant data to be collected: action is necessary under conditions that require guidance through reasoning, even if there is not a single rational answer to the problem posed.

DISCUSSION QUESTIONS

Discussion Question 1: What does Vico mean when he refers to a realm that is "midway between truth and falsity" and that serves as "the criterion of practical judgment?"

Vico urges his audience to promote these rhetorical capacities in the education that we design for our students. It is asking too much for young minds to adhere to rigorously logical and abstract modes of analysis, rather than harnessing and activating their imaginations. Before one may rigorously *test* a proposition, it is necessary to have the inventive capacity to *conceive* of the proposition in the first place. To develop this capacity of invention, Vico proposes to reinvigorate an "ingenious method" by which students argue cases from both sides. The lesson is not relativism but rather the ability to be persuasive when argumentation is grounded in probability and verisimilitude. The remnants of this "ingenious method" remain in the contemporary law school curriculum.

Discussion Question 2: How would Vico change contemporary legal education to promote wisdom and eloquence as well as scientific rigor?

Legal practice is premised on rhetoric. The radical democracy of Greece called upon citizens to press their own cases, but Vico emphasizes that even under the republican government in Rome there was need for argumentation based on probabilities. Politicians and judges quickly find that there is no firm, clear, and distinct rule to be applied without controversy to individual cases. As a result, consciously or not—and whether shaped by formal study or intuitions—they must reason rhetorically.

Discussion Question 3: Even if rhetoric is unavoidable, shouldn't judges strive to avoid its effects, which lead them away from objectivity and truth?

The opinions in *Transom Trucking* clearly reveal the unavoidable rhetorical nature of legal reasoning. Consider the elemental obligation to state the "facts" of the case. There is no ostensible dispute about the facts, but the two opinions tell very different stories. The majority opinion describes the "subzero" and "frigid" temperatures that led to the brakes freezing. The plaintiff waited for three hours without heat in the truck, becoming numb and confused, slurring his words and receiving no comfort from the supervisor's repeated assurances that help was on its way. He rejected his supervisor's suggestion to drag the load without working brakes and ultimately abandoned the load and drove the cab to shelter out of desperation. In contrast, Judge Gorsuch's dissent paints a very different picture. The plaintiff was "stranded . . . in cold weather" when he decided to ignore the options provided by his boss to address the problem of the disabled truck and the need to protect the cargo. On this bare account, Justice Gorsuch advises that we should not be distracted by questions of whether the employer's behavior was "wise" or "kind," because the case presents a simple question of whether a law was violated.

Discussion Question 4: Why would either judge characterize the weather and Mr. Maddin's condition? What does this have to do with whether the statutory test is met?

Having set the stage for the reader through the construction of competing stories, the majority addresses the seemingly straightforward legal question: Was the plaintiff illegally fired for refusing "to operate a vehicle . . . because of the vehicle's hazardous safety or security condition?" A simple focus on the semantic meaning of the phrase would appear to provide a certain answer. The plaintiff drove his cab away from the trailer, thereby "operating" his vehicle against his employer's instructions rather than refusing to operate the vehicle.

Discussion Question 5: Should the court consider the purpose of the statute, which appears to be to protect drivers who suffer adverse employment decisions because they refuse to act in an unsafe manner?

The majority refuses to conflate "operating" with "driving," concluding that such a narrow reading would undermine the remedial purpose of the statutes. This approach finds support in previous cases, including one in which the driver unloaded the overweight truck before continuing driving, and one in which the driver moved the vehicle to the shoulder of the road rather than following his employer's instructions not to move out of the dangerous and busy roadway. In these cases, the court had construed "operating" to mean refusing to exercise control over the vehicle in a manner that is unsafe. In the present case, the majority concluded that the plaintiff refused to "operate" his vehicle unsafely by dragging the load with locked brakes and instead uncoupling the load and driving away.

Judge Gorsuch puts on his grammarian spectacles and takes the majority to task for ignoring the dictionary definitions of "refuse" and "operate." He concludes that the driver did the opposite of "refusing to operate" his vehicle by deciding to drive his cab away from the trailer and so was beyond the literal scope of the protection of the statute. Judge Gorsuch chides the majority for transforming the statute into a general protection for drivers who choose to operate their vehicles in contravention to their employer's directives. He posits a choice between following the clear meaning of the statute as enacted (which Congress drafted almost certainly without the present case in mind) and converting the statute into a general "protect workers who do the right thing" provision.

Discussion Question 6: Should judges restrict themselves to objective interpretations of the law and eschew the rhetorical approach that is described by Vico?

Discussion Question 7: Is Vico assuming that we still live in the ancient polis of Athens? Is the "wisdom of the ancients" inextricably linked to certain forms of life that may no longer exist?

Defenders of Judge Gorsuch's literalist approach to interpretation would argue that it does not necessarily lead to outcomes with which conservatives would agree. Is it possible that Judge Gorsuch might arrive at a liberal, or even progressive, result when reading a statute literally? Consider Justice Gorsuch's majority opinion in *Bostock v. Clayton County*, 140 S. Ct. 1731 (2020), in which he concluded that the ban on discrimination "because of sex" in Title VII of the Civil Rights Act of 1964 protected gays, lesbians, and transgender persons because one must literally consider their "sex" to discriminate on these other grounds. More conservative Justices argued that Justice Gorsuch's literalism contrasted with Congress's intent in adopting Title VII in 1964.

Discussion Question 8: Does the result in *Bostock* establish that Justice Gorsuch in fact does follow a "neutral" approach to interpreting statutes? What would Vico say about adopting a "neutral" approach?

ADDITIONAL READINGS

Grassi, Ernesto. "The Priority of Common Sense and Imagination: Vico's Philosophical Relevance Today." *Social Research* 43, no. 3 (Fall 1976): 553–80.

Kelley, Donald R. "Vico's Road: From Philology to Jurisprudence and Back." *Giambattista Vico's Science of Humanity*, edited by Giorgio Tagliacozzo and Donald Philip Verene, 15–29. Baltimore: Johns Hopkins University Press, 1976.

Lilla, Mark. *G. B. Vico: The Making of an Anti-Modern*. Cambridge, MA: Harvard University Press, 1993.

Mooney, Michael. *Vico in the Tradition of Rhetoric*. New York: Lawrence Erlbaum Associates, 1994.

Mootz III, Francis J. "Vico and Imagination: An Ingenious Approach to Educating

Lawyers with Semiotic Sensibility." *International Journal for the Semiotics of Law* 22, no. 1 (2009): 11–22.
———. "Vico, Llewellyn and the Task of Legal Education." *Loyola Law Review* 57, no. 1 (2011): 135–56.
———. "Vico's "Ingenious Method" and Legal Education." *Chicago-Kent Law Review* 83, no. 3 (2008): 1261–302.
Verene, Donald Philip. "Vichian Moral Philosophy: Prudence as Jurisprudence." *Chicago-Kent Law Review* 83, no. 3 (2008): 1107–130.
Vico, Giambattista. *The Art of Rhetoric (Institutiones Oratoriae 1711–41)*. Edited and translated by Girogio A. Pinton and Arthur W. Shippee. Amsterdam: Rodopi, 1996.
———. *The New Science*. Edited by Guiseppe F. Mazzotta. Translated by Jason Taylor and Robert C. Miner. New Haven, CT: Yale University Press, 2020.
Witteveen, Willem J. "Reading Vico for the School of Law." *Chicago-Kent Law Review* 83, no. 3 (2008): 1197–223.

4

Chaïm Perelman and Lucie Olbrechts-Tyteca

Answering Vico's Lament

David A. Frank

INTRODUCTION

As Francis J. Mootz III observes in the previous chapter, Giambattista Vico, the eighteenth-century professor of rhetoric, lamented the failure of his contemporaries to value the classical tradition of rhetoric. This tradition, Vico argued, offers the intellectual and moral resources necessary for wisdom and just action. The twentieth-century contemporaries of Chaïm Perelman (1912–84) and Lucie Olbrechts-Tyteca (1899–1987) also devalued the rhetorical tradition. Perelman and Olbrechts-Tyteca offer a contemporary response to Vico's lament in their 1958 magnum opus *Traité de l'argumentation: La nouvelle rhétorique*, which was translated into English in 1969 under the title *The New Rhetoric: A Treatise on Argumentation*.[1] They cite Vico at sixteen different sections in their text.

Vico, Perelman, and Olbrechts-Tyteca offer an alternative to the thinking and philosophy of René Descartes (1596–1650). The intellectual leader of one interpretation of the Enlightenment, Descartes held that there could be no true knowledge unless it was "clear and distinct." Such knowledge resulted from the application of formal logic, mathematics, and geometry, which placed truth and understanding beyond the reach of time and the concrete experiences of human beings. Perelman and Olbrechts-Tyteca developed a system of rhetorical reasoning that recovered and updated the ancient tradition of rhetoric. Their rhetoric was "new" because it recaptured and renovated the classical rhetorical tradition by moving the human audience and informal logic expressed through argumentation and persuasion to the center of civil society.

A Belgian Jew, Perelman witnessed and experienced the horrors of the Nazi invasion of his homeland. In response, he launched a lifetime scholarly project designed to identify and then better anchor the roots of social justice. Perelman wrote the book *Justice*[2] while leading the Belgian Jewish underground during the Nazi occupation of Belgium. Lucie Olbrechts-Tyteca, who was a prominent member of the Belgian resistance against the Nazis, joined Perelman in 1947 in a ten-year scholarly collaboration to recover the role that reason should play in civil society. They rediscovered rhetoric and Vico as touchstones for their project.

Chaïm Perelman, alone and then in collaboration with Lucie Olbrechts-Tyteca, answered Vico's lament by drawing from and updating the classical rhetorical theories of Plato, Aristotle, and Cicero as well as the works of Vico to recover the humanistic tradition of rhetoric. Perelman and Olbrechts-Tyteca offered the "reasonable" as a check on and as a complement to the "rational." As defined by Descartes, the rational existed outside of time and human experience. Perelman and Olbrechts-Tyteca placed high value on the reasonable because it unfolds in human time and is a result of argument and deliberation. The methods of math and geometry, in contrast, require computation, not deliberation. Perelman and Olbrechts-Tyteca outline a system of rhetorical reason designed to navigate between the certainty of formal logic and the irrational.

Vico's lament centers on the arrogance of Descartes's assumption that all truths are clear and distinct, products of math and geometry. Importantly, Perelman and Olbrechts-Tyteca offer "confused notions" as an alternative to Descartes's "clear and distinct ideas" beyond the reach of human time. The principles of justice and equality, Perelman and Olbrechts-Tyteca maintained, were "confused notions," some that need to be strengthened and others that remain open to new and re-interpretations. Confused notions are those values, like justice, that have meanings that reveal themselves in and over time; they are responses to the concrete problems faced by humans.

Perelman and Olbrechts-Tyteca highlight the possibility of error, mistake, and moral impairment in decision-making that can be rectified through argumentation and deliberation. Argumentation, for both the classical rhetoricians and Perelman and Olbrechts-Tyteca, serves as a rhetorical expression of reason designed for audiences swayed by logic and emotion. This is the gist of their response to Vico's lament: in contrast to Descartes's system of reason, Perelman and Olbrechts-Tyteca's new rhetoric acknowledges and develops an informal logic, one rooted in human time and experience, expressed through argumentation and persuasion. This new rhetoric was yoked to audiences and confused notions.

The *New Rhetoric* identifies three audiences, a particular (an audience of homogenous values), composite (an audience of heterogenous values), and universal (an audience representing all reasonable people). Audiences in *The New Rhetoric* are tethered to a robust sense of reason and reasoning that includes all expressions of logic. The universal audience, which Perelman and Olbrechts-Tyteca take some pain to define, is a speaker's constructed image of an ideal audience open to argument and deliberation in making value choices. This audience is in process; it changes as reason and knowledge evolves and unfolds.

Perelman and Olbrechts-Tyteca's informal logic hosts "confused notions" (truth, justice, etc.) as the basis of accepted values. These can be developed and strengthened through epideictic discourse, which celebrates common values and precedent. They can be challenged through and with argumentation, and their meaning can be changed and improved, as illustrated in the subsequent case study. Their new rhetoric both answers Vico's lament and helps explain the moral breakthrough in *Lawrence v. Texas* (2003), a landmark decision that ruled unconstitutional a Texas law criminalizing sexual relations between persons of the same sex.

In this chapter, Perelman and Olbrechts-Tyteca's new rhetoric will serve as a lens designed to explain why *Lawrence*, in the words of the distinguished constitutional scholar Laurence Tribe, "may well be remembered as the *Brown v. Board* of gay and lesbian America." During the 2002 term of the US Supreme Court, the justices revisited the conclusions the court reached in the 1986 case *Bowers v. Hardwick*. In *Bowers*, the Supreme Court considered the following question: Does the constitution confer a fundamental right guaranteeing same-sex intimacy? The answer the court offered in *Bowers* was no. The states could pass laws criminalizing same-sex intimacy, the court ruled, because decriminalized same-sex intimacy was, according to the authorities the court cited, an "infamous crime against nature," an offense of "deeper malignity" than rape, and "a crime not fit to be named."

In *Lawrence v. Texas*, announced on June 26, 2003, the court ruled that "*Bowers* was not correct when it was decided, is not correct today, and is hereby overruled." The decision, written by Associate Justice Anthony Kennedy, declared that Texas had no good reason to treat same-sex intimacy differently than opposite-sex intimacy. Citizens engaging in same-sex intimacy, Kennedy insisted, deserved "dignity." In *Lawrence*, the Supreme Court interred the cruel reasoning in *Bowers*, marking an advance both for same-sex couples and the cause of constitutional justice. The moral advance in *Lawrence* is a result of rhetorical reasoning and can be illuminated by five concepts drawn from Perelman and Olbrechts-Tyteca's new rhetoric.

Lawrence v. Texas is a truly striking moment for the Supreme Court. For a majority opinion to claim that the Supreme Court was "not correct" in an important case and quite directly reverse a recent precedent makes that opinion deserving of close study with the tools provided by rhetoric. Kennedy uses rhetorical reason to explain why the court was "not correct" in *Bowers*. In so doing, he crafts a decision designed to honor and then plumb the US Constitution for values that are not expressed in the form of formal logic, mathematics, or a rationality untethered to human culture. He then seeks out evidence from a host of different and independent sources to challenge the conclusions of *Bowers* that same-sex intimacy can be criminalized. To be sure, the decision had its weaknesses, but Professor Tribe is right, *Lawrence v. Texas* should be joined with *Brown v. Board* as advances in moral thinking, a result of the proper use of rhetorical reason.

CHAÏM PERELMAN AND LUCIE OLBRECHTS-TYTECA, *THE NEW RHETORIC* (1958)

Editors' Note: The excerpts are from Chaïm Perleman and Lucie Olbrechts-Tyteca, *The New Rhetoric: A Treatise on Argumentation*. Translated by John Wilkinson and Purcel Weaver. Notre Dame, IN: University of Notre Dame Press, 1969. Permission granted. Internal footnotes are omitted.[3]

Frank Note: Among the many concepts in Perelman and Olbrechts-Tyteca's *New Rhetoric*, five help explain the power of Kennedy's reasoning in *Lawrence*: (1) the rule of justice, (2) confused notions, (3) epideictic discourse, (4) argumentation, and (5) the universal audience. What follows are explanations of these five concepts and excerpts from the *New Rhetoric* that then will help explain the rhetorical reasoning in *Lawrence*.

1. The Rule of Justice

Frank Note: Perelman and Olbrechts-Tyteca place the principles of equality and justice at the center of their new rhetoric. In so doing, they recapture the classical rhetorical tradition's understanding that values and judgments take place in time, that there are no immaculate methods to determine truth, and that the formal methods of math and geometry often do not produce wise decisions. The application of the rule of justice yields the best results through argumentation yoked to "foundations of concrete" human situations. In *Lawrence* the Supreme Court considered the best and most recent evidence on the status of same-sex intimacy, deciding that the evidence and reasoning set forth in *Bowers* did not justify treating people who engage in same-sex intimacy unequally.

> The rule of justice requires giving identical treatment to beings or situations of the same kind. The reasonableness of this rule and the validity that it is recognized as having derived from the principle of inertia, from which originates in particular the importance that is given to precedent. For the rule of justice to serve as the basis of a rigorous demonstration, the objects to which it applies ought to be identical, that is, completely interchangeable. However, this is never the case. These objects always differ in some respect, and the great problem,

which gives rise to most controversies, is to decide whether the observed differences are negligible or not, or, in other words, whether the objects differ in essential characteristics, that is in the only ones which must be taken into account in the administration of justice. The rule of justice recognizes the argumentative value of what one of us has called *formal justice*, according to which "beings in the same essential category should be treated in the same way." Formal justice does not tell when two objects belong to the same category; neither does it specify the treatment they should be given. Indeed, in every concrete situation, a prior classification of the objects and the existence of precedents as to the manner of treating them is indispensable. The rule of justice furnishes the foundation which makes it possible to pass from earlier cases to future cases. It makes it possible to present the use of precedent in the form of a quasi-logical argument. . . .

Application of the rule of justice, following upon a prior likening of two types of situations, can lead to results which are very different from those which were desired. The rule, which is purely formal, requires, for its application, a foundation in the concrete, anchored to opinions and agreements which are rarely beyond argument.

2. Confused Notions

Frank Note: Vico lamented the limited viewpoints of Descartes and other thinkers who narrowed all truths to definitive truths, beyond the reach of time. Descartes had no room or tolerance for ambiguity and sought a perfect fit between language and ideas. Perelman and Olbrechts-Tyteca's introduction of "confused notions" identified key values, like justice and equality, that were "plastic." They had meaning and an essence that lived in human time; they were open to evolution and reframing.

Univocal passage from the word to the idea it represents was seen by the theoreticians of the past as a phenomenon resulting from the good use of language. One assumes also that this idea can be precisely determined by resort to other ideas that are themselves expressed by univocal terms or that it can be the object of a rational intuition. For centuries, many good minds have found in the artificial language of mathematicians an ideal of clarity and univocity that natural languages, with their lesser development, should strive to imitate. From this viewpoint, any ambiguity, obscurity, or confusion is considered an imperfection that can be eliminated not only in theory but also in fact. Because of the univocity and the exactness of its terms, scientific language is held to be the best instrument for demonstration and verification, and one would like to impose these characteristics on all language.

But are all the functions of language linked in the same way to these qualities of univocity and exactness, and is it even possible to say that scientific language is really free from all ambiguity? Discussion in *Philosophy of Science* of an article by M. Black led A. Benjamin to the conclusion that vague ideas are an integral part of science and that any theory of meaning which denies their existence is not a theory of science.

How is this change to be explained? It seems to follow from the fact that one has come to see that a notion can be considered univocal only if its field of application is wholly determined, which is possible only in a formal system from which every unforeseen element has been excluded: the notion of "bishop" in the game of chess satisfies this condition. But the situation is different where one is dealing with notions developed within a scientific or juridical system and which must apply to future events whose nature cannot always be completely determined. . . .

To the extent that future experiences and the way in which they are to be examined are not entirely foreseeable, it is essential to conceive even the most precisely stated terms as surrounded by a fringe of indefiniteness sufficient to enable them to be applied to reality. A perfectly clear notion is one of which all cases of application are known, so that it does not admit of a new unforeseen use. Only divine knowledge or knowledge limited by conventions satisfies such a requirement.

For these reasons it is not possible to do as Bobbio suggests, and compare the exactness of law with that of mathematics. Nor can we follow Kelsen's proposal to regard law simply as a closed order. A judge cannot do as a formal logician does and limit the field of application of his system once and for all. He is in danger of being guilty of a denial of justice if he refuses to make a decision "on the ground of the silence, obscurity, or deficiency of the law" (Code Napoleon, art. 4). In each case, he must be able to decide whether or not the provision that is invoked can be used under the circumstances, even if these circumstances were not foreseen by the legislature. This compels him to make a decision based on specific reasons as to the way he will define one or another juridical category.

Frank Note: Perelman and Olbrechts-Tyteca cite the prominent Italian political scientist Norberto Bobbio's contention that law should seek the security and status of mathematics. They also cite Hans Kelman, well-known for developing a "pure theory" of the law, a theory that would treat legal principles as expressions of formal logic, protected from the influences of politics, emotions, and practical logic.[4]

When the use of notions has not been formalized, their application presents problems connected with the formulation and determination of the concepts.

These problems inevitably get more difficult as the notions used get vaguer and more woolly. This is the case, in particular, with notions which can be referred explicitly or implicitly to indeterminate groupings, such as negative phrases like "that which is not living" and "those who do not pay taxes." The difficulty is greatest with vague notions—*justice*, for example—which can be made precise and applied only by selecting and bringing to the fore certain of their aspects that are incompatible with others or with notions—of which merit is one—whose use can be conceived only in terms of their vagueness: an evaluation has to be made by referring both to the subject who acts and to the result obtained.

Use of the notions of a living language thus very often appears not as a simple choice of data applicable to other data, but as a construction of theories and as an interpretation of reality by means of the notions which they make it possible to develop. And that is not all. Language is not only a means of communication: it is also an instrument for acting on minds, a means of persuasion. Now, the influence of the needs of argumentation on the malleability of notions has not received the emphasis it deserves.

Where the basic notions of morality and philosophy are concerned, only argumentation and controversy can explain why nuances are introduced and why distinctions are brought in that show the ambiguity of what had previously been considered clear. And it is precisely because the notions used in argumentation are not univocal and have no fixed meaning that will not change that the conclusions of an argumentation are not binding.

3. Argumentation

Frank Note: Influenced by Vico's lament, Perelman and Olbrechts-Tyteca begin their *New Rhetoric* with this statement: "The publication of a treatise devoted to argumentation and this subject's connection with the ancient tradition of Greek rhetoric and dialectic constitutes a break with a concept of reason and reasoning due to Descartes which has set its mark on Western philosophy for the last three centuries." The concept of reason and reasoning they develop is based on the rule of justice, assumes that notions are confused, and is expressed in rhetorical argumentation. In their system, rhetoric is concerned with audiences and argumentation with informal reason and logic. Their new rhetoric is new because it breaks the hold of Descartes on Western philosophy by placing concrete and situated human audiences at the center of knowledge rather than formal mathematics, geometry, and logic, identifying human argumentation as an expression of reason and informal logic.

Although it would scarcely occur to anyone to deny that the power of deliberation and argumentation is a distinctive sign of a reasonable being, the study of the methods of proof used to secure adherence has been completely neglected by logicians and epistemologists for the last three centuries. This state of affairs is due to the noncompulsive element in the arguments adduced in support of a thesis. The very nature of deliberation and argumentation is opposed to necessity and self-evidence, since no one deliberates where the solution is necessary or argues against what is self-evident. The domain of argumentation is that of the credible, the plausible, the probable, to the degree that the latter eludes the certainty of calculations. Now Descartes's concept, clearly expressed in the first part of *The Discourse on the Method*, was to "take well nigh for false everything which was only plausible." It was this philosopher who made the self-evident the mark of reason, and considered rational only those demonstrations which, starting from clear and distinct ideas, extended, by means of apodictic proofs, the self-evidence of the axioms to the derived theorems.

Reasoning *more geometrico* was the model proposed to philosophers desirous of constructing a system of thought which might attain to the dignity of a science. A rational science cannot indeed be content with more or less probable opinions; it must elaborate a system of necessary propositions which will impose itself on every rational being, concerning which agreement is inevitable. This means that disagreement is a sign of error. "Whenever two men come to opposite decisions about the same matter," says Descartes, "one of them at least must certainly be in the wrong, and apparently there is not even one of them who knows; for if the reasoning of one was sound and clear he would be able so to lay it before the other as finally to succeed in convincing his understanding also."

What is important to the partisans of the experimental and inductive sciences is not so much the necessity of propositions as their truth, their conformity with facts. The empiricist considers as evidence not "that which the mind does or must yield to, but that which it ought to yield to, namely, that, by yielding to which, its belief is kept conformable to fact." The evidence which the empiricist recognizes is not that of rational but of sensible intuition, and the method he advocates is not that of the deductive but of the experimental sciences, but he is nonetheless convinced that the only valid proofs are those recognized by the natural sciences.

What conforms to scientific method is rational, in the broader sense of the word. Works on logic devoted to the study of the methods of proof, essentially limited to the study of deduction, usually supplemented by some remarks on inductive reasoning which merely consider the means not of constructing, but of verifying hypotheses, seldom venture to examine the proofs used in human sciences. The logician is indeed inspired by the Cartesian ideal and feels at ease only in studying those proofs which Aristotle styled analytic, since all other methods do not manifest the same characteristic of necessity. This tendency has been strongly reinforced during the last century, a period in which, under the influence of mathematical logicians, logic has been limited to formal logic, that is to the study of the methods of proof used in the mathematical sciences. The result is that reasonings extraneous to the domain of the purely formal elude logic altogether, and, as a consequence, they also elude reason. This reason, which Descartes hoped would, at least in principle, solve all problems set to man the solution of which is already possessed by the divine mind, has become more and more limited in its jurisdiction, to the point that whatever eludes reduction to the formal presents it with unsurmountable difficulties. . . .

Only the existence of an argumentation that is neither compelling nor arbitrary can give meaning to human freedom, a state in which a reasonable choice can be exercised. If freedom were no more than necessary adherence to a previously given natural order, it would exclude all possibility of choice; and if the exercise of freedom were not based on reasons, every choice would be irrational and would be reduced to an arbitrary decision operating in an intellectual void. It is because of the possibility of argumentation which provides reasons, but not compelling reasons, that it is possible to escape the dilemma: adherence to an objectively and universally valid truth, or recourse to suggestion and violence to secure acceptance for our opinions and decisions. The theory of argumentation will help to develop what a logic of value judgments has tried in vain to provide, namely the justification of the possibility of a human community in the sphere of action when this justification cannot be based on a reality or objective truth. And its starting point, in making this contribution, is an analysis of those forms of reasoning which, though they are indispensable in practice, have from the time of Descartes been neglected by logicians and theoreticians of knowledge.

4. Epideictic Discourse

Frank Note: The ancient rhetorical tradition, anchored in the writings of Aristotle and Cicero, called on speakers to adjust their speeches to the values of the audience. These values, in turn, serve as the truths accepted and acted upon by the audience before any effort is made to persuade. Aristotle introduced the term "epideictic" to designate speech designed to celebrate and reinforce the values held by an audience. Perelman and Olbrechts-Tyteca recast and update the epideictic to capture the function it serves to build a shared value frame for social conflict and to promote education. Importantly, Perelman and Olbrechts-Tyteca see the epideictic as argumentative, that it can seek to modify values and "a pre-existing state of affairs."

According to Aristotle, the speaker sets himself different goals depending on the kind of speech he is making: in deliberative oratory, to counsel what is expedient, that is, the best; in legal oratory to establish what is just; and in epideictic oratory, which is concerned with praise and blame, his sole concern is with what is beautiful or ugly. It is a question, then, of recognizing values. But in the absence of the concept of value judgment, and of that of intensity of adherence, the theoreticians of speech, from Aristotle on, readily confused the concept of the beautiful, as the object of the speech (which was, besides, equivalent to the concept of "good") with the aesthetic value of the speech itself. . . .

Our own view is that epideictic oratory forms a central part of the art of persuasion, and the lack of understanding shown toward it results from a false conception of the effects of argumentation.

The effectiveness of an exposition designed to secure a proper degree of adherence of an audience to the arguments presented to it can be assessed only in terms of the actual aim the speaker has set himself. The intensity of the adherence sought is not limited to obtaining purely intellectual results, to a declaration that a certain thesis seems more probable than another, but will very often be reinforced until the desired action is actually performed. Demosthenes, considered to be one of the models of classical eloquence, spent most of his efforts not just in getting the Athenians to make decisions in conformity with his wishes, but in urging them, by every means at his command, to carry out the decisions once they were made. . . .

The taking of a decision stands halfway, so to speak, between a disposition to take action and the action itself, between pure speculation and effective action.

The intensity of adherence, aiming at effective action, cannot be measured by the degree of probability attributed to the accepted argument, but rather by the obstacles overcome by the action and the sacrifices and choices it leads to and which can be justified by the adherence. The existence of an interval, whether long or short, between the time of adherence and the time of the action it was designed to stimulate explains the intervention into the debate, after it has supposedly ended, of values that had been overlooked or played down, or maybe of new elements that arose after the decision was made. This intervention, the likelihood of which is increased if in the meanwhile there has been a change in the situation, has a twofold result: on the one hand it is hazardous to evaluate the effectiveness of a speech, and, secondly, the adherence gained by a speech can always advantageously be reinforced. It is in this perspective that epideictic oratory has significance and importance for argumentation, because it strengthens the disposition toward action by increasing adherence to the values it lauds. . . .

Unlike the demonstration of a geometrical theorem, which establishes once and for all a logical connection between speculative truths, the argumentation in epideictic discourse sets out to increase the intensity of adherence to certain values, which might not be contested when considered on their own but may nevertheless not prevail against other values that might come into conflict with them. The speaker tries to establish a sense of communion centered around particular values recognized by the audience, and to this end he uses the whole range of means available to the rhetorician for purposes of amplification and enhancement.

In epideictic oratory every device of literary art is appropriate, for it is a matter of combining all the factors that can promote this communion of the audience. . . .

In epideictic oratory, the speaker turns educator.

5. The Universal Audience

Frank Note: Perelman and Olbrechts-Tyteca's universal audience is the speaker's psychological construction of how humans in general should reason and deliberate. This construction will vary with culture and time. The universal audience does establish a standard for argumentation; the speaker should strive to meet this standard. Justice Kennedy, in *Lawrence*, acknowledges that the reasoning in affected by culture and time in which advocates and audiences live, reflecting an implicit understanding of and the importance of adapting to the universal audience.

Argumentation aimed exclusively at a particular audience has the drawback that the speaker, by the very fact of adapting to the views of his listeners, might rely on arguments that are foreign or even directly opposed to what is acceptable to persons other than those he is presently addressing. This danger is apparent in the case of a composite audience, which the speaker has to resolve into its constituent parts for the purposes of his argumentation. For a composite audience, such as a parliamentary assembly, will have to be regrouped as a single entity to make a decision, and it is extremely easy for the opponent of an incautious speaker to turn against him all of the arguments he directed to the different parts of the audience, either by setting the arguments against each other so as to show their incompatibility or by presenting them to those they were not meant for. This explains the relative weakness of arguments that are accepted only by particular audiences and the value attached to opinions that enjoy unanimous approval, particularly approval by persons or groups who agree on very few matters.

Naturally, the value of this unanimity depends on the number and quality of those expressing it. Its highest point is reached when there is *agreement of the universal audience*. This refers of course, in this case, not to an experimentally proven fact, but to a universality, since for legitimate reasons, we need not take into consideration those which are not part of it. . . .

> Everyone constitutes the universal audience from what he knows of his fellow men, in such a way as to transcend the few oppositions he is aware of. Each individual, each culture, has thus its own conception of the universal audience. The study of these variations would be very instructive, as we would learn from it what men, at different times in history, have regarded as *real*, *true*, and *objectively valid*. . . .
>
> We believe, then, that audiences are not independent of one another, and that particular concrete audiences are capable of validating a concept of the universal audience which characterizes them. On the other hand, it is the undefined universal audience that is invoked to pass judgment on what is the concept of the universal audience appropriate to such a concrete audience, to examine simultaneously the manner in which it was composed, which are the individuals who comprise it, according to the adopted criterion, and whether this criterion is legitimate. It can be said that audiences pass judgment on one another.

LAWRENCE V. TEXAS, 539 U.S. 558 (2003)

Frank Note: The five concepts discussed in the previous section help illuminate the rhetorical reasoning powering *Lawrence*. In this section, Perelman and Olbrechts-Tyteca's new rhetoric will serve as a lens through which the four discrete arguments developed in *Lawrence* are viewed and explained. In his majority opinion Justice Kennedy uses the rule of justice to argue for the decriminalization of same-sex intimacy; he treats liberty as a confused notion, open to new interpretations and reinterpretations; he engages in epideictic argumentation, assuming that he and his audience share and endorse the search for constitutional justice; he disagrees and argues with colleagues who ratify the reasoning in *Bowers*, contesting their interpretation of history; and finally, he addresses his understanding of the universal audience, seeking to use it as a norm for argument evaluation.

This case deals with same-sex intimacy. Kennedy used the term "homosexual" in this excerpt. *Lawrence* deals specifically with the right of same-sex intimacy and serves as a precedent for granting rights to the broader LGBTQ+ community. Modern usage calls for the use of "LGBTQ+ individuals" rather than "homosexuals."

Editors' Note: Bracketed text indicates revisions here of text from the official reporter. Internal footnotes and some citations are omitted.

> The Court began its substantive discussion in *Bowers* [*v. Hardwick*, 478 U.S. 186 (1986)] as follows: "The issue presented is whether the Federal Constitution confers a fundamental right upon homosexuals to engage in sodomy and hence invalidates the laws of the many States that still make such conduct illegal and have done so for a very long time." That statement, we now conclude,

discloses the Court's own failure to appreciate the extent of the liberty at stake. To say that the issue in *Bowers* was simply the right to engage in certain sexual conduct demeans the claim the individual put forward, just as it would demean a married couple were it to be said marriage is simply about the right to have sexual intercourse. The laws involved in *Bowers* and here are, to be sure, statutes that purport to do no more than prohibit a particular sexual act. Their penalties and purposes, though, have more far-reaching consequences, touching upon the most private human conduct, sexual behavior, and in the most private of places, the home. The statutes do seek to control a personal relationship that, whether or not entitled to formal recognition in the law, is within the liberty of persons to choose without being punished as criminals.

This, as a general rule, should counsel against attempts by the State, or a court, to define the meaning of the relationship or to set its boundaries absent injury to a person or abuse of an institution the law protects. It suffices for us to acknowledge that adults may choose to enter upon this relationship in the confines of their homes and their own private lives and still retain their dignity as free persons. When sexuality finds overt expression in intimate conduct with another person, the conduct can be but one element in a personal bond that is more enduring. The liberty protected by the Constitution allows homosexual persons the right to make this choice.

Having misapprehended the claim of liberty there presented to it, and thus stating the claim to be whether there is a fundamental right to engage in consensual sodomy, the *Bowers* Court said: "Proscriptions against that conduct have ancient roots." *Id.* at 192. In academic writings, and in many of the scholarly *amicus* briefs filed to assist the Court in this case, there are fundamental criticisms of the historical premises relied upon by the majority and concurring opinions in *Bowers*. Brief for Cato Institute as *Amicus Curiae* 16–17; Brief for American Civil Liberties Union et al. as *Amici Curiae* 15n-21; Brief for Professors of History et al. as *Amici Curiae* 3–10. We need not enter this debate in the attempt to reach a definitive historical judgment, but the following considerations counsel against adopting the definitive conclusions upon which *Bowers* placed such reliance.

At the outset it should be noted that there is no longstanding history in this country of laws directed at homosexual conduct as a distinct matter. Beginning in colonial times there were prohibitions of sodomy derived from the English criminal laws passed in the first instance by the Reformation Parliament of 1533. The English prohibition was understood to include relations between men and women as well as relations between men and men. See, *e.g., King v. Wiseman*, 92 Eng. Rep. 774, 775 (K. B. 1718) (interpreting "mankind" in Act of 1533 as including women and girls). Nineteenth-century commentators similarly read

American sodomy, buggery, and crime-against-nature statutes as criminalizing certain relations between men and women and between men and men. See, e.g., 2 J. Bishop, Criminal Law § 1028 (1858); 2 J. Chitty, Criminal Law 47n–50 (5th Am. ed. 1847); R. Desty, A Compendium of American Criminal Law 143 (1882); J. May, The Law of Crimes § 203 (2d ed. 1893). The absence of legal prohibitions focusing on homosexual conduct may be explained in part by noting that according to some scholars the concept of the homosexual as a distinct category of person did not emerge until the late 19th century. See, e.g., J. Katz, The Invention of Heterosexuality 10 (1995); J. D'Emilio & E. Freedman, Intimate Matters: A History of Sexuality in America 121 (2d ed. 1997) ("The modern terms *homosexuality* and *heterosexuality* do not apply to an era that had not yet articulated these distinctions"). Thus early American sodomy laws were not directed at homosexuals as such but instead sought to prohibit non- procreative sexual activity more generally. This does not suggest approval of homosexual conduct. It does tend to show that this particular form of conduct was not thought of as a separate category from like conduct between heterosexual persons. . . .

To the extent *Bowers* relied on values we share with a wider civilization, it should be noted that the reasoning and holding in *Bowers* have been rejected elsewhere. The European Court of Human Rights has followed not *Bowers* but its own decision in *Dudgeon v. United Kingdom*. See *P. G. & J. H. v. United Kingdom*, App. No. 00044787/98, ¶56 (Eur. Ct. H. R., Sept. 25, 2001); *Modinos v. Cyprus*, 259 Eur. Ct. H. R. (1993); *Norris v. Ireland*, 142 Eur. Ct. H. R. (1988). Other nations, too, have taken action consistent with an affirmation of the protected right of homosexual adults to engage in intimate, consensual conduct. See Brief for Mary Robinson et al. as *Amici Curiae* 11–12. The right the petitioners seek in this case has been accepted as an integral part of human freedom in many other countries. There has been no showing that in this country the governmental interest in circumscribing personal choice is somehow more legitimate or urgent. . . .

The rationale of *Bowers* does not withstand careful analysis. In his dissenting opinion in *Bowers* Justice Stevens came to these conclusions:

> Our prior cases make two propositions abundantly clear. First, the fact that the governing majority in a State has traditionally viewed a particular practice as immoral is not a sufficient reason for upholding a law prohibiting the practice; neither history nor tradition could save a law prohibiting miscegenation from constitutional attack. Second, individual decisions by married persons, concerning the intimacies of their physical relationship, even when not intended to produce offspring, are a

> form of "liberty" protected by the Due Process Clause of the Fourteenth Amendment. Moreover, this protection extends to intimate choices by unmarried as well as married persons. 478 U.S. at 216 (footnotes and citations omitted).

Justice Stevens' analysis, in our view, should have been controlling in *Bowers* and should control here.

CRITICAL ASSESSMENT

Justice Kennedy uses the rule of justice to argue for equal treatment of gays and lesbians; he treats liberty as a confused notion, open to new and reinterpretations; he engages in epideictic argumentation, assuming that he and his audience share and endorse the search for constitutional justice; he disagrees and argues with colleagues who ratify the reasoning in *Bowers*, contesting their interpretation of history; he addresses his understanding of the universal audience, seeking to use it as a norm for argument evaluation.

In *Lawrence*, the court held that the notion of equality resists any one definition or understanding, which allowed Justice Kennedy to (1) acknowledge the court's mistake in *Bowers* and (2) broaden the definition of equal treatment to include homosexual conduct. Using the traditional mode of argumentation in Supreme Court decisions, Justice Kennedy employed the voice of educator. The Supreme Court in *Lawrence* uses rhetorical reason to admit the mistakes in *Bowers* and to make an argument in favor of a more expansive definition of equality. These notions provide a method and vocabulary for clarifying why *Lawrence* constitutes a significant advance for gays and lesbians. Using a principle quite similar to the rule of justice, Justice Kennedy, in a direct confrontation with the reasoning in *Bowers*, held that gays and lesbians should receive the same protections granted to all Americans, which turned on the assumption that justice and equality are confused notions. Here, he relied on epideictic discourse, drawing from his friendship with Gordon Schaber, a gay man, and the legal reasoning of Harvard law professor Laurence Tribe.[5] Tribe, in an amicus brief he wrote for the ACLU, offered a critique of *Bowers* in the conservative voice, allowing him to argue that the court in *Bowers* had erred in its understanding of tradition, which in turn, permitted Justice Kennedy to use epideictic discourse in making the case for gay equality and dignity. Justice Kennedy uses a rhetorically inflected sense of reason in *Lawrence* to persuade particular, composite, and universal audiences that *Bowers* was in error.

The following discussion questions are designed to demonstrate how the concepts offered by Perelman and Olbrechts-Tyteca help to explain the *Lawrence* decision.

DISCUSSION QUESTIONS

Discussion Question 1: Perelman and Olbrechts-Tyteca agree with Aristotle: truth and justice are stronger than their opposites. If they are right, then explain why Justice Stevens's dissent in *Bowers* failed to persuade the majority but Justice Kennedy was successful in *Lawrence*.

Discussion Question 2: Assume that you agree with Justice Antonin Scalia's dissent in *Lawrence*. He argued that "the matters appropriate for this Court's resolution are only three: Texas' prohibition of sodomy neither infringes a fundamental right (which the court does not dispute), nor is unsupported by a rational relation to what the Constitution considers a legitimate state interest, nor denies the equal protection of the laws." If Perelman, Olbrechts-Tyteca, and Aristotle are right, that truth and justice are stronger than their opposites, then explain why Justice Scalia's dissent in *Lawrence* failed to persuade the majority.

Discussion Question 3: If Perelman, Olbrechts-Tyteca, and Aristotle are right, that truth and justice are stronger than their opposites, then explain why Justice Kennedy in *Lawrence* failed to persuade those who dissented.

Discussion Question 4: Perelman and Olbrechts-Tyteca held that argumentation is an expression of nonformal reasoning, that it runs parallel with mathematical and more formal expressions of reason. Do you think it is possible to develop a mathematics of constitutional questions that might answer the questions raised in *Lawrence*?

Discussion Question 5: Perelman and Olbrechts-Tyteca's rule of justice is in use by Justice Kennedy in his decision. What are the risks of using the rule of justice with the principles of rhetoric?

Discussion Question 6: Justice Scalia disagrees with Justice Kennedy. Justice Scalia also uses the rule of justice, epideictic rhetoric, and other tools of rhetoric to argue with and against Justice Kennedy. Among the several arguments in his dissent, Scalia claims:

- Kennedy has invented "a brand-new 'constitutional right'" giving same-sex couples the right to sexual intimacy.
- Kennedy has, wrongly, given power to the courts rather than "to the people" and their legislatures to make decisions about the legality of same-sex intimacy.
- Kennedy does not support the claim that "laws prohibiting sodomy do not seem to have been enforced against consenting adults acting in private."

Given they both offer arguments that some audiences would find reasonable, how would you judge their arguments? What tools are needed to make sure you judge well?

Discussion Question 7: Justice Kennedy appeals to the universal audience in *Lawrence* by referring to and affirming how other countries deal with the issues facing him. He also appeals to an imaginary universal audience that evolves in its understanding of liberty and dignity. Do you think the universal audience is a useful concept?

ADDITIONAL READINGS

Aristotle. *On Rhetoric: A Theory of Civic Discourse.* Translated by George A. Kennedy. New York: Oxford University Press, 1991.

Bobbio, Norberto. "Scienza del diritto e analisi del linguaggio." *Rivista Trimestrale di Diritto e Procedura Civile* 4, no. 2 (1950): 342–67.

Bolduc, Michelle, and David A. Frank. "Chaïm Perelman and Lucie Olbrechts-Tyteca's 'On Temporality as a Characteristic of Argumentation:' Commentary and Translation." *Philosophy and Rhetoric* 43, no. 4 (2010): 308–15.

Crosswhite, James. *Deep Rhetoric: Philosophy, Reason, Violence, Justice, Wisdom.* Chicago: University of Chicago Press, 2013.

Frank, David A. "The New Rhetoric, Judaism, and Post Enlightenment Thought: The Cultural Origins of Perelmanian Philosophy." *Quarterly Journal of Speech* 83, no. 3 (1997): 311–31.

Frank, David A., and Michelle K. Bolduc. "Chaïm Perelman's 'First Philosophies and Regressive Philosophy:' Commentary and Translation." *Philosophy and Rhetoric* 36, no. 3 (2003): 177–88.

Kelsen, Hans. *Reine Rechtslehre: Einleitung in die rechtswissenschaftliche Problematik.* Leipzig: F. Deuticke, 1934.

Mootz, Francis J., III. "Introduction to Recalling Vico's Lament: The Role of Prudence and Rhetoric in Law and Legal Education." *Chicago-Kent Law Review* 83, no. 3 (2008): 1097–105.

Perelman, Chaïm. *The Idea of Justice and the Problem of Argument.* New York: Routledge, 1963.

———. *Justice.* 1945. Repr., New York: Random House, 1967.

Perelman, Chaïm, and Lucie Olbrechts-Tyteca. *The New Rhetoric: A Treatise on Argumentation.* Translated by John Wilkinson and Purcell Weaver. Notre Dame, IN: University of Notre Dame Press, 1969.

———. *Traité de l'argumentation: La nouvelle rhétorique.* 2 vols. Paris: Presses Universitaires de France, 1958.

Stolberg, Sheryl Gay. "Justice Anthony Kennedy's Tolerance Is Seen in His Sacramento Roots." *New York Times*, June 21, 2015.

Tribe, Laurence H. "Lawrence v. Texas: The Fundamental Right That Dare Not Speak Its Name." *Harvard Law Review* 117 (2003): 1893–956.

III

CLASSICAL RHETORIC AND CONTEMPORARY LAW

5

Antiphon the Athenian

Probability Arguments in Ancient Greece and Today

Michael Gagarin

INTRODUCTION

Because no amount of clear, direct evidence is ever in itself 100 percent probative, in any legal case there will always be some amount of uncertainty and thus a need for argument that lacks certainty and depends on probability or likelihood. Such arguments were of special interest to the Greek Sophists of the fifth century BCE and especially to Antiphon, a noted intellectual with a special interest in law. Because of the absence of forensic science in antiquity, in most cases no direct evidence was available except perhaps for witness testimony, and probability arguments thus dominated many forensic arguments. Similar arguments are common in most contemporary litigation, where they are categorized as circumstantial evidence. This chapter will examine the discussion and use of probability arguments in Antiphon's *First Tetralogy* and the discussion and use of circumstantial evidence in the closing arguments of the trial of O. J. Simpson. The same strengths and weaknesses of these arguments are evident in both cases.

Antiphon (ca. 480–11 BCE) was one of a number of fifth-century Greek intellectuals who have come to be grouped under the name Sophists, even though they had no formal association with one another. They did share some characteristics, including a spirit of inquiry and skepticism, which frequently manifested itself as a challenge to traditional ways of thinking. Their challenges were often provocative, sometimes paradoxical. Protagoras criticized Homer for beginning *the Iliad* with a feminine word "wrath" (*mēnin*) because "wrath" is something masculine; Gorgias argued that "nothing exists." In general, the Sophists were suspicious of absolute truths but nonetheless explored moral issues like justice, a special interest of Antiphon. In addition, all the Sophists were interested in logos in its many senses: "word," "language," "argument," "logic," "reason," "rationality." Prodicus specialized in making fine distinctions among near synonyms; Protagoras emphasized the importance of arguing both sides of a case; and Gorgias stressed the power of logos to influence the behavior of others.

Plato strongly opposed the Sophists' ideas, criticizing them for being moral relativists and having no concern for truth. He sharply distinguishes them from his teacher Socrates, though scholars recently have begun to treat Socrates, with his persistent, provocative, inquiring mind, as himself a Sophist. Plato saw himself as continuing the work of Socrates, but whereas Socrates famously said that the only thing he knew was that he knew nothing, Plato developed a theory of absolute truths (Forms) that stands in opposition to the views of Socrates and the Sophists. This led him to condemn the Sophists' use of probability arguments, claiming that they thought "probability arguments should be more honored than truths."[1] Although this claim is demonstrably false, it has been echoed by most modern scholars writing about the Sophists.[2]

Like the other Greek Sophists, Antiphon's writings exist today mostly in fragments, but six legal works survive in full, three cases written for litigants in actual trials and three Tetralogies. Each of the Tetralogies contains four speeches from a fictional homicide case, two each by the plaintiff and defendant, the same format as in actual homicide trials at the time. The *First Tetralogy* is a showcase for probability arguments. The facts are few: a man is found dead in the street late at night; his attendant was also killed, but the people who discovered the body reported that just before dying the attendant identified the accused as the killer. This is considered weak evidence, however, because the attendant knew that his master disliked the accused; he is also a slave and a slave's testimony was not normally admitted in court unless the slave had previously been interrogated under threat of torture, with both sides present. The plaintiff, therefore, relies primarily on probability arguments, as does the defendant. The plaintiff argues that no one else is likely to have killed the man and that the accused had a strong motive for the killing because he was being prosecuted by the victim in another case and was in danger of losing all his property. The defendant responds that there are other, more likely suspects, and that the alleged motive was insufficient to make him risk being caught and put to death. The plaintiff then rebuts the defendant's arguments; this is followed by a rebuttal by the defendant. Interspersed among these probability arguments is a kind of metadiscourse about the general nature and validity of probability arguments.

The O. J. Simpson case was a sensational murder trial that ran for eleven months in 1994–95 and ended with Simpson's acquittal on all counts. He had been accused of killing his former wife and another man, who was with her. There was very little hard evidence tying Simpson to the killings, and what little there was—a bloody glove that may or may not have been his, other traces of blood at the scene and in Simpson's car, some hairs found at the scene, and a bloody shoeprint—was in dispute. Both sides therefore made considerable use of circumstantial evidence, drawing inferences from various facts that were established during the trial. The prosecution, defense, and presiding judge also discussed the general nature and validity of circumstantial evidence vis-à-vis direct evidence.[3]

ANTIPHON THE ATHENIAN, *FIRST TETRALOGY*

Editors' Note: The excerpts from the four speeches of Antiphon's First Tetralogy (no. 2 in the corpus of Antiphon's speeches) are taken from Gagarin and MacDowell 1998, with slight modifications. Most of the introductions and final remarks are omitted from all four speeches, as they say nothing about probability.

Speech 1

Gagarin Note: The plaintiff begins his first speech by connecting his use of probability arguments to the difficulty of obtaining direct evidence in this case. He concludes by reasserting the need for probability arguments in cases like this.

> It is not difficult to obtain a conviction for crimes planned by ordinary people, but when those with natural ability and previous experience commit a crime at that point in their lives when their mental facilities are at their height, it is difficult to get any knowledge or proof of it. Because of the great risk involved, in their planning they pay close attention to security and do not undertake anything without first guarding against all possible suspicion. You should be aware of this and even if you accept a point as only probable, you should have confidence in it.
>
> Common criminals are not likely to have killed the man, for no one who went so far as to risk his life would abandon the gain he had securely in hand; and yet the victims were still wearing their cloaks when they were found.

Gagarin Note: At the time, a heavy cloak was usually the most valuable item a man had with him when walking outside in the cold.

> The killer wasn't someone who was drunk, for he would have been identified by his fellow drinkers. He wasn't killed in a quarrel, for they would not have been quarreling in the middle of the night in a deserted place. And no one would have killed him by accident when aiming at someone else, for then his attendant would not have been killed too. So all other suspicions are removed, and the circumstances of the death show that it was deliberately planned. Who is

more likely to have attacked him than someone who has already suffered great harm from him and expects to suffer even more? That person is the defendant, who is his old enemy and has prosecuted him many times on serious charges but never gained a conviction. In turn he was prosecuted even more often and on more serious charges, and since he never once won acquittal, he has lost most of his property. Most recently the defendant was indicted by him for theft of sacred property with a penalty of two talents. He knew full well he was guilty, he knew his opponent's ability from previous experience, and he harbored resentment from the earlier incidents. In all probability, therefore, he formed this plan and in all probability he killed the man to defend himself against this hostile action. Desire for revenge made him unmindful of the danger, and fear of impending disaster fired him with greater eagerness to attempt the crime. He hoped by this action to kill the man without being caught and to be free from that indictment, since without a prosecutor the case would be dropped.

Gagarin Note: There was no public prosecutor in Athens; all cases were brought by private individuals.

Even if he should be caught, he thought it more honorable to gain his revenge and suffer the consequences than to be a coward and do nothing but let himself be destroyed by the impending prosecution. He was quite certain he would be convicted in that case; otherwise he wouldn't have thought this trial offered him a better chance. These considerations forced him to commit this unholy crime. As for witnesses, if many had been present, we would have presented many here. But since only his attendant was present, those who heard him speak will testify. For he was still breathing when we picked him up and questioned him, and he said he recognized this man alone among those who attacked them.

Since, then, his guilt is established both by probability arguments and by those who were present, there is no way that his acquittal could be just or advantageous. For it would be impossible to convict those who plan crimes if they cannot be convicted either by the testimony of those present or by probability arguments.

Speech 2

Gagarin Note: The defendant begins his first speech with what we may call a "reverse-probability argument," namely that his strong motive would, in fact, make him unlikely to kill the man. He then argues that other suspects are likely to have killed the man and that the attendant's testimony is untrustworthy.

If the enormous hostility between us leads you [the jury] now to consider me the likely suspect, then it was even more likely that before committing the crime I would foresee that I was going to be the obvious suspect and far from committing the murder myself and willingly incurring the obvious suspicion, I would even prevent others from killing him if I learned that they were planning to do so. For if the deed itself showed that I was the killer, I was doomed, and even if I escaped detection, I was quite certain I would incur this suspicion. I am thus in this miserable position: not only am I forced to defend myself but I must also reveal the true killers. Still, I must try, for it seems that nothing is more bitter than necessity. I have no other way to proceed than with arguments the prosecutor used when he absolved others of the crime and claimed that the circumstances of the death show that I am the murderer. For if making them seem innocent makes the crime appear to be my doing, then it is only right that making them suspect should make me seem innocent.

It is not unlikely, as they claim, but likely that someone wandering around in the middle of the night would be killed for his cloak. That his cloak was not removed proves nothing. If the killers didn't remove it in time but left it there because they were frightened by others approaching, then they were acting prudently; they were not crazy to prefer their own safety to considerations of profit. If he wasn't killed for his cloak, perhaps he noticed others committing some crime and was killed so he wouldn't report it. Who knows? There are also many others who hated him almost as much as I did; surely one of these is more likely to have killed him. It was clear to them that I would be suspected, and I was quite certain that I would be blamed instead of them. As for the attendant's testimony, how can you believe it? Terrified by the danger, it is not likely that he recognized the killers, but it is likely he was persuaded to agree with his masters. Since the testimony of slaves in general is untrustworthy—otherwise we wouldn't torture them—how can it be right for you to believe this witness' testimony and destroy me?

If anyone thinks probability arguments carry as much weight against me as the truth, by the same reasoning he should consider that it was more probable that I would watch out for the safety of my plan, and would take care not to be present at the crime rather than let this man recognize me as he was being killed. Unless I was out of my mind, I did not think this crime presented less danger than the indictment I was facing, but rather far more, as I will show. If I was convicted in that case, I knew I would lose my property but I wouldn't lose my life or my city. I would survive, and even if I had to borrow money, I wouldn't have faced total destruction. But if I am convicted now and put to death, I shall leave a foul disgrace for my children; or if I go into exile, an old man without a country, I'll be a beggar in a foreign land.

Gagarin Note: The penalty for intentional homicide was death, but one could generally avoid this by going into exile.

Thus all their accusations are unconvincing. If it is probable, but not a fact, that I killed the man, then it is only just that I be acquitted. I was clearly defending myself against an enormous injustice; otherwise it wouldn't seem likely that I killed him. Your proper task is to convict killers, not those who have a reason to kill.

Speech 3

Gagarin Note: In his rebuttal speech the plaintiff first responds to the defendant's response concerning other probable killers and his claim that he did not have sufficient motive. Then he effectively refutes the defendant's reverse-probability argument. He concludes by returning to his initial point about the need for probability arguments.

If the killers had seen others approaching and had fled leaving the victims there without removing their cloaks, then those who discovered the victims would have gotten a clear story from the servant, who was still conscious when they found him even if his master was already dead, and they would have reported the culprits to us so that this man would not be blamed. Or if others had been seen committing a crime and had killed the victims so that they wouldn't be identified, then the other crime would have been reported at the same time as this murder and suspicion would have fallen on those others. And I don't know how those who were in less danger would have plotted against him more readily than those who had more to fear. For the latter, fear and the great wrong they had suffered overcame their caution; whereas for the former, the danger and disgrace of the crime outweighed their dispute and moderated the vehemence of their spirit, if they even contemplated such action. They are wrong to say you should not believe the attendant's evidence. For evidence like that we don't torture slaves, we free them. In cases where they deny a theft or conspire with their masters to conceal a crime, then we consider their testimony truthful only under torture.

And he is no more likely to have been absent than present: he would run the same risk absent as present, since anyone captured at the scene would have confirmed that he was the planner; but the execution of the crime would have suffered, since none of his agents would be as eager for it as he. I will also show that he thought the indictment posed not a smaller but a far greater risk than this trial. Let's assume he had the same expectation of conviction or acquittal in each case. He had no hope of avoiding trial on the indictment as long as this man was alive, for he would never agree to a settlement; but in this case he hoped to avoid trial, since he thought he could kill the man without being caught. If he thinks you should not suspect him because he is the obvious suspect, he is wrong. If the risk of suspicion was enough to deter this man from attacking when he faced the gravest danger, then no one would have planned the murder. Anyone in less danger would be even less likely than he to attempt the crime, since the fear of incurring suspicion would still outweigh the danger he was facing. . . . When he says that murderers are not those who are likely to have killed but those who actually did kill, he is correct about those who killed, if it were clear to us who his actual killers were. But if the actual killers have not been revealed, then, since his guilt is proven by the probability arguments, this man and no other would be the killer; for such things are not done in the presence of witnesses, but secretly.

Speech 4

Gagarin Note: In his rebuttal speech the defendant responds again concerning probable killers. He has no answer for the plaintiff's refutation of his reverse-probability argument, but it may not matter because he then abandons talk of probability and introduces a completely new element into the argument, an alibi that has thus far remained unmentioned. He then concludes by denying the plaintiff's initial observation about the difficulty of obtaining a conviction.

Their slanderous accusations are pure invention—or should I call them evil intention. They pretend to be prosecuting and punishing a case of murder, but they reject all valid suspicion and call me the murderer simply because they don't know who really killed him. Their duty is to punish the killer, but their goal is evidently just the opposite, to kill me unjustly. My proper course is only to defend myself against the attendant's testimony, for I am not obliged to reveal or convict the true killers, only to answer the charge against me. Nonetheless, I must do more if I am to make it entirely clear to you that these men are plotting against me, and that I am free of all suspicion. So I ask that my misfortune, which they use to criticize me, be turned to good fortune, and that you delight me with an acquittal rather than pity me after a conviction. They assert that anyone who happened on them during the attack would be more likely to investigate exactly who the killers were and report them when they reached home than to run away. But I don't think any man is so brave or reckless that if in the middle of the night he came upon corpses still quivering, he wouldn't turn and run away rather than risk his life trying to learn the identity of the criminals. And since they surely preferred to do what was reasonable, it would be unreasonable to let those who killed them for their cloaks go free. Thus I am no longer a suspect. Whether or not any other crimes were reported at the same time as the murder, who knows? No one took the trouble to look into this. So, since nothing is known of any such report, it is not implausible that he was killed by these criminals. And why should you believe the attendant's testimony rather than that of free men? If it is determined that the latter have testified falsely, they lose their civic rights and are fined, but this man furnished no proof and was not tortured, so how will he be punished? Indeed, what proof could there be? Since he faced no danger in testifying, it's not surprising he was persuaded by his owners, my enemies, to lie about me. But it would be a sacrilege if this untrustworthy testimony should cause you to destroy me.

They also assert that it is more credible that I was present at the scene of the murder than absent, but I shall prove my absence not as a matter of probability but as a fact. I offer you all my slaves for torture, male and female; if it becomes clear that I was not at home in bed that night or that I went out anywhere, then I admit I am the murderer. It was no ordinary night, for the man died the day of the Diipoleia.

Gagarin Note: The Diipoleia was a festival in honor of Zeus. A detail such as this would add credibility to the defendant's claim of an alibi.

As for their claim that it is likely that I killed him because I was afraid of losing my prosperity, the situation is just the opposite. It is those in misfortune who stand to gain by stirring up trouble, since in a time of change their own impoverished state can be expected to change. Those who are prosperous, on the other hand, stand to gain from preserving stability and protecting their present prosperity, for when conditions change, their fortune becomes misfortune.

Although they claim to establish my guilt on the basis of probability, they then assert that I am the man's killer not in probability but in fact. But it has been shown that the probability is on my side; moreover, the witness' testimony against me has been proven to be unconvincing, and it cannot be tested. Thus, I have shown that the evidence supports me not him, and that the tracks of the murder lead not to me but to those who are being set free by my opponents [i.e., the actual killers]. Since their entire case has proven unconvincing, my acquittal would not mean that criminals cannot be proved guilty, but my conviction would mean that no one facing prosecution can present a successful defense. Their prosecution is unjust; they claim to be pure while seeking to murder me in unholy fashion and then calling my actions unholy though I only urge you to respect the gods. Since I am innocent of all charges, for myself I implore you to respect the righteousness of those who have done no wrong.

THE TRIAL OF O. J. SIMPSON

Gagarin Note: The prosecution of former pro football star O. J. Simpson for the murder of his ex-wife and her companion was followed by people around the world. These excerpts are taken first from Judge Lance Ito's preliminary instructions to the jury and then from the closing arguments of each side. The prosecution's closing arguments are shared between two different prosecutors. The excerpts from Judge Ito's instructions to the jury are taken from the transcript of the proceedings for September 22, 1995. The trial was then adjourned, and so all the other excerpts come from a separate transcript of the proceedings on September 26–29, 1995.

Judge Lance Ito, Instructions to the Jury

Evidence is either direct or circumstantial. Direct evidence is evidence that directly proves a fact without the necessity of an inference. It is evidence which by itself, if found to be true, establishes that fact. Circumstantial evidence is evidence that, if found to be true, proves a fact from which an inference of the existence of another fact may be drawn. An inference is a deduction of fact that may logically and reasonably be drawn from another fact or group of facts established by the evidence.

It is not necessary that facts be proved by direct evidence. They may be proved also by circumstantial evidence or by a combination of direct evidence and circumstantial evidence. Both direct evidence and circumstantial evidence are acceptable as a means of proof. Neither is entitled to any greater weight than the other.

However, a finding of guilt as to any crime may not be based on circumstantial evidence unless the proved circumstances are not only (1) consistent with the theory that the Defendant is guilty of the crime, but (2) cannot be reconciled with any other rational conclusion. Further, each fact which is essential to complete a set of circumstances necessary to establish the Defendant's guilt must be proved beyond a reasonable doubt. In other words, before an inference essential to establish guilt may be found to have been proved beyond a reasonable doubt, each fact or circumstance upon which such inference necessarily rests must be proved beyond a reasonable doubt. Also, if the circumstantial evidence as to any particular count is susceptible of two reasonable interpretations, one of which points to the Defendant's guilt and the other to his innocence, you must adopt that interpretation which points to the Defendant's innocence and reject that interpretation which points to his guilt. If, on the other hand, one interpretation of such evidence appears to you to be reasonable and the other interpretation to be unreasonable, you must accept the reasonable interpretation and reject the unreasonable.

Deputy District Attorney Marcia Clark, closing argument
And the thumps themselves, just think about that.

Gagarin Note: The "thumps" were noises heard by Kato Kaelin, who lived in a guest cottage on Simpson's property.

Regardless of where or how they happened, just the fact that they happened shortly after the murders at the Defendant's house and just before the Defendant walked up his driveway in dark clothing, like the dark blue or black sweat outfit that Kato described, you just put those facts together and you realize what has happened. . . .

And it was just as simple as that. Simple common sense tells you that the thumping, the glove and the Defendant's appearance on the driveway almost immediately thereafter are all part of one set of events, all connected in time and space. You don't need science to tell you that; you just need reason and logic.

Gagarin Note: A glove found at the scene may or may not have belonged to Simpson.

And there's one other thing. It's kind of a simple common sense thing and something that it is your job as jurors to do. You use your common sense. You use your life experience. That's very important because that's part of evaluating the facts as a Judge and that's what you're here to do. . . .

This is the instruction [by Judge Ito] about circumstantial and direct evidence. There are a lot of words in this instruction, I must also say. Let me first say something to you about direct and circumstantial evidence. This instruction explains them both. I don't know how well. You know, I'm not a big fan of the way they are written. I think they could be a lot clearer, frankly. But they talk about direct and circumstantial evidence. This one is just circumstantial evidence. You have another instruction that distinguishes between the two. You are told in these instructions that: "Direct and circumstantial evidence are of equal weight. Neither one is better than the other." Now, an example of direct evidence would be an eyewitness, someone who would say, "I saw him, I saw that." We have an eyewitness in Allan Park, okay? His testimony, seeing the man we know to be the Defendant walking into the house at Rockingham. Allan Park testified to his observations. That is direct evidence, okay? Circumstantial evidence is evidence that leads you to infer, okay? For example, in this case, the blood, the blood at Bundy dripped by the killer next to the bloody shoeprints.

It is not direct. Somebody didn't see the murder being committed, didn't see the murderer leaving the crime, but you have the blood of the murderer left behind. Kind of like, well, you have the blood on the rear gate that actually identifies Mr. Simpson. That is kind of like a fingerprint. Okay? That is circumstantial evidence, as opposed to seeing it. Now, in terms of quality, there is no difference, the law has no favorites, but when you think about it, you think about it logically, circumstantial evidence has a lot of benefits that direct evidence doesn't. What is that? It gives you a lot of quality assurance. It gives you independent corroborating bases on which to believe that the Defendant is guilty. Instead of relying on one person's observation, one person who might be mistaken, who might be tired, who might not have observed very well, you know what happens because you saw it happen in this case.

Now, this instruction. Usually when I see lawyers argue this they take out one paragraph and they only talk about that one. I want to talk about the whole instruction here. Okay. Begins in the very first paragraph with: "A finding of guilt as to any crime may not be based on circumstantial evidence unless the proved circumstances are not only (1) consistent with the theory that the Defendant is guilty of the crime, but (2) cannot be reconciled with any other rational conclusion." You will see the words reasonable, rational throughout these jury instructions, because that is what it is all about; reason, common sense, logical, rational. All right. I'm going to jump around between this and I'm going to come back and forth to this instruction because there is a lot here, but in the third paragraph, this is what I told you about a little bit earlier. "If you have two reasonable interpretations"—remember I talked to you about—I gave you the example of the Bronco that could have been on Ashford or could have been gone completely at the time that Charles Cale was walking his dog. You had two reasonable interpretations from that evidence when he said he couldn't see the Bronco on Rockingham. At the point in time he testified based on his testimony you had two reasonable conclusions to draw; either that it was not there at all or that it was on Ashford and he didn't see it. "When you have two reasonable interpretations, one of which points to guilt and the other to innocence, you adopt the interpretation that points to the innocence and reject that interpretation which points to his guilt." That is when they're equally susceptible of two reasonable interpretations.

"If, on the other hand, one interpretation of the evidence appears to you to be reasonable and the other to be unreasonable, you must accept the reasonable interpretation and reject the unreasonable." Reasonable, rational. The Defense will argue to you many things; inferences that could be drawn, just like the possibilities I talked to you about. Ask yourself are they reasonable? Because if they are not, if those inferences are not reasonable, then you are to reject them and accept the reasonable. And that is why I keep referring to common sense; rational, logical. . . .

And I spoke to you before a little bit about direct and circumstantial evidence. . . . Well, this is a physical evidence case obviously and they call it circumstantial evidence. Now that I've reviewed all of the evidence, you can see what I'm talking about when I say a circumstantial evidence case gives you much more assurance of the guilt of the Defendant. And that is because of this. In a direct evidence case, you may have one eyewitness to tell you, "I saw it." That means you have one thing to rely on. But in a circumstantial evidence case, especially this one, you have many things to rely on.

Deputy District Attorney Christopher Darden, closing argument

When you get down to the bottom line, this case really is a simple case. All you have to do is use the tools God gave you, the tools he gave you to use or utilize whenever you're confronted with a problem or an issue. All you have to do is use your common sense. And the Defense would have you believe that this is a complex series of facts and evidence and law and science and all of that. Not really. Not really. You have to question or wonder how it is a lawyer can summarize a case in eight hours when presenting the case took eight months. It's a simple case, but there's been a lot of smoke, a lot of smoke screens, a lot of diversions, a lot of detractions, a lot of distractions, and in some respect, there's been an attempt to get you to lose focus of what the real issues are in this case. And that takes time. If I could give you any advice as jurors, any advice at all, I would say to you, use your common sense. When you get all of this evidence and go into the jury room and after you pick a Foreperson, take that common sense that God gave you, take the evidence that the Prosecution gave you and the Defense evidence, go into that jury room, sit down, spread it out. And using that common sense, ask yourself a question; what does the evidence show. What does the evidence show? And when you look at it in the simplest terms, what you are going to see is the blood in the Bronco, blood trail from Bundy, blood in his bathroom, blood on his socks. Simple evidence. . . .

Christian Reichardt was called by the Defense and he testified that he spoke to the Defendant at nine o'clock that night and that when he spoke to the Defendant that the Defendant was jovial, happier than he had been in weeks. He went from simmering anger at the recital to jovial at 9:00 p.m. that night. Well, what happened? Why is that? It is because the Defendant has developed a plan, he has come up with a plan to rid himself of the problem that has plagued him for seventeen years [i.e., his ex-wife]. . . .

Gagarin Note: That afternoon Simpson had attended a music recital by his daughter; his ex-wife also attended.

Johnny Cochran, Attorney for the Defense, closing argument

Gagarin Note: Cochran first quotes the excerpt of Judge Ito's instructions to the jury. He then continues:

I put that up at this very moment because you've just seen the timeline which is circumstantial evidence of O. J. Simpson's innocence because he couldn't have done the crime given this time. So under that scenario, even if the Prosecution's timeline was reasonable, if they're both reasonable—I think you must agree ours is reasonable—it becomes your duty to adopt that which points towards innocence. But even further, if theirs is unreasonable and ours is reasonable, he's still entitled to an acquittal. The only way they're entitled to a conviction is [if] ours is unreasonable and theirs is reasonable, and I think you can see and understand that's not true, that shouldn't happen, that's not the facts of this case. . . .

Then we know that at nine o'clock he [O. J. Simpson] talked to Christian Reichardt, his friend Dr. Christian Reichardt, and you saw Chris Reichardt come in here and talk to you. I thought he made a very, very, very good witness from the standpoint of what he had to say. He told you that O. J. Simpson sounded even happier than usual. He was more jovial, he got his life back together and he was moving on. Isn't that interesting? Isn't that an interesting way of looking at circumstantial evidence. Let me show you how we differ in this case. A doctor witness comes in and says O. J. Simpson is jovial at nine o'clock on June 12th. Pretty good evidence, wouldn't you say? I think you would love to have that. Anybody would in a case where you are supposedly in a murderous rage. Instead of Chris Darden standing here and saying, well, that is pretty tough evidence for us to overcome, he says O. J. Simpson was happy because he was going to kill his wife. Now, if you believe that, I suppose I might as well sit down now and I am probably wasting my time. I don't think any of you believe that. That is preposterous. It flies in the face of everything that is reasonable.

CRITICAL ASSESSMENT

The *First Tetralogy* establishes both the necessity and the limitations of probability arguments. The plaintiff acknowledges that the near total absence of direct evidence, which in this case consists only of a secondhand witness statement, makes it necessary to use probability arguments to convict the accused. Admittedly, a probability argument does not provide the same certainty as direct evidence, but without the use of probability arguments, most crimes would go unpunished. The plaintiff builds a strong case, adding the defendant's substantial motive and the absence of any other likely suspects to the reported witness testimony. The defendant responds by stressing the weakness of the witness testimony and argues that the presence of a motive in fact makes it unlikely that he killed the man, but the plaintiff effectively refutes this line of argument. The defendant also argues that the killer was probably one of the other possible suspects, but this line of argument also seems weak. Near the end of his second speech, therefore, the defendant introduces an alibi, which he claims can be supported by witnesses. Antiphon does not include the verdict, but it seems likely that the defendant's alibi, a matter of fact not probability, would outweigh all probability arguments.

In the Simpson trial, the prosecution tries to build a convincing case from circumstantial evidence within the limitations of Judge Ito's instructions. The case is complex and they must present a confusing tangle of circumstantial evidence in such a way as to be able to claim that it provides certainty, even though their conclusions are disputed by the defense. This requires presenting the details clearly and coherently, but the disorganized nature of their closing arguments, skipping back and forth among the various pieces of evidence, results in a less than compelling case. For its part, the defense only has to generate reasonable doubt about one of the prosecution's arguments, and they work hard to cast doubt on most of the essential facts and the inferences drawn from them. Their strongest point, in my view, is contained in the second excerpt quoted previously, that Simpson's jovial mood is inconsistent with his killing his wife later that evening. However one may judge their success in casting doubt on any particular point, the cumulative effect of their arguments is to make it almost certain that the jurors will be left with reasonable doubt.

DISCUSSION QUESTIONS

Discussion Question 1: In Plato's *Phaedrus* (267a), Socrates derides the Sophists' rhetoric, saying, "We will let Tisias and Gorgias rest in peace, who say that probabilities should be more honored than truths and who make small things appear great and great things appear small by the power of speech." Does Antiphon seem to you to honor probabilities more than truth? Does Ms. Clark, in her remarks excerpted in this chapter?

You might also set Antiphon's use of probability arguments against Plato's implied standard of (absolute) truth (see chapter 8). Could the Athenian legal system (or our own legal system) do without the use of probability arguments and rely only on truth? What kind of legal system might be able to do completely without probability arguments?

Discussion Question 2: In Athenian law, there was no statutorily defined standard of proof; the side with the stronger case won, and this could in practice mean the side whose argument was the more persuasive. In what way, if any, does this factor make the use of probability arguments different for the Athenians than it is for us today?

We do not know how Athenian jurors actually decided on their vote, but it is possible that, especially in a capital case, they would only vote for conviction if they felt that the prosecution's case was quite strong, not just slightly more probable. But they did not need to be certain beyond reasonable doubt in order to convict (or acquit) someone.

Discussion Question 3: In criminal prosecutions today the standard of proof is "beyond reasonable doubt." In practice, is "reasonable" equivalent to "in all probability"? Does this mean that our standard of proof today may not be so different in practice from what it was for the Athenians, only with an added veneer of objectivity?

Note that Ms. Clark distinguishes between science on the one hand and reason and logic on the other. Does she wish to imply that "reason and logic" belong in the realm of common sense (which she repeatedly insists is all one needs), but at the same time that common sense is a process using tools (reason and logic) that are more often associated with science? Does our current standard of proof force prosecutors in criminal cases to claim greater certainty than the circumstantial evidence warrants? Could one say that a good defense attorney should be able to cast enough doubt to secure an acquittal in any case that depends on circumstantial evidence?

Discussion Question 4: Do you share Mr. Cochran's incredulous reaction to Mr. Darden's argument that Simpson's reported happiness on the night of the killings indicates that he had decided to kill his ex-wife? If we assume that the opposite reactions of these two lawyers to this probability argument was probably shared by members of the audience, some agreeing with one side some with the other, how would this factor affect one's view of probability arguments? Are some kinds of probability arguments more likely than others to receive universal agreement?

Discussion Question 5: To what extent do probability arguments depend on shared experiences? Would differences in race, gender, religion, and other types of backgrounds affect a juror's receptivity to different probability argument? Do such considerations make the composition of the jury especially important? Would large juries such as there were in Athens (two hundred to five hundred members) help compensate for such differences?

ADDITIONAL READINGS

Gagarin, Michael. *Antiphon the Athenian: Law and Oratory in the Age of the Sophists.* Austin: University of Texas Press, 2002.

———. "Probability and Persuasion: Plato and Early Greek Rhetoric." *Persuasion: Greek Rhetoric in Action,* edited by Ian Worthington, 46–68. London: Routledge Press, 1994.

Gagarin, Michael, and Douglas MacDowell, trans. *Antiphon and Andocides.* Austin: University of Texas Press, 1998.

Gagarin, Michael, and Paul Woodruff, eds. *Early Greek Political Thought from Homer to the Sophists.* Cambridge, UK: Cambridge University Press, 1995.

Guthrie, W. K. C. *The Sophists.* Cambridge, UK: Cambridge University Press, 1971.

Kerferd, George B. *The Sophistic Movement.* Cambridge, UK: Cambridge University Press, 1981.

Toobin, Jeffrey. *The Run of His Life. The People v. O. J. Simpson.* New York: Random House, 1996.

Vickers, Brian. *In Defence of Rhetoric.* Oxford: Clarendon Press, 1989.

Worthington, Ian, ed. *A Companion to Greek Rhetoric.* Oxford: Blackwell, 2007.

Yunis, Harvey. "The Rhetoric of Law in Fourth-Century Athens." In *The Cambridge Companion to Ancient Greek Law,* edited by Michael Gagarin and David Cohen, 191–208. Cambridge, UK: Cambridge University Press, 2005.

6

Dissoi Logoi

Speaking on Both Sides of a Question

Elizabeth C. Britt

INTRODUCTION

Law schools in the United States teach students to speak on both sides of a question, seeing the practice as a central component of learning to think like a lawyer. Through this training, students learn not just to produce contrary claims but to recognize and evaluate them. The practice is an ancient one, and so is its connection to legal rhetoric. The idea that any given experience can be described in opposing ways (a concept called *dissoi logoi*) is widely credited to the Sophist Protagoras. During the fifth century BCE, Sophists taught rhetoric, politics, and ethics as Athens was shifting from an aristocracy to a democracy. To participate fully in civic life, Athenian citizens (free, native-born men) needed to learn to speak well. This need was perhaps greatest in the law courts, as ancient Athens had no lawyers. Sophists responded to this need, teaching their students how to deliver the long speeches that constituted Athenian trials.

The Sophists were popular and successful but not admired by everyone. Among their most vocal detractors was Plato, who claimed that teaching students to speak on both sides of a question was tantamount to teaching them to ignore or subvert the truth, which he characterized as constant, timeless, and independent of human perception. But for the Sophists, truth could not be separated from human perceptions and descriptions. For them, the closest a person could come to the truth of any given matter was to look at it from multiple perspectives. Regardless, Plato's criticism of the Sophists echoes even today, as lawyers have a reputation for being willing to make any argument that will help a client's case. In fact, studies confirm that the signature pedagogies of contemporary legal education do not pay enough attention to morality and ethics.[1] But rather than distancing students from moral and ethical concerns, the sophistic practice of speaking on both sides of a question has the potential to help students attend more closely to them.

This chapter presents a sophistic text (ca. 400 BCE) that embodies the concept of speaking on both sides of a question. Originally untitled, it has come to be known as the *Dissoi Logoi*. Although discovered appended to the manuscripts of the Greek skeptic Sextus Empiricus, the *Dissoi Logoi* is believed to be the work of a different, unnamed author. The text appears as a fragment and has nine sections, the first four of which (included here) are statements about pairs of terms: (good/bad, seemly/disgraceful, just/unjust, truth/falsehood). In each of these sections, the author makes claims on both sides of the same question: whether the two terms being discussed are the same or different. The remaining sections (not included here) cover whether all things are the same or different, whether virtue can be taught, how public offices are assigned, what makes a good speaker, and how to train the memory.

The legal texts paired with the *Dissoi Logoi* are from a child custody case heard by the Massachusetts Supreme Judicial Court, *Malachi M. v. Quintana Q.*, 483 Mass. 725 (2019). The case concerned how courts use evidence of domestic violence when determining child custody. Included are excerpts from the briefs of each party, demonstrating modern arguments on either side of a question. In appellate cases, attorneys for each side submit briefs on the merits of the case before they appear for oral argument.

ANONYMOUS, *DISSOI LOGOI*

Editors' Note: The following open-access translation is from Sebastiano Molinelli, "Dissoi Logoi: A New Commented Edition" (PhD diss., Durham University, 2018), available at Durham E-Theses Online. Brackets are used by the translator to indicate words that have been added to clarify meaning implied by the original Greek text. Paragraphing has been altered for readability. Ellipses are added by the chapter author. Readers should be aware that violence is depicted in this text.

1. On What Is Good and What Is Bad

(1) Contrasting speeches are made in Hellas by those who philosophize about what is good and what is bad. For some say that that which is good is one thing, that which is bad is another; others say that they are the same, and that for some people it is good, for others bad, and for the same man sometimes good, sometimes bad. (2) I too agree with the latter. I will reflect, then, starting from human life, whose business is food, drinking and sexual pleasures. These things, in fact, are bad for those who are sick, but good for one who is in health and needs them. (3) And incontinence in these things is something

bad for the incontinent, but good for those who trade in them and earn wages by them. Illness, further, is bad for patients, but good for physicians. Death is something bad for those dying, but good for undertakers and grave-diggers. (4) When farming produces a successful harvest, it is a good thing for farmers, but bad for merchants. And the fact that the trading vessels shatter and smash is bad for the ship-owners, but good for the ship-builders. . . .

(11) But another speech says that what is good is one thing, what is bad another one, differing as much in name as in fact. I myself make a distinction in this way. For I believe that one could not recognize what sort is good and what sort bad, if the one were the same as the other and not different; and in fact that would be surprising. (12) I also think that not even he who says these things would be able to answer if thus asked: "Tell me, then, have your parents ever done good to you?" He could reply: "Many and important ones." "Therefore, you owe them many and important evils, if it is true that what is good is the same as what is bad." . . . And let this apply in every subject. (16) But I shall come to them individually as well, starting from eating, drinking and having sex. For it is good alike for people who are ill to follow these practices, if indeed the same thing is good and bad. And ailing is bad and good for the sick, if indeed what is good is the same as what is bad. (17) All the other cases mentioned in the previous speech are in accordance with this one. And I do not mean to say what the good thing is, but this I endeavour to show, that the same thing is not good and bad, but the one thing is different from the other.

2. On What Is Seemly and What Is Shameful

(1) Contrasting speeches are made also about what is seemly and what is shameful. In fact, some say that what is seemly is one thing, what is shameful is another, differing as much in name as in body; other people say that the same thing is seemly and shameful. (2) I too shall attempt to expound the matter in this way. . . . (5) [For the woman] having sexual intercourse with her own husband is seemly, with another woman's one is very shameful. And for the man too having sexual intercourse with his own wife is seemly, with another man's one shameful. (6) Adorning oneself, painting oneself with white lead, and covering oneself with gold leaves for the man is shameful, but is seemly for the woman. (7) Doing good to friends is seemly, to those hostile to us shameful. And fleeing from the enemies is shameful, but the competitors in the running race seemly. (8) Killing friends and fellow citizens is shameful, but enemies seemly. And that applies in everything. (9) I next move on to those behaviours which cities and peoples deem shameful. For example, to Lacedaemonians that girls practice gymnastic exercises and show themselves without sleeves and chiton is seemly, to Ionians shameful. (10) And to the former that youngsters do not learn the

music and the letters is seemly, whereas to Ionians it is shameful not to know all these things. . . . (13) To Thracians that women get tattooed is orderly, whereas to the other peoples tattoos are a punishment for those who do wrong. Scythians deem it seemly that he who has killed a man, after having flayed his head, carries his scalp about on the forehead of his horse, and having gilded and silvered the skull, that he drinks from it and makes libations to the gods. Among Hellenes one would not wish even to come together at the same house with him who has performed such actions. (14) Massagetae devour their parents once having chopped them [*sic*] and to them being buried inside their children seems a marvellous burial, whereas in Hellas if one did these things, he would die in misery, banished from there, as perpetrator of shameful and terrible actions. . . .

(21) But it is said also about what is shameful and what is seemly that they differ from one other. For, if someone asked those who say that the same thing is shameful and seemly whether anything seemly has ever been done to them, they would acknowledge that as shameful, if it is true that what is shameful and what is seemly are the same. (22) And if they know some man as seemly, they know that this same one is shameful too. . . . And if it is seemly to worship the gods, it is also shameful to worship the gods, if indeed the same thing is shameful and seemly. (23) And let this reasoning of mine apply in every case; but I will turn to the speech of theirs which they make. (24) If, in fact, it is seemly that the woman adorns herself, it will be shameful that the woman adorns herself, if indeed the same thing is shameful and seemly; and all the other cases go this same way. (25) In Lacedaemon it is seemly that children exercise, in Lacedaemon it is shameful that children exercise, and so it is for all the other cases. . . .

3. On What Is Just and What Is Unjust

(1) Contrasting speeches are made also about what is just and what is unjust, and some people [say] that what is just is one thing, what is unjust is another; other people say that the same thing is just and unjust. I too shall try to defend the latter thesis. (2) And to begin with, I shall say that it is just to lie and deceive. People may assert that [it is] ugly and base to do these things to one's enemies, but not to the people dearest to one, for instance parents. For if it were necessary for one's father or mother to drink or eat a medication, and they were not willing to do it, would it not be just to give it to them in the gruel or in the drink, without saying that it is inside? (3) Therefore, [it is] already just to lie to parents and to deceive them, and besides to steal the belongings of one's friends and to use force against one's most beloved people. (4) For example, if someone who is grieved and vexed by some private issue were about to kill themselves with a sword, or a rope, or something else, it would be just

to take these away, if possible; and if one happened to arrive late and found him with those, it would be just to remove them with force. . . . (6) And to break an oath: if a man, captured by his enemies, indicated under solemn oath that, once set free, he would betray his city, would he act justly by keeping it? (7) For I personally do not think so, but rather that he should save his city, his friends and the temples of his fathers, by breaking it. It immediately follows that [it is] just to break one's oath too. . . .

(13) But also a speech opposite to this one is made, to the effect that what is just is one thing, what is unjust is another, differing as much in name as in fact. For if one asked those who say that the same thing is unjust and just whether they have ever performed a just action towards their parents, they will answer in the affirmative. Then, that [will be] unjust too. For they admit that the same thing is unjust and just. (14) But take another case: if you know someone as a just man, then you will know the same person as unjust (and, further, as big and small, on the same principle). And, mark you, if he has performed many unjust actions let him be put to death also for having carried out many and just actions! (15) Now, enough about these cases. I come to the things saying which they claim that they show that the same thing [is] just and unjust. (16) For if ever their speech [is] true, it shows that robbing one's enemies [is] just and that this same action [is] unjust, and the same applies to the rest. . . .

4. On Truth and Falsehood

(1) Also about falsehood and truth contrasting speeches are made, of which one asserts that false speech is one thing, and true speech another; other people, instead, say that they are the same thing. (2) I too say the latter: firstly, because false and true speeches are said with the same words; secondly, when a speech is uttered, if what happened is as it is said, the speech is true; if not, the same speech is false. (3) For example, accuse someone of temple-robbery: if the action has occurred, the speech is true, if it has not, false. And so it is for the speech of him who defends himself. The Courts too judge the same speech false and true. (4) And indeed, if we, when we sit next to one another, should say "I am an initiate," we shall all say the same thing, but I shall be the only truthful one, as I also am [an initiate]. (5) It is, then, clear that the same speech, when falsehood is present to it, is false, but when truth is, is true, just as a man is only one thing as a child, a youngster, an adult, and when old.

(6) However, it is also said that the false speech is one thing, the true another, differing as much in name as in fact. For if someone asked those who claim that the same speech is false and true which is the one they are saying, and the person answered "the false one," then it is clear that the speeches would be two; if, instead, he answered "the true one," then this same speech would be false too.

> And if he ever said or testified something true, then these same words would be false too. And if he knows some man as truthful, he will know the same person as lying too. . . .

OVERVIEW OF *MALACHI M. V. QUINTANA Q.*

Background

In *Malachi M. v. Quintana Q.*, the Massachusetts Supreme Judicial Court (SJC) considered the issue of how evidence of domestic violence could be used in child custody cases. Massachusetts law presumes that it is not in the best interests of the child to award custody to a perpetrator of abuse, but this presumption can be challenged (hence it is called a "rebuttable presumption"; see chapter 2). In this case, a divorcing couple received joint legal and physical custody of their eight-year-old daughter. As part of the divorce decree, the judge found that evidence of the father's "particularly egregious" act of domestic violence against the mother did not preclude granting joint custody to him along with the mother.

Less than a year later, the father filed for sole custody of his daughter. He claimed that the mother was attempting to interfere with his relationship with his daughter by making false allegations. The mother had alleged that, *after* the divorce, the father had engaged in some additional instances of abuse. But, importantly, the mother also alleged for the first time that an additional incident of abuse had occurred *before* the divorce; she said that during their marriage, the father had squeezed her arm "extremely hard" and had thrown keys at her, not hitting her but striking and cutting the child instead.

During the custody modification proceeding, the family court judge allowed witness testimony about events that happened *after* the divorce but allowed only documentary evidence about the "key-throwing" incident. But the judge refused to allow the mother to testify about the father's history of domestic violence *during* their marriage, which she sought to offer as explanation for her current concerns about her daughter. Specifically, the judge did not allow the mother to testify about the new allegations of the key-throwing incident. The documentary evidence about this incident had to stand alone.

In light of this evidence, the family court judge ruled in favor of the father, allowing the mother to retain physical custody of the daughter but giving all legal custody to the father. The judge found that there was no basis for the mother's abuse allegations, stating that "the Court finds that Mother is still attempting to punish Father and has not been able to separate their prior relationship with that of his relationship with the child." Accordingly, the judge wrote, "it is in the child's best interests that Father shall have sole legal custody of the child."

The mother appealed the family court's ruling to the highest court in

Massachusetts. Her attorneys argued that the family court judge erred in two ways. First, the judge erred in refusing to allow testimony about the key-throwing incident. And second, the judge erred in failing to consider all of the evidence—including the new allegations of abuse—when applying the rebuttable presumption against awarding custody to a perpetrator of abuse.

The high court affirmed the lower court and allowed the modified custody arrangement to stand. The SJC found that the family court judge had considered all acts of abuse prior to the divorce, including the key-throwing incident. The court reasoned that even though the family court judge had prohibited witness testimony and cross-examination on events before the divorce, she had admitted into evidence a document from the original divorce proceedings about the father's abuse during the marriage. The court further found that, even though the wife's lawyer had argued otherwise, the judge's opinion showed that she had applied the rebuttable presumption law and had implicitly found that the father had rebutted it.

The Lawyers' Briefs to the High Court

In their briefs to the high court, attorneys for both parents addressed how the lower court treated both the rebuttable presumption and evidence. One might expect the attorneys to argue the facts of the case, with the mother's side arguing that the key-throwing incident had occurred and the father's side arguing that it had not (or that it had happened in a different way). But in an appeal, the court does not make independent determinations about the facts of the case. Instead, the court considers whether the judge in the lower court erred in how it applied the law to the facts of the case or whether there were procedural errors. Accordingly, the lawyers in this case spoke on either side of this question about judicial error: did the trial judge fail to apply the rebuttable presumption when modifying custody to give sole legal custody to the father?

How to Read the Brief Excerpts

The excerpts contain fairly complex arguments about the law. As you read, focus first on how each side argues about the issue of "rebuttable presumption." The mother's attorney argues that the judge in the custody modification proceeding needed but *failed to apply* this presumption. Conversely, the father's attorney argues that this judge *did not need to apply* the presumption. Note how the reasoning for each side depends on how one interprets the timing of the application of the rebuttable presumption. The mother's attorney argues that Massachusetts law did not specify a timeframe during which the presumption had to be applied; the father's attorney argues that the presumption would need to be applied only if new evidence of abuse had surfaced *after* the original custody decision.

Next focus on how each side argues about the issue of how the judge in the custody modification proceeding treated the evidence. The mother's attorney focuses on evidence regarding the key-throwing incident, arguing that the judge should have allowed the mother to testify about the incident, rather than allowing only documentary evidence, so that she could provide a complete picture of how the father's violence might affect the child. Conversely, the father's attorney focuses on the absence of any new evidence of domestic violence *after* the divorce: without this new evidence, the lawyer argues, the rebuttable presumption does not apply.

BRIEFS FROM *MALACHI M. V. QUINTANA Q.*, 483 MASS. 725 (2019)

Editors' Note: Internal citations have been removed without indication. Bracketed text and ellipses indicate Britt's amendments of the text. Minor punctuation changes have been made without indication. All italics are original.[2]

Brief for Mother, Appellant

II. THE TRIAL JUDGE ERRED IN FAILING TO APPLY THE REBUTTABLE PRESUMPTION THAT IT IS NOT IN THE BEST INTEREST OF A CHILD TO PLACE SOLE CUSTODY IN AN ABUSIVE PARENT.

For several decades this Court has recognized the potential impact of domestic violence in child custody situations and has required careful examination of the possible consequences. In growing recognition of this issue, the legislature has established a requirement that when domestic violence has been involved in a relationship, the Court must apply a rebuttable presumption against placing sole custody of a child with the perpetrator of the abuse. This provision does not violate the alleged abuse perpetrator's due process rights since it is in the child's best interest to be free from abuse.

The presumption is not preclusive and can be rebutted. The judge must enter comprehensive findings on the subject because it is the child's best interest which is paramount.

In this case, the judge refused to recognize this presumption because the physical violence had occurred during the marriage. Application of the statutory requirement is not so limited. The statute does not contain any such limiting language.

Where abuse has been involved the Court must provide for the safety and well-being of the child. The impacts of abuse are not limited to the direct impact of physical abuse or more recent events. In training court personnel to evaluate the concerns raised by domestic violence, the Legislature has identified several factors which must be considered. With respect to this case, two of them are worth special consideration: psychological effects on children who witness abuse and dynamics of coercive controlling behavior that increases dangerousness even when such patterns of behavior are not themselves violent.

The father claimed that the violence in the marriage had largely resolved after he had taken anger management classes in 2011. The mother documented in relating the 2013 incident that this claim was not accurate.

The judge could not assess the impact of the child's observation of abuse if she could not consider the specific incidents. The 2013 event was particularly poignant because the parties' version of the incident differed and it unequivocally occurred in the presence of the child who was sitting in the back seat of the mother's car. In the mother's version, the father fired the car keys angrily at the mother but missed and struck their daughter, who received cuts. The child also related this version to the person appointed by the court to represent the interests of the child, known as the guardian ad litem (GAL), who credited this account. Even in the father's version of an angry argument without a hostile key toss, the judge was at least required to address whether this may have affected the child's manner of interacting with her respective parents. The seizure of the car keys to prevent the mother from terminating an angry argument was itself an assertion of dominance and control. The child had also witnessed other violent incidents but neither the GAL in the divorce litigation nor the GAL in this modification action evaluated whether or how it had affected her.

The absence of more recent violent episodes could not be adequately evaluated without also considering the patterns of behavior from both before and after the divorce. Because the judge in the original divorce litigation had been unaware of the true nature of the domestic violence in the marriage, she adopted an explanation that the mother had not been able to separate the child's issues from the parents' issues. The father continued this narrative in the modification to facilitate his own campaign to separate the mother from her daughter and control the mother's behavior.

One example of this was the requirement in the modification judgment that the parties were required to mutually agree on any religious education. The judge did not permit the mother to explain the past history of agreement which the father chose to reject following the divorce. In effect, since the father disdains all religion this grants him the authority to impose his will and prevent any religious training.

Where domestic violence has been involved in the relationship and particularly where the alleged perpetrator of the violence is seeking to increase his custodial role and minimize the role of the other parent a strict limitation of the evidence only to events which have occurred since the previous judgment can prevent the judge from obtaining an accurate picture of the parties' behavior.

A determination of a custodial arrangement which provides the best interests of the child necessarily involves evaluation of the parties' interactions with each other and the reasons for their responses. Parties' actions are based upon their entire experience with the individual and not limited to a specific period of time.

By imposing a time limit on the consideration of events involving the parties the judge hampered the mother from providing a complete explanation for her actions and allowed the father to characterize her responses as inappropriate overreactions to recent events.

Brief for Father, Appellee

II. WHEN DOMESTIC VIOLENCE HAS ALREADY BEEN ADDRESSED IN A PRIOR CHILD CUSTODY JUDGMENT, A COURT CONSIDERING A COMPLAINT FOR MODIFICATION WILL ONLY REASSESS THE APPLICATION OF THE REBUTTABLE PRESUMPTION AGAINST AWARDING CUSTODY TO AN ABUSIVE PARENT BASED ON A MATERIAL OR SUBSTANTIAL CHANGE IN CIRCUMSTANCES.

Standard of Review

This issue requires the court to interpret the provisions of [the child custody statute]. Questions of statutory interpretation or construction are reviewed de novo,[3] as are pure questions of law. To the extent this issue involves mixed questions of law and fact, the trial judge's fact findings must be accepted unless they are clearly erroneous, but the judge's ultimate conclusion will be reviewed de novo. Mother, as the appellant, bears the burden of demonstrating an error below.

The Two-Step Analysis for the Rebuttable Presumption under [the Statute]

In child custody cases involving allegations of domestic violence, the court is required to "consider evidence of past or present abuse toward a parent or child as a factor contrary to the best interest of the child." Toward that objective, [the statute] creates "a rebuttable presumption that it is not in the best interests of the child to be placed in sole custody, shared legal custody or shared physical custody with the abusive parent." Thus, the first step of the [statutory] analysis is to determine whether the rebuttable presumption is established. The presumption is established when the evidence shows "by a preponderance of the evidence, that a pattern or serious incident of abuse has occurred." The proponent of the presumption bears the burden of proving that a pattern or serious incident of abuse has occurred.

If this threshold is not met—if the evidence does not demonstrate that a pattern or serious incident of abuse has occurred—there is no rebuttable presumption, and the inquiry ends. If, however, the threshold is met, the second step of the [statutory] analysis requires the court to determine whether the presumption can be rebutted. This requires the court to decide, by a preponderance of the evidence, that granting custody to the abusive parent is nevertheless in the best interests of the child. The party seeking to rebut the presumption bears the burden of proving that a custody award to the abusive parent is in the child's best interest.

The Divorce Judgment Conclusively Established Father's Right to Custody under [the Statute] as of August 2015.

There is no question that the trial court considered the allegations of domestic violence at the time of the parties' August 2015 divorce judgment because the court made express findings on the issue of physical assaults between the parties during their marriage. Whether the August 2015 findings rose to the level of detail required by [the statute] and the case law is not a question before the court in this appeal. As discussed above, Mother did not pursue an appeal of the August 2015 divorce judgment and, at this point, that judgment is presumed to be correct.

Notwithstanding the domestic violence evidence offered during the divorce trial, the court ultimately concluded that it was in the Child's best interest to be placed in the joint custody of the parents. Whether the divorce judgment was based on a finding that the presumption did not apply, or whether it was based on a finding that the presumption had been rebutted, the judgment conclusively determined that joint custody was in the Child's best interests despite any domestic violence that had occurred up to that point in time. And for the reasons discussed above, that conclusive determination was [final] with respect to the claims of custody over the Child. Any future dispute over the custody of the Child would, thereafter, be subject to the modification standards set forth in [the statute] requiring a material and substantial change in circumstances.

In the Modification Action, Mother Bore the Burden of Establishing a New Rebuttable Presumption Based on New Evidence of a Pattern or Serious Incident of Abuse.

The parties' custody rights were fixed by the August 2015 divorce judgment. For those fixed and established rights to thereafter be modified, the proponent of the change was required to demonstrate that "a material and substantial change in the circumstances of the parties has occurred and the judgment of modification is necessary in the best interests of the child." Thus, Father's fixed and established right to custody of the Child—which was determined to be in the Child's best interests notwithstanding consideration of the past allegations of domestic violence against Father—cannot be vulnerable to the very same rebuttable presumption that was already addressed in 2015. If any rebuttable presumption could be applied against Father after the divorce judgment, it would have to be a *new* rebuttable presumption derived from *new* domestic violence allegations. . . .

> The first step toward applying a new rebuttable presumption against Father placed the burden squarely on Mother as the proponent of the presumption. Mother was required to present new evidence of a pattern or serious incident of abuse. But as the trial court's modification judgment, findings, and rationale demonstrate, Mother fell far short of her burden. There was absolutely no evidence of domestic violence occurring since the time of the parties' August 2015 divorce judgment. Thus, no new rebuttable presumption applied. Father was still not precluded from having custody of the Child under [the statute] because *nothing had changed* with respect to domestic violence since the divorce. Mother was not entitled to a second bite of the apple without any credible new allegations of abuse. . . .

CRITICAL ASSESSMENT

Most scholars in rhetoric evaluate the *Dissoi Logoi* as a pedagogical artifact, possibly lecture notes compiled by a teacher or student. The text is designed to help students consider important questions from multiple perspectives. The questions it presents are ones we still grapple with today: How do we judge something as good or bad? Seemly or disgraceful? Just or unjust? True or false? These are questions that the litigants and court in *Malachi* also grapple with. Was it good or bad to adjust this child custody agreement? Was it seemly or disgraceful for the father to seek sole legal custody or for the mother to disclose abuse that happened before their divorce was final? Who is telling the truth about the domestic violence? Which outcome is just?

The briefs from *Malachi* included here are excerpts; each of the briefs makes many more claims and includes much more detail, and so these excerpts tell only part of the story. But even if we included the texts in their entirety, those accounts are still only part of the story. Recognizing the partiality of knowledge claims is a primary insight of the *Dissoi Logoi*. There is no position from which absolute knowledge can be ascertained; we always occupy a particular position in relation to the things we seek to know, and that position influences how and what we understand. Recognizing all knowledge claims as partial opens them up to critique so that we don't automatically accept an account at face value. Such skepticism is especially warranted when a knowledge claim is presented as "the whole truth" or "unbiased."

DISCUSSION QUESTIONS

Discussion Question 1: Can you identify any pattern to the claims made in the *Dissoi Logoi*? Which claims do you find most and least compelling?

One way to examine the claims in the *Dissoi Logoi* is to look at the relationship between the pairs of terms and the things in the world they describe, the terms' referents. The text uses two kinds of claims: those asserting that the terms are the same and those asserting that the terms are different. The "sameness" claims sometimes say that the same referent can wear the label of either term depending on perspective or situational context. For example, in the case of good and bad, one claim says that the referent *death* is bad for the person who dies but good for the undertaker. Other times, the "sameness" claims say that the same term can apply to seemingly opposite referents. For example, in the case of just and unjust, one claim asserts that the term "just" can apply to both *stealing from one's enemies* and *stealing from one's friends*. The "difference" claims all assert that both terms can never apply to the same referent. These claims take the form of exposing the paradox of calling a referent two opposite things at the same time, for example, calling a man both handsome and ugly. Most scholars agree that the "sameness" claims are the stronger, and some scholars say that the "difference" claims are formulated to help students learn to evaluate weak claims.

Discussion Question 2: How might you evaluate the claims made in the *Malachi* briefs? Do they fit any of the patterns of the *Dissoi Logoi*?

Laying the two briefs side by side allows us to see the contrast in how each deals with the question of whether to place the child with an allegedly abusive parent. Each brief must address the tension between the parental rights of the father and the requirement to act in the best interests of the child. As you might expect, the mother's attorney emphasizes the best interests of the child, while the father's attorney emphasizes his client's parental rights. Closer inspection shows how each side achieves this emphasis, especially regarding the key-throwing incident that had occurred during the marriage but was not revealed until after the divorce was finalized.

The mother's attorney chooses to address the competing versions of this incident as a way of arguing that both are evidence of abusive behavior. The attorney sets up this argument by explaining that the legislature requires court personnel in child custody cases to consider "dynamics of coercive controlling behavior" even when that behavior is not violent. In the mother's (and the child's) version of the key-throwing incident, the father threw the keys at the mother, missed, and hit the child. In the father's version, the father took the keys away from the mother to keep her from ending an argument. To define the father as an abuser according to the legislative requirements, the mother's attorney characterizes the father's action of taking the keys but not throwing them as "an assertion of dominance and control." In other words, the mother's attorney argues that even if the father's version is true, a judge should consider him an abuser.

The father's brief treats the key incident differently. The father's attorney does not address the key-throwing incident in this section of the brief, although earlier, in a part of the brief not included in the excerpt, he dismisses the mother's allegations as unbelievable: "It does not follow that Mother would have suffered such 'fear and trauma' over a set of keys allegedly being thrown in 2013 that she could not raise the allegations at the 2015 divorce trial, while she freely offered evidence during the divorce trial of other, more serious abuse allegations against Father about events that occurred in 2011. But whatever the excuse, Mother waived it by not adequately raising it below."

Emphasizing that this incident occurred before the divorce was finalized allows the attorney to later make the following argument regarding the tension between the child's best interests and the father's parental rights: (1) The original family court judge considered all of the evidence before her, which included allegations of domestic violence, when the court gave custody to the father. (2) The law allows for modifying custody decisions (and invoking the rebuttable presumption) only when there is a new or material change in circumstances after the divorce judgment. (3) Since no domestic violence occurred after the divorce was finalized (and the father was determined to be a suitable custodian), he retains his parental rights.

Discussion Question 3: Speaking on both sides of a question presumes the existence of a question. What is the role of the speaker in creating and framing a question?

In appellate briefs, attorneys must succinctly present the issues or questions they are asking the court to consider. These questions appear early in the brief, even before the facts of the case or the legal history. In law school, attorneys are taught that these questions must combine the important facts of the case with the relevant law.

In legal and nonlegal contexts, questions persuasively frame issues; while some questions may seem more obviously biased toward one viewpoint or answer, it's impossible to ask any question in a completely neutral way. Consider the question corresponding to each of the arguments excerpted previously. These are known as "issue statements":

> Mother's attorney: "[Did] the trial judge [err] by failing to apply the rebuttable presumption under [the statute] that it is not in the best interest of the child to be placed in the sole custody of an abusive parent?"

> Father's attorney: "The rebuttable presumption against awarding child custody to an abusive parent applies only when evidence establishes a pattern or serious incident of domestic violence. Here, the court determined at the time of the parties' divorce that Father was entitled to custody of the Child despite domestic violence allegations. In this modification action, there was no evidence of new domestic violence demonstrating changed circumstances. Was the judge correct not to reassess the rebuttable presumption?"

Each attorney frames the question favorably for their desired answer. The mother's attorney emphasizes that the trial judge "erred by failing to apply" the rebuttable presumption, while the father's attorney emphasizes that the judge was "correct not to reassess" it. Note that the lawyers use different styles to frame the issues. The father's attorney prefaces the question with a full sentence explaining the relevant law, a full sentence giving the pertinent facts, and another sentence applying the law to the facts. The mother's attorney included no such preface. Do you think one strategy is more effective than the other?

Discussion Question 4: The *Dissoi Logoi* assumes that every dispute has only two sides, an assumption sometimes evident in contemporary legal procedures. What are the limitations of this assumption?

The *Dissoi Logoi* frames each section in terms of a binary (good and bad, seemly and shameful, just and unjust, truth, and falsehood) and then takes a binary approach to each pair of terms by saying that an argument can be made on either side. This binary way of approaching the world has influenced not just law but also philosophy and the social sciences. In the late nineteenth century, structural linguist Ferdinand de Saussure proposed that binary terms organized language at a fundamental level.[4] Building on his work, anthropologist Claude Lévi-Strauss claimed that binaries were a natural phenomenon of human thinking and therefore of all cultures.[5] This approach has not gone unchallenged. Contesting binaries and binary thinking is a central project of critical theories from poststructuralism to feminist and queer theory to critical race theory. For example, the man/woman binary denies humanity to those who do not identify as either, while also assuming a fundamental commonality among individuals of the same gender, regardless of other facets of identity, such as race. The interplay among multiple facts of identity has been termed "intersectionality" by legal scholar Kimberlé Crenshaw.[6]

Formal legal procedures structured along adversarial lines can contribute to binary thinking for law students and lawyers, creating a tendency to believe that "I'm completely right" and "the other side is completely wrong." But this outcome is not inevitable. The *Dissoi Logoi* offers an example of how speaking on both sides of a question can help you see another's viewpoint. The Sophists traveled extensively through Greece, giving them a window into how customs and values differed. The section called "On What Is Seemly and What Is Shameful" illustrates that the speaker had either traveled to these various places or heard about them. The claims in this section show a recognition that values are rooted in culture, with the implication being that other cultures are worth listening to, not just for the purpose of attempting to persuade them but also for deeper understanding (in this case, of what seemly and shameful *are*).

Paying attention not just to claims but to the cultural logics informing them is central to what contemporary rhetorical theorist Krista Ratcliffe calls rhetorical listening, an approach to conducting oneself across cultural boundaries.[7] In the *Dissoi Logoi*, one claim is that, according to the Massagetae, eating one's dead parents is seemly. A piece of the cultural logic of this claim is stated explicitly: "Being buried inside their children seems a marvelous burial." We could attempt to further understand this logic by asking questions: in what ways is this practice a "burial"? How is it like and unlike other kinds of burials with which we are familiar? Why might a parent or child find this practice comforting rather than abhorrent?

A cultural logic can identify the assumptions of not only whole societies and cultures but also people with particular experiences. In the *Malachi* briefs, we might listen rhetorically for the assumptions of someone who has been abused by an intimate partner, particularly regarding why the mother didn't reveal the key-throwing incident until after the divorce was finalized. The father's brief implies that the incident was revealed so that the mother could get a "second bite of the [custody arrangement] apple." It wasn't plausible, the father's attorney reasoned, that "fear and trauma" would have kept the mother from reporting this event at the time of the divorce. Yet the mother's attorney does not use the language of "fear and trauma," explaining in a different section of the brief that the mother "only sought to have the event documented since it contradicted the father's narrative that domestic violence had ended two years earlier." The mother's lawyer presents a coherent logic about why the mother acted the way that she did, in contrast to the father's argument of implausibility; she argued that the mother knew the father's patterns of abuse against her and saw similar patterns in his behavior with their daughter.

The family court judge's opinion showed little understanding of domestic violence, ultimately adopting the father's view that the mother was attempting to punish him. Relying substantially on the report of a GAL with no training in domestic violence, the judge's opinion characterized the mother's behavior as "overreactions." This case illustrates the need for judges to have cultural competence in the social problems they see evidenced in court. Judges first need to recognize the partiality of their own perspectives; what seems like common sense to them may not be common sense to others.

What are the best ways to help judges recognize the partiality of their own perspectives? How can judges become more competent in the social problems they help to address?

ADDITIONAL READINGS

Anonymous. "Dissoi Logoi or Dialexeis." In *The Older Sophists*, edited and translated by Rosamond Kent Sprague, 279–93. Columbia: University of South Carolina Press, 1972.

Gagarin, Michael. *Antiphon the Athenian: Oratory, Law, and Justice in the Age of the Sophists*. Austin: University of Texas Press, 2002.

Kerferd, G. B. *The Sophistic Movement*. Cambridge, UK: Cambridge University Press, 1981.

Mendelson, Michael. *Many Sides: A Protagorean Approach to the Theory, Practice, and Pedagogy of Argument*. Dordrecht: Kluwer Academic Publishers, 2002.

Molinelli, Sebastiano. "Dissoi Logoi: A New Commented Edition." PhD diss., Durham University, 2018.

Poulakos, John. *Protagoras and Logos: A Study in Greek Philosophy and Rhetoric*. 2nd ed. Columbia: University of South Carolina Press, 2003.

———. *Sophistical Rhetoric in Classical Greece*. Columbia: University of South Carolina Press, 1995.

Robinson, Thomas M. *Contrasting Arguments: An Edition of the "Dissoi Logoi."* New York: Arno Press, 1979.

———. "The *Dissoi Logoi* and Early Greek Scepticism." In *Scepticism in the History of Philosophy*, edited by Richard H. Popkin, 27–36. Dordrecht: Kluwer Academic Publishers, 1996.

Scallen, Eileen A. "Evidence Law as Pragmatic Legal Rhetoric: Reconnecting Legal Scholarship, Teaching and Ethics." *Quinnipiac Law Review* 21, no. 4 (2003): 813–91.

Schiappa, Edward. "*Dissoi Logoi*." In *Classical Rhetorics and Rhetoricians: Critical Studies and Sources*, edited by Michelle Ballif and Michael G. Moran, 146–48. Westport, CT: Greenwood, 2005.

Sloane, Thomas O. *On the Contrary: The Protocol of Traditional Rhetoric*. Washington, DC: Catholic University of America Press, 1997.

Tindale, Christopher W. *Reason's Dark Champions: Constructive Strategies of Sophistical Argument*. Columbia: University of South Carolina Press, 2010.

7

Isocrates

Fear of the "Other" in Classical and Modern Times

Nick J. Sciullo and Craig A. Meyer

INTRODUCTION

Isocrates (436–338 BCE) was a Greek rhetorician often cited for his contributions to legal rhetoric, argumentation, education, and democratic theory. His teachers were Prodicus (465–395 BCE) and Gorgias (483–375 BCE), and he was also well-acquainted with Socrates (470–399 BCE). While Isocrates never formally defined his understanding of rhetoric, Quintilian suggests Isocrates would report that "rhetoric is the craftsman of persuasion."[1] Much of Isocrates's existing work demonstrates rhetoric should be used to address the practical problems of the day. His work was motivated by civic involvement, and as such, he is noted for making rhetoric more practical and expansive than many of his contemporaries. To that charge, Isocrates founded the first permanent school of rhetoric in the Lyceum of Athens, a change from the first generations of roaming Sophists who taught rhetoric.

The *Panegyricus* is a speech that attempts to unite Athenians against a perceived Persian threat.[2] This threat came from the Achaemenid Empire, which battled regularly with Greece over territorial expansion that saw the Achaemenid Empire conquer much of central and northern Greece, only to fall later to Alexander the Great. In the *Panegyricus*, Isocrates makes the argument that it is not simply enough to be Greek; rather, one must have a Greek education, including, of course, in rhetoric, lest Greeks risk their culture being overtaken by "barbarians."[3] The use of this term is exclusionary rhetoric that was both linguistically and culturally based (and biased). While there has been some disagreement about what Isocrates meant in the *Panegyricus*[4] (Was he discussing the need for a unified Greek culture? Was he only referring to Persians? Was this simply a response to the threat of Persians?), the term nonetheless suggests his feeling about the superiority of Athenian culture and the negation of Persian or barbarian culture, which posed a threat to Greece militarily as well as culturally.

In making his speech, Isocrates relies on two types of rhetoric: forensic and epideictic. Forensic, or judicial, rhetoric focuses on past events and establishes the facts about them. These "facts" strengthen a position and provide historical evidence to further the position. Epideictic rhetoric focuses on the present and generates a sense of shared values and community. In addition, epideictic rhetoric is used to celebrate virtuous actions, condemn unethical actions, and, most importantly, craft a narrative to tell the story.

Isocrates's forensic and epideictic rhetoric exhibits a deep-seated distrust of others, specifically, the Persians, in deference to his fellow Greeks, whom he calls "Hellenes." This "othering" of Persians creates a classical "us vs. them" mindset that emboldens exclusionary discourse and action. In some of his other works, Isocrates expresses concern about barbarians and the threat they pose to Hellenes. In his letter "To Phillip," for example, he writes of his efforts against the barbarians: "Wherefore I might justly be praised on every hand, because throughout my whole life I have constantly employed such powers as I possess in warring on the barbarians, in condemning those who opposed my plan, and in striving to arouse to action whoever I think will best be able to benefit the Hellenes in any way or to rob the barbarians of their present prosperity."[5] As he applauds himself, he also illustrates the importance of protecting those like him at the expense of those *not* like him.

In *Trump v. Hawaii*, the US Supreme Court case excerpted here, Chief Justice John Roberts's majority opinion invites consideration of Isocrates's rhetorical approach in the context of contemporary law. Justice Roberts *legally* grounded his majority opinion in a rational basis analysis, assessing whether government action—here, action by former President Donald Trump in an executive order restricting entry into the United States by foreign nationals from certain countries—was "rationally related" to a "legitimate" government interest. Ultimately, Justice Roberts's majority opinion held that the executive order met the rational basis test.

But *rhetorically*, what is important about Roberts's opinion is *how* he discusses President Trump's messaging around the executive order. Trump was known for divisive language about marginalized people, political rivals, and others, thus creating an "us-them" dichotomy between *his* supporters and everyone else. Isocrates created this same dichotomy between the Hellenes and the barbarians. Roberts, through analyzing Trump's discourse, must wrestle with who is American to provide a justification for the court's decision. More specifically, both Trump (via Roberts) and Isocrates created a narrative (epideictic speech) and weaved in historical tidbits (forensic speech) to establish the need to (re)act a specific way to a perceived threat.

With a deeper understanding of the rhetorical relationship between the *Panegyricus* and *Trump v. Hawaii*, we can better understand the contemporary fear of others as having classical antecedents. That is, does Isocrates's rhetoric clearly articulate a fear of "others" that justified collective opposition? How does Roberts articulate a collective American identity in similar or different ways? Can (or, even better, *should*) Isocrates's speech be modeled as a justification for government action?

The relationship between epideictic and forensic rhetoric is also important to understanding the connection between Isocrates's *Panegyricus* and Roberts's *Trump v. Hawaii*. Isocrates uses both types of rhetoric in his attempt to construct a collective Athenian identity and encourage Athenians to oppose the Persian threat. The two forms of rhetoric function together to make Isocrates's argument stronger. In other words, as Isocrates details historical events, he connects Greeks to those events to show how "we" endured them and established a culture despite collective challenges. It is this culture he wants to not only protect but also advance.

Roberts's opinion arguably does similar work. Unlike Isocrates, however, who expressly talks about a Greek identity, Roberts does not explicitly address an American identity for readers but rather presupposes one. By avoiding this discussion, Roberts's opinion attempts to avoid an "us vs. them" positionality. Thus, the opinion rhetorically appears to avoid any moral or ethical judgments about the president, foreign nationals, and the president's executive order. Nevertheless, though Roberts seems to rhetorically focus on forensic rather than epideictic rhetoric, the opinion also imparts elements of epideictic discourse by noting, for example, "the interests of the United States," which hints at the group of insiders that the opinion is meant to address.

We encourage readers, as they work through these excerpts, to note how both Isocrates's and Roberts's rhetorical choices create a community of insiders and a group of outsiders that help them both to explain their positions and to address the perceived threats. Isocrates does so by reminding Greeks of their collective community; Roberts does so by deferring to what he believes is understood about the collective "American" community.

ISOCRATES, *PANEGYRICUS*

Sciullo and Meyer Note: The *Panegyricus* is so named for a formal, public speech also called a "panegyric." With this speech, Isocrates sought to bring unity to Greece and use it as an opportunity to provoke war with Persia. In reporting his view of the great history of Greece, Isocrates expresses his belief that such a war is the only means to protect Greece, more specifically Athens, and to maintain its legacy for the ages.

Editors' Note: The following are excerpts from *Isocrates with an English Translation in Three Volumes*, translated by George Norlin (1882–1942), originally published in 1928. This version is available at the Perseus Digital Library hosted by Tufts University's website. Unless otherwise noted, ellipses indicating omissions have been added by the chapter authors, and bracketed numbers represent the sections that appear in the translated text. Footnotes appearing in the original excerpt have been removed. Some minor grammatical changes have been made to improve readability.

> [3] . . . I have come before you to give counsels on the war against the barbarians and on concord among ourselves. . . .
>
> [15] . . . The speakers . . . inform us that we must compose our enmities against each other and turn against the barbarian, rehearsing the misfortunes which have come upon us from our mutual warfare and the advantages which will result from a campaign against our natural enemy—these men do speak the truth. . . . [16] For the Hellenes are subject, some to us, others to the Lacedaemonians, the polities by which they govern their states having thus divided most of them. . . .

Sciullo and Meyer Note: Lacedaemonians were inhabitants of Lacedaemon, an area of ancient Greece that included Sparta and its surroundings.

> [17] No, the man who does not aim merely to make an oratorical display . . . must seek out such arguments as will persuade these two states to share and share alike with each other, to divide the supremacy between them, and to wrest from the barbarians the advantages which at the present time they desire to seize for themselves at the expense of the Hellenes. . . .
>
> [19] . . . I . . . am justified by a twofold motive in devoting most of my attention to these points: first and foremost, in order that some good may come of it, and that we may put an end to our mutual rivalries and unite in a war against the barbarian; [20] and, secondly, if this is impossible, in order that I may show who they are that stand in the way of the happiness of the Hellenes. . . .
>
> [23] . . . For it is admitted that our city is the oldest and the greatest in the world and in the eyes of all men the most renowned.
>
> [24] [W]e are of a lineage so noble and so pure that throughout our history we have continued in possession of the very land which gave us birth, since we are sprung from its very soil and are able to address our city by the very names which we apply to our nearest kin; [25] for we alone of all the Hellenes have the right to call our city at once nurse and fatherland and mother.

[31] [A]bout what I should like to know, can we more surely exercise our faith than about matters as to which the oracle of Apollo speaks with authority, many of the Hellenes are agreed, and the words spoken long ago confirm the practice of today, while present events tally with the statements which have come down from the men of old? [32] . . . [I]f we waive all this and carry our inquiry back to the beginning, we shall find that those who appeared upon the earth did not at the outset find the kind of life which we enjoy today, but that they procured it little by little through their own joint efforts. . . . [33] Would it not be those who are admitted by all men to have been the first to exist, to be endowed with the greatest capacity for the arts, and to be the most devoted in the worship of the gods?

[34] [Athens], our city, seeing the barbarians in possession of most of the country, while the Hellenes were confined within a narrow space and, because of the scarcity of the land, were conspiring and making raids against each other, and were perishing, some through want of daily necessities, others through war, [35]—our city, I say, was not content to let these things be as they were, but sent out leaders to the several states, who, enlisting the neediest of the people, and placing themselves at their head, overcame the barbarians in war, founded many cities on either continent, settled colonies in all the islands, and saved both those who followed them and those who remained behind; [36] for to the latter they left the home country—sufficient for their needs—and for the former they provided more land than they had owned since they embraced in their conquests all the territory which we Hellenes now possess. And so they smoothed the way for those also who in a later time resolved to send out colonists and imitate our city; for these did not have to undergo the perils of war in acquiring territory, but could go into the country marked out by us and settle there.

[43] [A]s we make our prayers and sacrifices in common, we are reminded of the kinship which exists among us and are made to feel more kindly towards each other for the future, reviving our old friendships and establishing new ties. [44] And neither to common men nor to those of superior gifts is the time so spent idle and profitless. . . . Since, then, the benefits which accrue to us from our assembling together are so great, . . . [45] for [Athens] affords the most numerous and the most admirable spectacles, some passing all bounds in the outlay of money, some highly reputed for their artistic worth, and others excelling in both these regards; and the multitude of people who visit us is so great that, whatever advantage there is in our associating together, this also has been compassed by our city, Athens. . . .

[51] . . . I think that honor is due to our ancestors no less for their wars than for their other benefactions; [52] for not slight, nor few, nor obscure, but many and dread and great, were the struggles they sustained, some for their own territories,

some for the freedom of the rest of the world; for at all times, without ceasing, they have offered the city as a common refuge and as a champion to the Hellenes whenever oppressed. [53] . . . For it was not because we failed to appreciate how much more advantageous great alliances are in point of security that we pursued this policy in regard to the weak; no, although we realized much more exactly than our rivals the consequences of such a course, we nevertheless preferred to stand by the weaker even against our interests rather than to unite with the stronger in oppressing others for our own advantage. . . .

[57] [I]t is easy to see that even at that time our city was in the position of a leader; for who would venture an appeal for help to those who were weaker than themselves, or to those who were subject to others, passing by those who had greater power, especially in matters not of personal but of public interest which none would be likely to take in hand but those who claimed to stand first among the Hellenes? [58] And, in the next place, the suppliants were manifestly not disappointed in the hopes which caused them to take refuge with our ancestors; for the Athenians went to war against the Thebans . . . and when the Peloponnesians, led by Eurystheus, had invaded our territory, they marched out against them, conquered them in battle, and put an end to their leader's insolence. [59] And though they already commanded admiration for their other deeds, these exploits enhanced their fame still more; for they did not do things by halves, but so completely revolutionized the fortunes of either monarch that Adrastus, who had seen fit to throw himself on our mercy, went his way, having in despite of his foes won all that he had asked, while Eurystheus, who had expected to overpower us, was himself made captive and compelled to sue for mercy; [60] . . . [W]hen Eurystheus offended against us, he suffered so complete a reverse that he fell into the power of Heracles' sons and came to a shameful end.

[61] Many are the services which we have rendered to the state of the Lacedaemonians, but it has suited my purpose to speak of this one only; for, starting with the advantage afforded by our succor of them . . . the progenitors of those who now reign in Lacedaemon—returned to the Peloponnese, took possession of Argos, Lacedaemon, and Messene, settled Sparta, and were established as the founders of all the blessings which the Lacedaemonians now enjoy. [62] These benefits they should have held in grateful remembrance, and should never have invaded this land. . . . [63] [A]ssuredly it is not ancestral custom for immigrants to set themselves over the sons of the soil, or the recipients of benefits over their benefactors, or refugees over those who gave them asylum. . . .

[66] [I]t seems to me fitting that I should speak also of the city's achievements against the barbarians. . . . [67] Let us single out, then, the races which have the strongest instinct for domination and the greatest power of aggression—the Scythians and the Thracians and the Persians; it so happens that these

have all had hostile designs upon us and that against all these our city has fought decisive wars. And yet what ground will be left for our opponents . . . and that those among the barbarians who purpose to enslave the Hellenes make us the first object of their attacks?

[68] Now, while the most celebrated of our wars was the one against the Persians, yet certainly our deeds of old offer evidence no less strong for those who dispute over ancestral rights. For while Hellas was still insignificant, our territory was invaded by the Thracians, led by Eumolpus, . . . and by the Scythians, led by the Amazons, . . . during the period when both races were trying to extend their dominion over Europe; for though they hated the whole Hellenic race, they raised complaints against us in particular, thinking that in this way they would wage war against one state only, but would at the same time impose their power on all the states of Hellas. [69] Of a truth they were not successful; nay, in this conflict against our forefathers alone they were as utterly overwhelmed as if they had fought the whole world. . . . [70] We are told regarding the Amazons that of all who came not one returned. . . . [W]e are told regarding the Thracians that, whereas at one time they dwelt beside us on our very borders, they withdrew so far from us in consequence of that expedition that in the spaces left between their land and ours many nations, races of every kind, and great cities have been established.

[71] Noble indeed are these achievements—yea. . . . But of the same breed as those which have been mentioned, and of such a kind as would naturally be expected of men descended from such ancestors, are the deeds of those who fought against Darius and Xerxes. For when that greatest of all wars broke out and a multitude of dangers presented themselves at one and the same time, . . . we outdid them both, [72] surpassing each . . . and having proved our superiority in meeting all dangers, . . . and we obtained, not long after, the sovereignty of the sea by the willing grant of the Hellenes at large and without protest from those who now seek to wrest it from our hands.

[73] And let no one think that I ignore the fact that during these critical times the Lacedaemonians also placed the Hellenes under obligations for many services; nay, for this reason I am able the more to extol our city because, in competition with such rivals, she so far surpassed them. But I desire to speak a little more at length about these two states, and not to hasten too quickly by them, in order that we may have before us reminders both of the courage of our ancestors and of their hatred against the barbarians. . . .

[75] Now the men who are responsible for our greatest blessings and deserve our highest praise are, I conceive, those who risked their bodies in defense of Hellas; and yet we cannot in justice fail to recall also those who lived before this war and were the ruling power in each of the two states; . . . and made of

them stern foemen of the barbarians. [76] For they did not slight the commonwealth, . . . [77] neither did they vie with one another in temerity, nor did they cultivate recklessness in themselves, but thought it a more dreadful thing to be charged with dishonor by their countrymen than to die honorably for their country. . . . [80] In the same spirit . . . [t]hey treated the Hellenes with consideration and not with insolence, regarding it as their duty to command them . . . but not to tyrannize over them, desiring rather to be addressed as leaders than as masters, and rather to be greeted as saviors than reviled as destroyers; they won the Hellenic cities to themselves by doing kindness instead of subverting them by force, . . . [81] . . . while they regarded their home cities as their several places of abode, yet they considered Hellas to be their common fatherland.

[82] Because they were inspired by such sentiments, and educated the young in such habits of conduct, they produced in the persons of those who fought against the Asiatic hordes. . . . And I can well excuse them, for it is quite as difficult to praise those who have excelled the exploits of the rest of the world as to praise those who have done no good thing at all; for in the case of the latter the speaker has no support in deeds, and to describe the former there exist no fitting words. [83] For what words can match the measure of such men, who so far surpassed the members of the expedition against Troy that, whereas the latter consumed ten years beleaguering a single city they, in a short space of time, completely defeated the forces that had been collected from all Asia, and not only saved their own countries but liberated the whole of Hellas as well? And from what deeds or hardships or dangers would they have shrunk so as to enjoy men's praise while living—these men who were so ready to lay down their lives for the sake of the glory they would have when dead? [84] Methinks some god out of admiration for their valor brought about this war in order that men endowed by nature with such a spirit should not be lost in obscurity nor die without renown, but should be deemed worthy of the same honors as are given to those who have sprung from the gods . . . for while the gods surrendered the bodies even of their own sons to the doom of nature, yet they have made immortal the memory of their valor.

TRUMP V. HAWAII, 585 U.S. ___ (2018)

Sciullo and Meyer Note: This is a selection from Chief Justice Roberts's opinion for the court, in which Justices Kennedy, Thomas, Alito, and Gorsuch joined.

Editors' Note: Footnotes in the original opinion have been omitted without indication. Unless otherwise noted, ellipses have been added by the chapter authors, not the court.

Under the Immigration and Nationality Act, foreign nationals seeking entry into the United States undergo a vetting process to ensure that they satisfy the numerous requirements for admission. The Act also vests the President with authority to restrict the entry of aliens whenever he finds that their entry "would be detrimental to the interests of the United States." 8 U. S. C. §1182(f). Relying on that delegation, the President concluded that it was necessary to impose entry restrictions on nationals of countries that do not share adequate information for an informed entry determination, or that otherwise present national security risks. Presidential Proclamation No. 9645, 82 Fed. Reg. 45161 (2017) (Proclamation). The plaintiffs in this litigation, respondents here, challenged the application of those entry restrictions to certain aliens abroad. We now decide whether the President had authority under the Act to issue the Proclamation, and whether the entry policy violates the Establishment Clause of the First Amendment.

I.

A.

Shortly after taking office, President Trump signed Executive Order No. 13769, Protecting the Nation From Foreign Terrorist Entry Into the United States. 82 Fed. Reg. 8977 (2017) (EO–1). EO–1 directed the Secretary of Homeland Security to conduct a review to examine the adequacy of information provided by foreign governments about their nationals seeking to enter the United States. §3(a). Pending that review, the order suspended for 90 days the entry of foreign nationals from seven countries—Iran, Iraq, Libya, Somalia, Sudan, Syria, and Yemen—that had been previously identified by Congress or prior administrations as posing heightened terrorism risks. . . .

[T]he President revoked EO–1, replacing it with Executive Order No. 13780, which again directed a worldwide review. 82 Fed. Reg. 13209 (2017) (EO–2). Citing investigative burdens on agencies and the need to diminish the risk that dangerous individuals would enter without adequate vetting, EO–2 also temporarily restricted the entry (with case-by-case waivers) of foreign nationals from six of the countries covered by EO–1: Iran, Libya, Somalia, Sudan, Syria, and Yemen. §§2(c), 3(a). The order explained that those countries had been selected because each "is a state sponsor of terrorism, has been significantly compromised by terrorist organizations, or contains active conflict zones." §1(d). The entry restriction was to stay in effect for 90 days, pending completion of the worldwide review. . . .

On September 24, 2017, after completion of the worldwide review, the President issued the Proclamation before us—Proclamation No. 9645. . . .

The Proclamation described how foreign states were selected for inclusion based on the review undertaken pursuant to EO–2. As part of that review, the Department of Homeland Security (DHS), in consultation with the State Department and several intelligence agencies, developed a "baseline" for the information required from foreign governments to confirm the identity of individuals seeking entry into the United States, and to determine whether those individuals pose a security threat. §1(c). . . .

After consulting with multiple Cabinet members and other officials, the President adopted the Acting Secretary's recommendations and issued the Proclamation. Invoking his authority under 8 U. S. C. §§1182(f) and 1185(a), the President determined that certain entry restrictions were necessary to "prevent the entry of those foreign nationals about whom the United States Government lacks sufficient information"; "elicit improved identity management and information-sharing protocols and practices from foreign governments"; and otherwise "advance [the] foreign policy, national security, and counterterrorism objectives" of the United States. Proclamation §1(h). The President explained that these restrictions would be the "most likely to encourage cooperation" while "protect[ing] the United States until such time as improvements occur." . . .

B.

Plaintiffs in this case are the State of Hawaii, three individuals (Dr. Ismail Elshikh, John Doe #1, and John Doe #2), and the Muslim Association of Hawaii. . . .

Plaintiffs challenged the Proclamation—except as applied to North Korea and Venezuela—on several grounds. As relevant here, they argued that the Proclamation contravenes provisions in the Immigration and Nationality Act (INA), 66 Stat. 187, as amended. Plaintiffs further claimed that the Proclamation violates the Establishment Clause of the First Amendment, because it was motivated not by concerns pertaining to national security but by animus toward Islam. . . .

III.

Plaintiffs argue that the Proclamation is not a valid exercise of the President's authority under the INA. In their view, §1182(f) confers only a residual power to temporarily halt the entry of a discrete group of aliens engaged in harmful conduct. They also assert that the Proclamation violates another provision of the INA—8 U. S. C. §1152(a)(1)(A)—because it discriminates on the basis of nationality in the issuance of immigrant visas.

By its plain language, §1182(f) grants the President broad discretion to suspend the entry of aliens into the United States. The President lawfully exercised that discretion based on his findings—following a worldwide, multi-agency review—that entry of the covered aliens would be detrimental to the national interest. And plaintiffs' attempts to identify a conflict with other provisions in the INA, and their appeal to the statute's purposes and legislative history, fail to overcome the clear statutory language.

A.

The text of §1182(f) states:

> "Whenever the President finds that the entry of any aliens or of any class of aliens into the United States would be detrimental to the interests of the United States, he may by proclamation, and for such period as he shall deem necessary, suspend the entry of all aliens or any class of aliens as immigrants or nonimmigrants, or impose on the entry of aliens any restrictions he may deem to be appropriate."

By its terms, §1182(f) exudes deference to the President in every clause. It entrusts to the President the decisions whether and when to suspend entry . . . , whose entry to suspend . . . ; for how long . . . ; and on what conditions. . . . It is therefore unsurprising that we have previously observed that §1182(f) vests the President with "ample power" to impose entry restrictions in addition to those elsewhere enumerated in the INA. . . .

The Proclamation falls well within this comprehensive delegation. The sole prerequisite set forth in §1182(f) is that the President "find[]" that the entry of the covered aliens "would be detrimental to the interests of the United States." The President has undoubtedly fulfilled that requirement here. He first ordered DHS and other agencies to conduct a comprehensive evaluation of every single country's compliance with the information and risk assessment baseline. The President then issued a Proclamation setting forth extensive findings describing how deficiencies in the practices of select foreign governments—several of which are state sponsors of terrorism—deprive the Government of "sufficient information to assess the risks [those countries' nationals] pose to the United States." Proclamation §1(h)(i). Based on that review, the President found that it was in the national interest to restrict entry of aliens who could not be vetted with adequate information. . . . The Proclamation therefore "craft[ed] . . . country-specific restrictions that would be most likely to encourage cooperation given each country's distinct circumstances," [ellipsis in original] while securing the Nation "until such time as improvements occur." . . .

Like its predecessors, the Proclamation makes clear that its "conditional restrictions" will remain in force only so long as necessary to "address" the identified "inadequacies and risks" within the covered nations. Proclamation Preamble, and §1(h); see *ibid.* (explaining that the aim is to "relax[] or remove[]" the entry restrictions "as soon as possible"). To that end, the Proclamation establishes an ongoing process to engage covered nations and assess every 180 days whether the entry restrictions should be modified or terminated. §§4(a), (b). Indeed, after the initial review period, the President determined that Chad had made sufficient improvements to its identity management protocols, and he accordingly lifted the entry suspension on its nationals. . . .

Finally, the Proclamation properly identifies a "class of aliens"—nationals of select countries—whose entry is suspended. Plaintiffs argue that "class" must refer to a well-defined group of individuals who share a common "characteristic" apart from nationality. . . . But the text of §1182(f), of course, does not say that, and the word "class" comfortably encompasses a group of people linked by nationality. Plaintiffs also contend that the class cannot be "overbroad." . . . But that simply amounts to an unspoken tailoring requirement found nowhere in Congress's grant of authority to suspend entry of not only "any class of aliens" but "all aliens." . . .

. . . Plaintiffs seek to locate additional limitations on the scope of §1182(f) in the statutory background and legislative history. Given the clarity of the text, we need not consider such extra-textual evidence. . . . At any rate, plaintiffs' evidence supports the plain meaning of the provision.

Drawing on legislative debates over §1182(f), plaintiffs suggest that the President's suspension power should be limited to exigencies where it would be difficult for Congress to react promptly. Precursor provisions enacted during the First and Second World Wars confined the President's exclusion authority to times of "war" and "national emergency." . . . When Congress enacted §1182(f) in 1952, plaintiffs note, it borrowed "nearly verbatim" from those predecessor statutes, and one of the bill's sponsors affirmed that the provision would apply only during a time of crisis. According to plaintiffs, it therefore follows that Congress sought to delegate only a similarly tailored suspension power in §1182(f). . . .

If anything, the drafting history suggests the opposite. . . .

C.

Plaintiffs' final statutory argument is that the President's entry suspension violates §1152(a)(1)(A), which provides that "no person shall . . . be discriminated against in the issuance of an immigrant visa because of the person's race, sex, nationality, place of birth, or place of residence." They contend that we should interpret the provision as prohibiting nationality-based discrimination throughout the entire immigration process, despite the reference in §1152(a)(1)(A) to the act of visa issuance alone. Specifically, plaintiffs argue that §1152(a)(1)(A) applies to the predicate question of a visa applicant's eligibility for admission and the subsequent question whether the holder of a visa may in fact enter the country. Any other conclusion, they say, would allow the President to circumvent the protections against discrimination enshrined in §1152(a)(1)(A).

As an initial matter, this argument challenges only the validity of the entry restrictions on immigrant travel. Section 1152(a)(1)(A) is expressly limited to the issuance of "immigrant visa[s]" while §1182(f) allows the President to suspend entry of "immigrants or nonimmigrants." At a minimum, then, plaintiffs' reading would not affect any of the limitations on nonimmigrant travel in the Proclamation.

In any event, we reject plaintiffs' interpretation because it ignores the basic distinction between admissibility determinations and visa issuance that runs throughout the INA . . .

The Proclamation is squarely within the scope of Presidential authority under the INA. . . .

IV.

A.

We now turn to plaintiffs' claim that the Proclamation was issued for the unconstitutional purpose of excluding Muslims. . . .

We need not decide whether the claimed dignitary interest establishes an adequate ground for standing. The three individual plaintiffs assert another, more concrete injury: the alleged real-world effect that the Proclamation has had in keeping them separated from certain relatives who seek to enter the country. See *ibid.*; *Town of Chester v. Laroe Estates, Inc.*, 581 U. S. ___, ___–___ (2017) (slip op., at 5–6) ("At least one plaintiff must have standing to seek each form of relief requested in the complaint."). We agree that a person's interest in being united with his relatives is sufficiently concrete and particularized to form the basis of an Article III injury in fact. This Court has previously considered the merits of claims asserted by United States citizens regarding violations of their personal rights allegedly caused by the Government's exclusion of particular foreign nationals. . . . Likewise, one of our prior stay orders in this litigation recognized that an American individual who has "a bona fide relationship with a particular person seeking to enter the country . . . can legitimately claim concrete hardship if that person is excluded." (Ellipsis in original.) *Trump v. IRAP*, 582 U. S., at ___ (slip op., at 13). . . .

B.

Plaintiffs believe that the Proclamation violates this prohibition by singling out Muslims for disfavored treatment. . . . Relying on Establishment Clause precedents . . . plaintiffs allege that the primary purpose of the Proclamation was religious animus and that the President's stated concerns about vetting protocols and national security were but pretexts for discriminating against Muslims. . . .

At the heart of plaintiffs' case is a series of statements by the President and his advisers casting doubt on the official objective of the Proclamation. For example, while a candidate on the campaign trail, the President published a "Statement on Preventing Muslim Immigration" that called for a "total and complete shutdown of Muslims entering the United States until our country's representatives can figure out what is going on." App. 158. That statement remained on his campaign website until May 2017. Id., at 130–31. Then-candidate Trump also stated that "Islam hates us" and asserted that the United States was "having problems with Muslims coming into the country." Id., at 120–21, 159. Shortly after being elected, when asked whether violence in Europe had affected his plans to "ban Muslim immigration," the President replied, "You know my plans. All along, I've been proven to be right." Id., at 123.

One week after his inauguration, the President issued EO–1. In a television interview, one of the President's campaign advisers explained that when the President "first announced it, he said, 'Muslim ban.' He called me up. He said, 'Put a commission together. Show me the right way to do it legally.'" Id., at 125. The adviser said he assembled a group of Members of Congress and lawyers that "focused on, instead of religion, danger. . . . [The order] is based on places where there [is] substantial evidence that people are sending terrorists into our country." Id., at 229. [Ellipsis in original.]

Plaintiffs also note that after issuing EO–2 to replace EO–1, the President expressed regret that his prior order had been "watered down" and called for a "much tougher version" of his "Travel Ban." Shortly before the release of the Proclamation, he stated that the "travel ban . . . should be far larger, tougher, and more specific," but "stupidly that would not be politically correct." Id., at 132–33. [Ellipsis in original.] . . .

But the issue before us is not whether to denounce the statements. It is instead the significance of those statements in reviewing a Presidential directive, neutral on its face, addressing a matter within the core of executive responsibility. In doing so, we must consider not only the statements of a particular President, but also the authority of the Presidency itself. . . .

C.

For more than a century, this Court has recognized that the admission and exclusion of foreign nationals is a "fundamental sovereign attribute exercised by the Government's political departments largely immune from judicial control." *Fiallo v. Bell*, 430 U. S. 787, 792 (1977); see *Harisiades v. Shaughnessy*, 342 U. S. 580, 588–89 (1952) ("[A]ny policy toward aliens is vitally and intricately interwoven with contemporaneous policies in regard to the conduct of foreign relations [and] the war power.")....

D.

Given the standard of review, it should come as no surprise that the Court hardly ever strikes down a policy as illegitimate under rational basis scrutiny. On the few occasions where we have done so, a common thread has been that the laws at issue lack any purpose other than a "bare . . . desire to harm a politically unpopular group." *Department of Agriculture v. Moreno*, 413 U. S. 528, 534 (1973). [Ellipsis in original.] . . .

Under these circumstances, the Government has set forth a sufficient national security justification to survive rational basis review. We express no view on the soundness of the policy. We simply hold today that plaintiffs have not demonstrated a likelihood of success on the merits of their constitutional claim.

V.

Because plaintiffs have not shown that they are likely to succeed on the merits of their claims, we reverse the grant of the preliminary injunction as an abuse of discretion. *Winter v. Natural Resources Defense Council, Inc.*, 555 U. S. 7, 32 (2008). The case now returns to the lower courts for such further proceedings as may be appropriate. Our disposition of the case makes it unnecessary to consider the propriety of the nationwide scope of the injunction issued by the District Court.

The judgment of the Court of Appeals is reversed, and the case is remanded for further proceedings consistent with this opinion.

It is so ordered.

CRITICAL ASSESSMENT

While the Roberts decision does not adjudicate the merits of the president's position on immigration, the opinion indicated that the plaintiffs had not established enough of a case to justify the Supreme Court's intervention. This rationale is a kind of distancing that allows Roberts's opinion to be neither politically motivated nor racially or otherwise biased in its express language. That is, Roberts's mostly forensic-focused opinion appears to avoid any moral or ethical judgment that can be present in epideictic discourse. Similarly, Isocrates utilized forensic rhetoric to enhance the epideictic use of the term "barbarians" and as such explicitly distinguished the Persian enemy from his people. For example, Isocrates retells the historical record of Athens sending out leaders to create support against the barbarian incursions. He also articulates concepts of belonging, (shared) culture, cultural distinctiveness, inclusion, group membership, difference, and diversity to make distinctions. These are partly evident in the Roberts decision, too. Roberts, deferring to the community (i.e., "interests of the United States") and precedent from World War I and World War II and times of "national emergency," saw no need to explicitly generate support for that community and precedent because in the court's view the president is already granted that authority. But the concepts Isocrates uses continue to circulate in today's political and legal discussions about immigration. Perceived fear of an "other" justifies many exclusionary policies and laws, but expressing such a fear can often be politically or legally unwise, which might explain why the Roberts decision indicates that the order was not racially or religiously based.

In sum, Isocrates showed how exclusionary rhetoric can function under the guise of theoretically promising values: patriotism, pride, national cohesion, civic virtue and participation, and democracy. While Isocrates is occasionally direct in his criticism of Persians or at least non-Athenians, he does so for seemingly higher purposes of constructing a nation. Isocrates also frames his construction of Athenians positively instead of constructing Athenians simply against Persians. The Athenians are "noble," and it is their ancestors that deserve "honor." The Athenians have produced many great "achievements." So, one then begins to understand how one's rhetoric can be used to promote specific goals while obscuring others (e.g., degrading Persians).

Roberts, on the other hand, deferred an examination of the exclusionary practice of "othering" to focus on the legality of the argument; in effect, the opinion omits a moral or ethical judgment of the "other" in favor of focusing on technicalities, which avoids Roberts explicitly stating the decision's resultant othering.

Consequently, contemporary readers must look for the historical basis for fearing an "other." Although it is easy to focus on recent legislation and case history—the USA PATRIOT ACT,[6] *Hamdi v. Rumsfield*,[7] *Rasul v. Bush*,[8] *Hamdan v. Rumsfeld*,[9] *Al-Aulaqi v. Panetta*,[10] and *Shelby County v. Holder*,[11] among others—to do so denies the classical roots of modern-day exclusionary rhetoric that, as Roberts's decision seems to suggest, presupposes community and an understanding of "our" collective ideals. The following questions consider classical and contemporary examples of othering that encourage thinking about the relationship between rhetoric, law, and politics in a multicultural world built on difference.

DISCUSSION QUESTIONS

Discussion Question 1: In what ways does Isocrates demean or devalue those not from Athens? Why does he choose to make these claims in the manner he does? What rhetorical techniques are at play?

Isocrates sought to steel Athenians against a perceived threat from foreign invaders. One way he does so is by establishing that Athenians are different from and better than those who threaten Athenians. The use of "barbarian" creates a narrative designed to differentiate and devalue. This discourse of contrast, Athenians against barbarous Persians, is a persuasive tool that helps constitute a collective subject. One might also observe this in legal rhetoric where one must constitute a class of plaintiffs or constitute a collective identity that would suffer harm based on a judicial decision to justify a public policy rationale.

Discussion Question 2: How does Roberts preempt arguments that his decision and the executive orders he discusses are about race or religion? What legal references and legal theories does he use to support these positions?

Roberts seems aware the decision will be perceived as exclusionary to specific groups. In part 4 of the opinion, he addresses these concerns by emphasizing the importance of the law and the court and the court's appreciation for the national security interests outlined by President Trump. This response is itself rhetorical, not just legal. Had he not responded to the dissent, his argument would have appeared weaker. Roberts preempts what he likely anticipates as a rhetorical weakness. Isocrates, too, responds to the opposing argument by establishing and reinforcing the community and the history of his people. The counterargument is not to go to war, but through his discourse, Isocrates details why they must go to war. As he details the history, he reminds his listeners of the commonality they share, deepens that commonality, and thus, negates the counter by directing attention to their community.

Discussion Question 3: Is Isocrates's speech a better example of forensic rhetoric or epideictic rhetoric? Does it have to be one or the other? Since legal rhetoric is traditionally understood as forensic rhetoric, in what ways does Roberts's decision exemplify a forensic approach?

The Roberts opinion is legally well-constructed even if one might disagree with the result. There is an easy reading of this decision as a vindication of President Trump as much as it is an affirmation of, but also distancing from, his executive orders. For example, in the first third of his opinion, Roberts focused on President Trump and his justifications for his policies.

Isocrates is helpful in this respect because although he does a fair amount of honoring Greek history and accomplishments, he also measures them with advancing his own arguments and responding to counterarguments. As such, after reading Isocrates, one is not left with the sense that

Isocrates's speech functions not only epideictically but also forensically. By understanding how both types of rhetoric can appear in a text, one develops a better understanding of a text's overall rhetorical approach as well as the relationship between forensic and epideictic rhetoric.

Roberts uses both forensic and epideictic rhetoric in his opinion. There is a chance that one, when reading Roberts's opinion, struggles to make sense of his forensic rhetoric or thinks it is only in service of his defense of Trump, given the epideictic rhetoric of the first third of the decision. One might have the sense that Roberts simply does not want to be involved; he writes as much at the end of part 4. Roberts seems to only engage the more forensic-based questions present to build a more convincing argument. This differs from Isocrates's direct appeal to Athenian identity and against the Persians.

Discussion Question 4: Which groups are included and excluded in the excerpts? How are they excluded? What similarities are there between Roberts's understanding of who is American and Isocrates's understanding of who is Athenian? How does the decision address the harm to several plaintiffs' "relatives"? How is Isocrates invocation of the "fatherland" and the use of the collective pronoun "we" similar to or different from Roberts's understanding of "relatives"?

Roberts makes note of the individual plaintiffs' claiming harm because they are unable to connect with their families. Isocrates, too, raises these questions by theorizing who gets included in Athens and what constitutes a Greek culture. The understanding of who is included in a group matters greatly in law and rhetoric to enhance persuasion and build community. Each author utilizes collective identity to make their arguments (i.e., Greeks/Athenians, foreign nationals/terrorists), and analyzing group identity provides insight into a rhetor's objectives and arguments.

ADDITIONAL READINGS

Beydoun, Khaled A. *American Islamophobia: Understanding the Roots and Rise of Fear.* Oakland: University of California Press, 2018.

Haskins, Ekaterina V. *Logos and Power in Isocrates and Aristotle.* Columbia: University of South Carolina Press, 2010.

Malik, Maleiha, ed. *Anti-Muslim Prejudice: Past and Present.* New York: Routledge, 2010.

Too, Yun Lee. *The Rhetoric of Identity in Isocrates: Text, Power, Pedagogy.* Cambridge, UK: Cambridge University Press, 2009.

8

Plato

Legal Argument as the Distortion of Reality

Kristen K. Tiscione

INTRODUCTION

The three branches of government at both the federal and state level rely on argument to make important decisions. Members of Congress and state legislators debate the merits of proposed laws, government agencies invite the public to comment on proposed administrative regulations, and lawyers argue on behalf of their clients for justice. The assumption is that in a democracy, "the truth will out," meaning that the open exchange of multiple viewpoints ultimately leads to truth or at least the best possible truth under the circumstances.

Despite the explicitly adversarial nature of our legal system, we are often skeptical of argument as a proper or viable tool for decision-making. Particularly in the political sphere, our instinct is to doubt the credibility of arguments born of self-interest, from campaign promises to the impetus for new legislation. Lawyers and clients alike know that judges, tasked with resolving legal disputes by applying what may be differing accounts of what the law *is* to differing accounts of facts, sometimes frame decisions so as to achieve the desired result. What's surprising, though, is when the judiciary itself acknowledges the rhetoricity of law and claims to be suspicious of legal argument, the sine qua non of its existence.

The mistrust of legal argument as a distortion of reality can be traced back, at the least, to ancient Greece and Plato's dialogues. Plato (ca. 428–348 BCE) was born in Athens of wealthy parents and studied with Socrates (ca. 470–399 BCE) from the time he was a young man until Socrates was convicted of impiety and the corruption of youth (including Plato) and sentenced to commit suicide (which he did by drinking hemlock). In 386 BCE Plato founded his Academy in Athens. His student Aristotle studied with him for nearly twenty years, establishing his own school after Plato's death. Plato died at about the age of eighty, but his Academy survived another nine hundred years.

Plato's dialogues are written using the question-and-answer method Socrates used for teaching. According to Plato, this form of reasoning, known as dialectic or the Socratic Method, was the sole instrument for gaining true knowledge (in contrast to rhetoric). In several dialogues, Plato uses the voice of Socrates to criticize the Sophists of his day, such as Gorgias of Leontini (ca. 485–390 BCE) and his student, Isocrates (ca. 436–338 BCE), who Plato criticized for teaching rhetoric as a means for distorting truth.[1] Having grown up during the Peloponnesian War and experienced Athens's defeat, Plato attributed the corruption of Greek society in part to rhetoric's ability to dupe the public. He was most critical of the Sophists, such as Gorgias, who performed in public to large audiences.

The subsequent excerpt from *Gorgias* illustrates Plato's view that rhetoric manipulates truth to gain advantage. According to Plato, rhetoric—the so-called art of persuasion—is the false art of justice. In one of the most recognized passages of the dialogue, Plato compares rhetoric to cookery, the false art of medicine. Medicine determines what is truly healthy for the body, whereas cookery simulates what is good for us by tasting good. Just as cookery simulates what is good for the body, rhetoric simulates what is good for the soul. Thus, rhetoric produces only the appearance of truth and cannot lead to justice.

This ancient distinction between rhetoric and truth played a significant role in a controversial campaign finance case called *Citizens United v. Federal Election Commission* (FEC), 588 U.S. 310 (2010). Prior to this case, the Bipartisan Campaign Reform Act of 2002 (BCRA) prohibited corporations from using general funds to contribute directly to political campaigns or advocate for or against candidates through certain media during certain federal elections. To be clear, corporations could still engage in these activities, but BCRA required they do so using funds donated specifically for that purpose to a political action committee or PAC. The goal, in part, was to prevent corporations from spending shareholder money to wield political power without shareholder consent.

In 2007 Citizens United, a nonprofit conservative organization, produced a movie for cable television to dissuade the public from voting for Hillary Clinton in the 2008 presidential primary elections. Citizens United then filed suit seeking a declaration that BCRA, which prohibited it from distributing the movie on cable television, violated its free speech rights. The case made its way to the Supreme Court, which agreed with Citizens United. As you will read, the court repeatedly expressed concern that the arguments for upholding BCRA were designed to obscure what was really going on—the suppression of political speech of millions of associations of citizens (i.e., corporations) and not, as the government had argued, the attempt to prevent corporations from enjoying an unfair advantage in the political arena from using "resources amassed in the economic marketplace."

OVERVIEW OF PLATO'S *GORGIAS*

The dialogue begins with Socrates meeting Callicles, an Athenian aristocrat, outside his house in Athens. Callicles informs him that he has just missed a public speech given by Gorgias. Socrates is disappointed, not because he wanted to hear Gorgias display his rhetorical skill but because he wishes to question Gorgias about rhetoric in general. Callicles invites Socrates inside to meet Gorgias and his student, Polus.

Socrates begins the dialogue by asking Gorgias and Polus about the nature of rhetoric. Gorgias explains that rhetoric is the art of discourse that relates to justice; it relates to "the greatest" and "the best of human affairs" because it gives men the ability to persuade "judges in the law courts," "the statesmen in the council-chamber," and the citizens "in the Assembly." Gorgias explains that this power is greater than the knowledge of any expert, such as a physician, who lacks the power to motivate action. When prompted by Socrates, Gorgias acknowledges that such power should not be abused.

Socrates counters with three main arguments. First, he points out (and Gorgias concedes) that rhetoric produces belief, not knowledge, which may be either true or false. Second, Socrates points out (and Gorgias concedes) that only an ignorant audience can be persuaded by one with great oratory skills but no knowledge of the subject matter at hand. Third, Socrates rejects Gorgias's claim that rhetoric relates to justice because Gorgias has already admitted that rhetoric can be used to argue as much for an unjust result as much as for a just one.

In the excerpt that follows, Polus attempts to defend Gorgias by questioning Socrates about his definition of rhetoric, and Gorgias quickly reenters the conversation.

PLATO, *GORGIAS* (CA. 380 BCE)

Editors' Note: Walter R. M. Lamb first translated Plato's *Gorgias* in 1925. Lamb (1882–1961) was a British classical lecturer, author, and translator. This translation is available from the Perseus Digital Library Project at Tufts University and publicly available under a Creative Commons license. Ellipses indicate the omission of text, and numbers in brackets correspond to Stephanus numbers that will help the reader locate the text in the original source. Stephanus numbers denote the page (number) and paragraph (letter) where the text appears in an earlier and well-known translation from 1578 by Henri Estienne (1528–98), also known as Henricus Stephanus. These numbers allow readers to locate the same text in any translation.

PERSONS OF THE DIALOGUE: Callicles, Socrates, Gorgias, Polus.
SCENE: The house of Callicles.

[462b] Polus: . . . So answer me this, Socrates: since you think that Gorgias is at a loss about rhetoric, what is your own account of it?

Socrates: Are you asking what art I call it?

Polus: Yes.

Socrates: None at all, I consider, Polus, if you would have the honest truth.

Polus: But what do you consider rhetoric to be?

[462c] Socrates: A thing which you say—in the treatise which I read of late—"made art."

Polus: What thing do you mean?

Socrates: I mean a certain habitude.

Tiscione Note: "Habitude" is translated by others as "knack" or "experience."

Polus: Then do you take rhetoric to be a habitude?

Socrates: I do, if you have no other suggestion.

Polus: Habitude of what?

Socrates: Of producing a kind of gratification and pleasure.

Polus: Then you take rhetoric to be something fine—an ability to gratify people?

Socrates: How now, Polus? Have you as yet heard me tell you [462d] what I say it is, that you ask what should follow that—whether I do not take it to be fine?

Polus: Why, did I not hear you call it a certain habitude?

Socrates: Then please—since you value "gratification"—be so good as gratify me in a small matter.

Polus: I will.

Socrates: Ask me now what art I take cookery to be.

Polus: Then I ask you, what art is cookery?

Socrates: None at all, Polus.

Polus: Well, what is it? Tell me.

[462e] Socrates: Then I reply, a certain habitude.

Polus: Of what? Tell me.

Socrates: Then I reply, of production of gratification and pleasure, Polus.

Polus: So cookery and rhetoric are the same thing?

Socrates: Not at all, only parts of the same practice.

Polus: What practice do you mean?

Socrates: I fear it may be too rude to tell the truth; for I shrink from saying it on Gorgias' account, lest he suppose I am making satirical fun of his own profession. Yet indeed I do not know [463a] whether this is the rhetoric which Gorgias practices, for from our argument just now we got no very clear view as to how he conceives it; but what I call rhetoric is a part of a certain business which has nothing fine about it.

Gorgias: What is that, Socrates? Tell us, without scruple on my account.

Socrates: It seems to me then, Gorgias, to be a pursuit that is not a matter of art, but showing a shrewd, gallant spirit which has a natural bent for clever dealing with mankind, and I sum up its substance in the name flattery. [463b] This practice, as I view it, has many branches, and one of them is cookery; which appears indeed to be an art but, by my account of it, is not an art but a habitude or knack. I call rhetoric another branch of it, as also personal adornment and sophistry[2]—four branches of it for four kinds of affairs. So if Polus would inquire, let him inquire: he has not yet been informed to what sort of branch of flattery [463c] I assign rhetoric; but without noticing that I have not yet answered that, he proceeds to ask whether I do not consider it a fine thing. But I am not going to reply to the question whether I consider rhetoric a fine or a base thing, until I have first answered what it is; for it would not be fair, Polus: but if you want the information, ask me what sort of branch of flattery I assert rhetoric to be.

Polus: I ask you then; so answer, what sort of branch it is.

Socrates: Now, will you understand when I answer? Rhetoric, [463d] by my account, is a semblance [counterfeit] of a branch of politics.

Polus: Well then, do you call it a fine or a base thing?

Socrates: A base one, I call it—for all that is bad I call base—since I am to answer you as though you had already understood my meaning.

Gorgias: Nor do I myself, upon my word, Socrates, [463e] grasp your meaning either.

Socrates: And no wonder, Gorgias, for as yet my statement is not at all clear; but Polus here is so young and fresh![3]

Gorgias: Ah, do not mind him; but tell me what you mean by rhetoric being a semblance of a branch of politics.

Socrates: Well, I will try to express what rhetoric appears to me to be: if it is not in fact what I say, Polus here will refute me. There are things, I suppose, that you call body and soul?

[464a] Gorgias: Of course.

Socrates: And each of these again you believe to have a good condition?

Gorgias: I do.

Socrates: And again, a good condition that may seem so, but is not? As an example, let me give the following: many people seem to be in good bodily condition when it would not be easy for anyone but a doctor, or one of the athletic trainers, to perceive that they are not so.

Gorgias: You are right.

Socrates: Something of this sort I say there is in body and in soul, which makes the body or the soul seem to be in good condition, though it is none the more so in fact.

[464b] Gorgias: Quite so.

Socrates: Now let me see if I can explain my meaning to you more clearly. There are two different affairs to which I assign two different arts: the one, which has to do with the soul, I call politics; the other, which concerns the body, though I cannot give you a single name for it offhand, is all one business, the [care] of the body, which I can designate in two branches as gymnastic [i.e., exercise] and medicine. Under politics I set legislation in the place of gymnastic, and justice to match medicine.[464c] In each of these pairs, of course—medicine and gymnastic, justice and legislation—there is some intercommunication, as both deal with the same thing; at the same time they have certain differences. Now these four, which always bestow their care for the best advantage respectively of the body and the soul, are noticed by the art of flattery which, I do not say with knowledge, but by speculation, divides herself into four parts, and then, insinuating herself into each of those branches, [464d] pretends to be that into which she has crept, and cares nothing for what is the best, but dangles what is most pleasant for the moment as a bait for folly, and deceives it into thinking that she is of the highest value. Thus cookery assumes the form of medicine, and pretends to know what foods are best for the body; so that if a cook and a doctor had to contend before boys, or before men as foolish as boys, as to which of the two, the doctor or the cook, understands the question of sound and noxious foods, [464e] the doctor would starve to death. Flattery, however, is what I call it, [465a] and I say that this sort of thing is a disgrace, Polus—for here I address you—because it aims at the pleasant and ignores the best; and I say it is not an art, but a habitude, since it has no account to give of the real nature of the things it applies, and so cannot tell the cause of any of them. I refuse to give the name of art to anything that is irrational: if you dispute my views, I am ready to give my reasons. [465b] However, as I put it, cookery is flattery disguised as medicine; and in just the same manner self-adornment personates gymnastic: with its rascally, deceitful, ignoble, and illiberal nature it deceives men by forms and colors, polish and dress so as to make them, in the effort of assuming an extraneous beauty, neglect the native sort that comes through gymnastic. Well, to avoid prolixity, I am willing to put it to you like a geometer [i.e., a mathematician] for by this time I expect you can follow me:

> [465c] as self-adornment is to gymnastic, so is sophistry to legislation; and as cookery is to medicine, so is rhetoric to justice.

But although, as I say, there is this natural distinction between them [meaning sophistry and rhetoric], they are so nearly related that sophists and orators are jumbled up as having the same field and dealing with the same subjects, and neither can they tell what to make of each other, nor the world at large what to make of them. For indeed, if the soul were not in command of the body, but the latter had charge of itself, and so cookery and medicine were not surveyed [465d] and distinguished by the soul, but the body itself were the judge, forming its own estimate of them by the gratifications they gave it, we should have a fine instance of what Anaxagoras described, my dear Polus,—for you are versed in these matters: everything would be jumbled together, without distinction as between medicinal and healthful and tasty concoctions.[4] Well now, you have heard what I state rhetoric to be—the counterpart of cookery in the soul, acting here as that does on the body. . . .

CITIZENS UNITED V. FEDERAL ELECTION COMMISSION, 558 U.S. 310 (2010)

Tiscione Note: In *Citizens United v. Federal Election Commission (FEC)*, the Supreme Court had to decide whether Section 441b of the Bipartisan Campaign Reform Act of 2002 (BCRA) violated the First Amendment rights of Citizens United, a nonprofit corporation. Justice Kennedy, writing for the majority, expressed the view that the government's position in defending the law was rhetoric, designed to distort the fact that Section 441b unlawfully acted to suppress political speech on the basis of the speaker's identity as a corporation.[5] This decision has been harshly criticized for expanding the political influence of wealthy donors, corporations, and special-interest groups without adequate notice to the public.

Editors' Note: Brackets indicate text modified in the official reporter, and ellipses indicate omitted text. Most internal citations are omitted to improve readability.

Federal law prohibits corporations and unions from using their general treasury funds to make independent expenditures for speech defined as an "electioneering communication" or for speech expressly advocating the election or defeat of a candidate. 2 U.S.C. § 441b.[6] Limits on electioneering communications were upheld in *McConnell v. Federal Election Comm'n*, 540 U.S. 93 (2003). The holding of *McConnell* rested to a large extent on an earlier case, *Austin v. Michigan Chamber of Commerce*, 494 U.S. 652 (1990). *Austin* had held that political speech may be banned based on the speaker's corporate identity.

In this case we are asked to reconsider *Austin* and, in effect, *McConnell*. It has been noted that "*Austin* was a significant departure from ancient First Amendment principles." . . . We agree . . . and hold that . . . [t]he Government may regulate corporate political speech through disclaimer and disclosure requirements, but it may not suppress that speech altogether. We turn now to the case before us.

I.

A.

Citizens United is a nonprofit corporation. . . .

Citizens United has an annual budget of about $12 million. Most of its funds are from donations by individuals; but, in addition, it accepts a small portion of its funds from for-profit corporations.

In January 2008, Citizens United released a film entitled *Hillary: The Movie*. . . . a 90–minute documentary about then-Senator Hillary Clinton, who was a candidate in the Democratic Party's 2008 Presidential primary elections. *Hillary* mentions Senator Clinton by name and depicts interviews with political commentators and other persons, most of them quite critical of Senator Clinton. *Hillary* was released in theaters and on DVD, but Citizens United wanted to . . . mak[e] it available through video-on-demand.

Video-on-demand allows digital cable subscribers to select programming from various menus, including movies, television shows, sports, news, and music. The viewer can watch the program at any time. . . . In December 2007, a cable company offered, for a payment of $1.2 million . . . to make *Hillary* available on a video-on-demand channel . . . free of charge.

To implement the proposal, Citizens United was prepared to pay for the video-on-demand; and to promote the film . . . by running advertisements on broadcast and cable television.

B.

Before BCRA, federal law . . . prohibited—and still does prohibit—corporations and unions from using general treasury funds to make direct contributions to candidates or independent expenditures that expressly advocate the election or defeat of a candidate, through any form of media, in connection with certain qualified federal elections. 2 U.S.C. § 441b. BCRA amended § 441b to prohibit any "electioneering communication" as well . . . [which it] defined as "any broadcast, cable, or satellite communication" that "refers to a clearly identified candidate for Federal office" and is made within 30 days of a primary or 60 days of a general election. . . . Corporations and unions . . . may establish, however, a "separate segregated fund" (known as a political action committee, or PAC) for these purposes. . . .

C.

Citizens United wanted to make *Hillary* available . . . within 30 days of the 2008 primary elections. It feared, however, that both the film and the ads would be covered by the ban on corporate-funded independent expenditures . . . In December 2007, Citizens United sought declaratory and injunctive relief against the FEC. It argued that (1) § 441b is unconstitutional as applied to *Hillary*; and (2) [that the] disclaimer and disclosure requirements are unconstitutional as applied to *Hillary* and to the three ads for the movie.

The [United States] District Court [for the District of Columbia] denied Citizens United's motion for a preliminary injunction . . . and then granted the FEC's motion for summary judgment. . . . The court held that § 441b was facially constitutional under *McConnell*, . . . [and] constitutional as applied to *Hillary* . . . The court also rejected Citizens United's challenge to BCRA's disclaimer and disclosure requirements. . . .

We noted probable jurisdiction. . . .

II.

Tiscione Note: In this section, omitted in its entirety, the court rejected the parties' arguments that the court did not need to reach the First Amendment issue.

III.

The First Amendment provides that "Congress shall make no law . . . abridging the freedom of speech." . . .

The law before us is an outright ban [on speech], backed by criminal sanctions. . . .

Section 441b is a ban on corporate speech notwithstanding the fact that a PAC created by a corporation can still speak. . . . [T]he option to form PACs does not alleviate the First Amendment problems with § 441b. PACs are burdensome alternatives; they are expensive to administer and subject to extensive regulations. . . .

PACs have to comply with these regulations just to speak. This might explain why fewer than 2,000 of the millions of corporations in this country have PACs. . . . Given the onerous restrictions, a corporation may not be able to establish a PAC in time to make its views known regarding candidates and issues in a current campaign.

Section 441b's prohibition on corporate independent expenditures is thus a ban on speech . . . [that] "reduces the quantity of expression by restricting the number of issues discussed, the depth of their exploration, and the size of the audience reached." *Buckley v. Valeo*, 424 U.S. 1, 19 (1976) (*per curiam*). . . . If § 441b applied to individuals, no one would believe that it is merely a time, place, or manner restriction on speech.[7] Its purpose and effect are to silence entities whose voices the Government deems to be suspect.

Speech is an essential mechanism of democracy, for it is the means to hold officials accountable to the people. . . . The right of citizens to inquire, to hear, to speak, and to use information to reach consensus is a precondition to enlightened self-government and a necessary means to protect it. The First Amendment "'has its fullest and most urgent application' to speech uttered during a campaign for political office." . . .

For these reasons, political speech must prevail against laws that would suppress it, whether by design or inadvertence. Laws that burden political speech are "subject to strict scrutiny," which requires the Government to prove that the restriction "furthers a compelling interest and is narrowly tailored to achieve that interest." . . .

By taking the right to speak from some and giving it to others, the Government deprives the disadvantaged person or class of the right to use speech to strive to establish worth, standing, and respect for the speaker's voice. . . .

The Court has upheld a narrow class of speech restrictions . . . , but these rulings were based on an interest in allowing governmental entities to perform their functions. *See, e.g.*, *Bethel School Dist. No. 403 v. Fraser* (1986) (protecting the "function of public school education"). . . . The corporate independent expenditures at issue in this case, however, would not interfere with governmental functions, so these cases are inapposite. . . .

We find no basis for the proposition that, in the context of political speech, the Government may impose restrictions on certain disfavored speakers. Both history and logic lead us to this conclusion.[8]

A.

. . .The Court has recognized that First Amendment protection extends to corporations. . . .

This protection has been extended by explicit holdings to the context of political speech. . . .

[S]ince the latter part of the 19th century, . . . laws of some States and of the United States imposed a ban on corporate direct contributions to candidates. Yet not until 1947 did Congress first prohibit independent expenditures by corporations and labor unions . . .

For almost three decades thereafter, the Court did not reach the question whether [such] restrictions . . . are constitutional. . . .

Tiscione Note: The court summarized the relevant case law, beginning with *Buckley*, which invalidated a ban on independent expenditures applicable to individuals (as well as to corporations and labor unions). Recognizing a "sufficiently important" governmental interest in preventing the potential for quid pro quo corruption, the court upheld limits on direct contributions to candidates by individuals but invalidated the limits on independent expenditures because they failed to serve the government's stated interest.

In *First Nat. Bank of Boston v. Bellotti*, the court struck down a state-law prohibition on corporate independent expenditures related to referenda issues on the ground that speech cannot be restricted based on the speaker's identity.[9]

In contrast, *Austin* upheld a Michigan law that prohibited corporate independent expenditures that supported or opposed any candidate for state office. Kennedy described Austin as recognizing "a new governmental interest" [the antidistortion rationale] in preventing "the corrosive and distorting effects of immense aggregations of wealth that are accumulated with the help of the corporate form and that have little or no correlation to the public's support for the corporation's political ideas."

B.

The Court is thus confronted with conflicting lines of precedent: a pre-*Austin* line that forbids restrictions on political speech based on the speaker's corporate identity and a post-*Austin* line that permits them. . . .

In its defense of . . . § 441b, the Government notes the antidistortion rationale on which *Austin* and its progeny rest in part, yet it all but abandons reliance upon it. It argues instead that two other compelling interests [in anticorruption and protecting shareholders] support *Austin's* holding. We consider the three points in turn. . . .

If [*Austin*'s] antidistortion rationale were to be accepted, . . . it would permit Government to ban political speech simply because the speaker . . . has taken on the corporate form. . . . If *Austin* were correct, the Government could prohibit a corporation from expressing political views in media beyond those presented here, such as by printing books. The Government responds "that the FEC has never applied this statute to a book," and if it did, "there would be quite [a] good as-applied challenge." This troubling assertion of brooding governmental power cannot be reconciled with the confidence and stability in civic discourse that the First Amendment must secure.

Political speech is "indispensable to decisionmaking in a democracy, and this is no less true because the speech comes from a corporation rather than an individual." . . . This protection for speech is inconsistent with *Austin's* antidistortion rationale. *Austin* sought to defend the antidistortion rationale as a means to prevent corporations from obtaining "'an unfair advantage in the political marketplace'" by using "'resources amassed in the economic marketplace.'" But *Buckley* rejected the premise that the Government has an interest "in equalizing the relative ability of individuals and groups to influence the outcome of elections." . . .

The rule that political speech cannot be limited based on a speaker's wealth is a necessary consequence of the premise that the First Amendment generally prohibits the suppression of political speech based on the speaker's identity. . . .

It is irrelevant for purposes of the First Amendment that corporate funds may "have little or no correlation to the public's support for the corporation's political ideas." All speakers, including individuals and the media, use money amassed from the economic marketplace to fund their speech. . . .

Austin's antidistortion rationale would produce the dangerous, and unacceptable, consequence that Congress could ban political speech of media corporations. . . . Media corporations are now exempt from § 441b's ban on corporate expenditures. Yet [they] accumulate wealth with the help of the corporate form, the largest media corporations have "immense aggregations of wealth," and [their] views . . . often "have little or no correlation to the public's support" for those views. Thus, under the Government's reasoning, wealthy media corporations could have their voices diminished to put them on par with other media entities. There is no precedent for permitting this under the First Amendment. . . .

The law's exception for media corporations is . . . all but an admission of the invalidity of the antidistortion rationale . . . [and] results in a further, separate reason for finding this law invalid: . . . the law exempts some corporations but covers others . . . [E]ven assuming . . . that a news organization has a right to speak when others do not, the exemption would allow a conglomerate that owns both a media business and an unrelated business to influence or control the media in order to advance its overall business interest. At the same time, some other corporation, with an identical business interest but no media outlet . . . would be forbidden to speak or inform the public about the same issue. This differential treatment cannot be squared with the First Amendment. . . .

Austin interferes with the "open marketplace" of ideas protected by the First Amendment. It permits the Government to ban the political speech of millions of associations of citizens. Most of these are small corporations without large amounts of wealth. This fact belies the Government's argument that the statute is justified on the ground that it prevents the "distorting effects of immense aggregations of wealth." It is not even aimed at amassed wealth.

The censorship we now confront is vast in its reach. The Government has "muffle[d] the voices that best represent the most significant segments of the economy." And "the electorate [has been] deprived of information, knowledge and opinion vital to its function." By suppressing the speech of manifold corporations, both for-profit and nonprofit, the Government prevents their voices and viewpoints from reaching the public and advising voters . . . . Factions should be checked by permitting them all to speak, and by entrusting the people to judge what is true and what is false.

The purpose and effect of this law is to prevent corporations, including small and nonprofit corporations, from presenting both facts and opinions to the public. This makes *Austin's* antidistortion rationale all the more an aberration. . . . An *amici* brief . . . notes that lobbying and corporate communications with elected officials occur on a regular basis. When that phenomenon is coupled with § 441b, . . . smaller or nonprofit corporations cannot raise a voice to object when other corporations, including those with vast wealth, are cooperating with the Government. That cooperation may sometimes be voluntary, or it may be at the demand of a Government official who uses his or her authority, influence, and power to threaten corporations to support the Government's policies. Those kinds of interactions are often unknown and unseen. The speech that § 441b forbids, though, is public, and all can judge its content and purpose. References to massive corporate treasuries should not mask the real operation of this law. Rhetoric ought not obscure reality.

Even if § 441b's expenditure ban were constitutional, wealthy corporations could still lobby elected officials, although smaller corporations may not have the resources to do so. And wealthy individuals and unincorporated associations can spend unlimited amounts on independent expenditures. Yet certain disfavored associations of citizens—those that have taken on the corporate form—are penalized for engaging in the same political speech.

When Government seeks to use its full power . . . to command where a person may get his or her information or what distrusted source he or she may not hear, it uses censorship to control thought. This is unlawful. The First Amendment confirms the freedom to think for ourselves.

Tiscione Note: The court rejected the government's stated interest in avoiding the appearance or reality of corruption on several grounds: that *Buckley*'s concern with quid pro quo corruption (bribery) was limited to direct contributions to candidates, that the chilling effect of the independent expenditure restriction was disproportionate to its stated interest, and by definition, an independent expenditure, unlike a direct contribution, is speech that is not coordinated with a candidate and thus poses no corruption risk.

The court also rejected the government's stated interest in preventing shareholders from being forced to fund political speech because this rationale would permit Congress to restrict the speech of media corporations as well.

The court further declined to address the government's stated interest in preventing foreign individuals or associations from influencing the political process on the ground that Section 441b was not limited to foreign contributions.

III.C-E and IV.A-C

Tiscione Note: These sections, omitted in their entirety, discussed the propriety of overruling *Austin* and upheld BCRA's disclosure and disclaimer requirements.

V.

When word concerning the plot of the movie *Mr. Smith Goes to Washington* reached the circles of Government, some officials sought, by persuasion, to discourage its distribution.[10] Under *Austin*, though, officials could have done more than discourage its distribution—they could have banned the film. After all, it, like *Hillary*, was speech funded by a corporation that was critical of Members of Congress. *Mr. Smith Goes to Washington* may be fiction and caricature; but fiction and caricature can be a powerful force. . . .

Governments are often hostile to speech, but under our law and our tradition it seems stranger than fiction for our Government to make this political speech a crime. Yet this is the statute's purpose and design. . . .

"The First Amendment underwrites the freedom to experiment and to create in the realm of thought and speech. Citizens must be free to use new forms, and new forums, for the expression of ideas. The civic discourse belongs to the people, and the Government may not prescribe the means used to conduct it."

The judgment of the District Court is reversed with respect to the constitutionality of § 441b's restrictions on corporate independent expenditures.

The judgment is affirmed with respect to BCRA's disclaimer and disclosure requirements. The case is remanded for further proceedings consistent with this opinion.

It is so ordered.

CRITICAL ASSESSMENT

Although § 441b aimed to protect the public from political speech distorted by the power of large corporations, the majority focused primarily on BCRA's unfairness to smaller and nonprofit corporations. Noting that "[p]olitical speech is 'indispensable to decisionmaking in a democracy,'" Kennedy concluded "this is no less true because the speech comes from a corporation rather than an individual."[11] Indeed, the only way to know "what is true and what is false" is by permitting all factions to speak.[12] Ignoring Congress's attempt to create a level playing field in the marketplace of ideas, Kennedy concluded that the FEC's stated concerns were rhetorical distractions that obscured the reality that 441b unlawfully suppressed speech.[13]

Plato might say that the FEC's arguments amounted to flattery or the counterfeit of justice. Although these arguments might satisfy an ignorant audience, the court was able to discern the truth that 441b deprived Citizens United the right to speak based on its identity. As Kennedy stated, it "'muffle[d] the voices that best represent the most significant segments of the economy'" and deprived the public of "'information, knowledge and opinion vital to its function.'"[14] To deny corporations the right to speak was neither constitutional nor just.

Justice Stevens's dissent[15] laid out a different view: "[t]he real issue in this case concern[ed] how, not if," Citizens United could finance and engage in political speech.[16] Citizens United was and is a wealthy nonprofit corporation with its own PAC, which could have paid to televise and promote *Hillary*. The only dispute was "whether Citizens United had a right to use the funds in its *general treasury* to pay for broadcasts during the 30–day period [before the presidential primary]."[17] Thus the court did not need "to rewrite the law relating to campaign expenditures by *for-profit* corporations and unions to decide this case."[18] And "its ruling threaten[ed] to undermine the integrity of elected institutions across the Nation."[19]

As to the court's inability to do other than invalidate § 441b, Stevens countered that the court could have held that the issue had been waived, that televising *Hillary* on cable television on demand did not constitute an electioneering communication, that an exception should be made for corporations with de minimus for-profit contributions, or that the statute was unconstitutional as applied in this case.[20] Stevens also argued that instead of a ban on speech, 441b operated as a permissible time, manner, and place restriction.[21] The majority's suggestion that 441b might apply to the media or be used to ban books or other works of fiction such as *Mr. Smith Goes to Washington* was "nonsense."[22]

Using Kennedy's words against him, Stevens took issue with the assertion that speech cannot be restricted on the basis of the speaker's identity, stating "the Court's denunciation of identity-based distinctions may have rhetorical appeal but it obscures reality."[23] As Stevens pointed out, the court has held that compelling government interests justify restrictions on several categories of speakers, including students, prisoners, and even government employees.[24]

More important, though, was the extent to which Kennedy ignored the longstanding regulation of corporate campaign speech (since 1907) and cases upholding the statute at issue.[25] What these precedents underscored was "the need to regulate corporate participation in candidate elections to '[p]reserv[e] the integrity of the electoral process, preven[t] corruption, . . . sustai[n] the active, alert responsibility of the individual citizen,' protect the expressive interests of shareholders, and '[p]reserv[e] . . . the individual citizen's confidence in government.'"[26] A wealthy corporation may be powerful, but that power "'may be no reflection of the power of its ideas.'"[27]

DISCUSSION QUESTIONS

Discussion Question 1: Why is the court suspicious of legal argument but not the viability of an "open marketplace" of ideas?

In this case, Justice Kennedy played the role of Socrates in *Gorgias* when he accused the FEC of using rhetoric to obscure its true motive to suppress corporate speech. Kennedy's approach seems inconsistent with the underlying premise of our adversarial system, in which competing arguments are thought to help the judge and jury find truth or the best truth possible under the circumstances. Why did the court use this device to question the FEC's credibility? If rhetoric can be used to distort truth in the judicial process, why doesn't the rhetoric of powerful corporations pose a similar risk in the marketplace of ideas? To what extent is the distinction between rhetoric and reality helpful in either context?

Discussion Question 2: Can there be one version of truth in a multicultural and pluralistic society? Among competing truths, whose truth matters most?

In this case, Justice Kennedy speaks about truth as though it were universal, as if the court's role is to discern the one truth that leads to justice in the case before it. In modern-day society, the notion of Truth with a capital T is plainly problematic. Since the early twentieth century, legal realists have acknowledged that judges make decisions based on the rule of law, precedent, public policy, and personal bias. But why should a particular judge's views control the outcome and to what extent do judges' views represent the broad spectrum of society? As critical legal scholars have made clear, the law often perpetuates the viewpoint of those in power, excluding or silencing the voices of underrepresented groups. To what extent does the majority opinion perpetuate traditional notions of justice and the status quo? Whose voices and viewpoints does it exclude?

Discussion Question 3: Why was the majority so concerned about the free speech rights of corporations?

The majority took the view that corporations are no different from individuals when it comes to political speech rights. Justice Kennedy rejected the idea that corporate wealth might be used to distort public opinion, concluding that Congress may not "restrict the speech of some elements of our society in order to enhance the relative voice of others."[28] In sharp contrast, Justice Stevens thought the court had a responsibility to "'equalize[] the relative ability of individuals and groups to influence the outcome of elections.'"[29] Why was the court primarily concerned with treating corporations fairly and giving them an equal voice without regard to their potential for distorting public opinion? In what ways do corporations resemble individual citizens and in what ways do they not?

Discussion Question 4: Did the majority engage in the same distortion of truth it accused the FEC of committing?

What was the truth in *Citizens United*? Justice Kennedy claimed that § 441b constituted an "outright ban" on corporate speech even though corporations could engage in the same prohibited speech as long as they used PAC donations to fund it. In that sense, did § 441b operate more as a permissible time, place, and manner restriction? Were you convinced that the end result was to protect all speaker's rights to engage equally in political speech, or did it "undermine the integrity of elected institutions across the Nation"?[30] Reread the court's concern that one of the stated goals of § 441b—to prevent undue influence on public opinion—could be used to prohibit media corporations (e.g., producers of news and entertainment) from engaging in political speech. Given that media corporations were already exempt from § 441b, was the court's concern convincing? Why does Justice Kennedy go so far as to say the FEC's rationale would ban the fictional movie *Mr. Smith Goes to Washington*?

Discussion Question 5: If you were deciding this case, how would you have framed the issue? What would you have ultimately decided?

Whether Congress can ban speech based solely on the identity of the speaker was not the only way to frame the issue in this case. Thus framed, the issue focused on the rights of the parties as opposed to the nature of their speech, their effect on public opinion, and the ultimate fairness of elections. As between the rights of the speaker and the effect of exercising those rights, which concern is paramount? Is there a different way to view the competing demands in this case? How would you have resolved them?

Discussion Question 6: Do competing versions of truth yield the best truth?

Having read the competing views of the parties and justices in this case, do you think you have a better sense of the truth than you would have had otherwise? How does this case affect your view of rhetoric and its role in judicial decision-making?

ADDITIONAL READINGS

Barnett, Randy, and Josh Blackmun. "Citizens United v. Federal Election Comm'n." In *An Introduction to Constitutional Law: 100 Supreme Court Cases Everyone Should Know*. Web.

Berger, Linda L. "What Is the Sound of a Corporation Speaking? Just Another Voice, According to the Supreme Court." *Administrative and Regulatory Law News* 35, no. 3 (2010): 8–9, 15.

Cairns, Huntington. "Introduction" to "Gorgias." In Hamilton and Cairns, *Plato: Plato's Dialogues*, xiii–xxv.

Heerwig, Jennifer A., and Katherine Shaw. "Through a Glass, Darkly: The Rhetoric and Reality of Campaign Finance Disclosure." *Georgetown Law Journal* 102 (2014): 1443–500.

Jowett, Benjamin. "Introduction" to "Gorgias." In *Plato: Plato's Dialogues*, edited and translated by Benjamin Jowett. Chapel Hill: Project Gutenberg, 2022 (1871).

Plato, *Plato's Dialogues*. Edited by Edith Hamilton and Huntington Cairns. Princeton, NJ: Princeton University Press, 1961.

Robertson, Christopher, D. Alex Winkelman, Kelly Bergstrand, and Darren Modzelewski. "The Appearance and the Reality of *Quid Pro Quo Corruption*: An Empirical Investigation." *Journal of Legal Analysis* 8, no. 3 (2016): 375–438.

Schotland, Roy A. "The Post-Citizens United Fantasy-land." *Cornell Journal of Law and Public Policy* 20 (2011): 753–60.

9

Aristotle

Persuasion and Practical Reason

EUGENE GARVER

INTRODUCTION

From its beginnings, the practice of rhetoric has always attracted suspicion, as well as paying customers. Many people don't think that persuasion has anything to do with reason but is instead a matter of manipulating people's emotions, or distracting or charming them with a style that convinces people of the speaker's intelligence, moral goodness, or that she's on our side. It's hard to see how to refute such an attitude, since one can assemble endless evidence against the rationality of rhetoric, and against the idea of any connection between rhetorical persuasion and practical reasoning. It might help a little to notice that the same accusations of irrationality of persuasion can be leveled against the pretense to rationality of the practical decision-making of a single individual; people are especially good at self-deception and thinking that we are more intelligent and morally good than we are. Modern discussions of free speech mirror this same ambivalence.

Aristotle's *Rhetoric* and the dissent by Oliver Wendell Holmes Jr. in *Abrams v. U.S.*—only a year after he spoke for a unanimous court in *Schenck v. U.S.* reaching the opposite conclusion—address exactly this problem.[1] Aristotle's art of rhetoric has an ambiguous relation to what he conceives good decisions and good institutions to be, and the *Rhetoric* can be a useful and challenging way to think about legal argument—not only the persuasive activity of the advocate but the deliberation and opinions of judges, and even the conversations between lawyer and client. This chapter includes excerpts from the first three chapters of the *Rhetoric*. These first chapters present Aristotle's orientation to the subject as a whole, as well as the relation between persuasion and its wider political context.

Think of Aristotle's project this way. What are the conditions under which the most persuasive argument *should* be the argument that persuades? The conditions under which the most persuasive argument most embodies and leads to good practical reasoning?

Aristotle's *Rhetoric* stands out among ancient treatments of persuasive speech by putting reasoning at the center of persuasion. Holmes's image of the marketplace of ideas proposes to substitute triumph in the market for triumph on the battlefield. Both are concerned, in very different ways, with the place of persuasive speech in a democracy and the ways in which argumentation can be a substitute for, and another form of, coercion. Aristotle's *Rhetoric* is an art of character: rational persuasion is a part of the ethical life of a citizen. In Holmes's vision, speakers and the state are rational actors pursing their own purposes.

Aristotle was born in Stagira in northern Greece in 384 BCE. He went to Athens when he was seventeen to study at Plato's academy, and continued there for twenty years until Plato's death in 347, so he was never an Athenian citizen. When Plato died, Aristotle moved to Assos in what is now Turkey, and then in 345 to the island of Lesbos, where he made detailed biological field work. Two years later he moved to Macedonia, at the request of King Philip II of Macedon to tutor his son, who would become Alexander the Great. In 335 he moved back to Athens and founded his own school, the Lyceum. But after Alexander died in 323, anti-Macedonian feeling made things unsafe for him in Athens and he moved one last time, to Chalcis, where he died a year later.

Aristotle, like Plato, published dialogues, none of which has survived. What we have instead are lecture notes from the courses he taught in his twelve years at the Lyceum. One reason they are hard to read is that they weren't intended to be read on their own but along with the lectures themselves. Those surviving works are from lectures he gave, ranging from logic through physics and psychology, biology, ethics and politics, and finally rhetoric and drama. The second reason his surviving works are hard to understand is that to understand one you need to understand them all, or at least it's unpredictable what else you need to read.

In particular, the *Rhetoric* has been read as allied with his logical works, with ethics and politics, and with his *Poetics*, the analysis of tragedy. For the purposes of this book, it is probably most useful to think of the *Rhetoric* as connected, in some way, with ethical and political problems and considerations.

The opening of the *Rhetoric* invites reflection on the relation between the activity of persuasion and the goods (or bads) it produces, as well as the relation between the kind of person one presents in the legal context and one's "real" self, and whether persuasive activity has any intrinsic value or is just unfortunately necessary, but nothing to be proud of being good at. It nicely pairs with Justice Oliver Wendell Holmes's dissent in *Abrams v. U.S.*, which is both about what to do with the defendants (and the law under which they were prosecuted and convicted) and with the place of persuasive activity in a democracy.

Aristotle distinguishes three kinds of rhetoric: deliberative oratory about decisions of what will be useful in the future; forensic or judicial decisions about the justice of past actions; and demonstrative or epideictic exhibitions about current values, both the noble and the base. The rest of book 1 shows how to construct arguments leading to those different kinds of judgments. The first part of book 2 is devoted to showing the role of emotions in those decisions—in spite of his saying in our selection that emotions should play no role in good decisions—and the rest of book 2 examines formal structures of practical reasoning. Book 3 completes the *Rhetoric* by showing the proper arrangement and style of a persuasive speech.

ARISTOTLE, *ON RHETORIC*

Editors' Note: The excerpt by Aristotle is drawn from Aristotle, *Rhetoric*, trans. W. Rhys Roberts (New York: Modern Library, 1954). Numbers in this excerpt in parentheses are in this translation. Omissions are indicated by ellipses.

Chapter 1

(1) The framers of the current treatises on rhetoric have constructed but a small portion of that art. The modes of persuasion [or proof] are the only true constituents of the art: everything else is merely accessory. These writers, however, say nothing about enthymemes, which are the substance of rhetorical persuasion, but deal mainly with non-essentials. The arousing of prejudice, pity, anger, and similar emotions has nothing to do with the essential facts, but is merely a personal appeal to the man who is judging the case. (2) Consequently if the rules for trials which are now laid down in some states—especially in well-governed states—were applied everywhere, such people would have nothing to say. . . . (3) It is not right to pervert the judge by moving him to anger or envy or pity—one might as well warp a carpenter's rule before using it.

(4) Again, a litigant has clearly nothing to do but to show that the alleged fact is so or is not so, that it has or has not happened. As to whether a thing is important or unimportant, just or unjust, the judge must surely refuse to take his instructions from the litigants: he must decide for himself all such points as the law-giver has not already defined for him. (5) Now, it is of great moment that well-drawn laws should themselves define all the points they possibly can and leave as few as may be to the decision of the judges; and this for several reasons. First, to find one man, or a few men, who are sensible persons and capable of legislating and administering justice is easier than to find a large number. Next, laws are made after long consideration, whereas decisions in the courts are given

at short notice, which makes it hard for those who try the case to satisfy the claims of justice and expediency. The weightiest reason of all is that the decision of the lawgiver is not particular but prospective and general, whereas members of the assembly and the jury find it their duty to decide on definite cases brought before them. They will often have allowed themselves to be so much influenced by feelings of friendship or hatred or self-interest that they lose any clear vision of the truth and have their judgement obscured by considerations of personal pleasure or pain. In general, then, the judge should, we say, be allowed to decide as few things as possible. But questions as to whether something has happened or has not happened, will be or will not be, is or is not, must of necessity be left to the judge, since the lawgiver cannot foresee them. . . .

(6) Hence it comes that, although the same systematic principles apply to political [or deliberative] as to forensic oratory, and although the former is a nobler business, and fitter for a citizen, than that which concerns the relations of private individuals, these authors say nothing about political oratory, but try, one and all, to write treatises on the way to plead in court. The reason for this is that in political oratory there is less inducement to talk about nonessentials. Political oratory is less given to unscrupulous practices than forensic, because it treats of wider issues. In a political debate the judge who is forming a judgement is making a decision about his own vital interests. There is no need, therefore, to prove anything except that the facts are what the supporter of a measure maintains they are. In forensic oratory this is not enough; to conciliate the listener is what pays here. It is other people's affairs that are to be decided, so that the judges, intent on their own satisfaction and listening with partiality, surrender themselves to the disputants instead of judging between them. . . .

(7) Persuasion is clearly a sort of demonstration, since we are most fully persuaded [convinced] when we consider a thing to have been demonstrated. The orator's demonstration is an enthymeme, and this is, in general, the most effective of the modes of persuasion. The enthymeme is a sort of syllogism, and the consideration of syllogisms of all kinds, without distinction, is the business of dialectic, either of dialectic as a whole or of one of its branches. It follows plainly, therefore, that he who is best able to see how and from what elements a syllogism is produced will also be best skilled in the enthymeme, when he has further learnt what its subject-matter is and in what respects it differs from the syllogism of strict logic. (8) The true and the apparently true are apprehended by the same faculty; it may also be noted that men have a sufficient natural instinct for what is true, and usually do arrive at the truth. Hence the man who makes a good guess at truth is likely to make a good guess at probabilities. It has now been shown that the ordinary writers on rhetoric treat of non-essentials; it has also been shown why they have inclined more towards the forensic branch of oratory.

(9) Rhetoric is useful (a) because things that are true and things that are just have a natural tendency to prevail over their opposites, so that if the decisions of judges are not what they ought to be, the defeat must be due to the speakers themselves, and they must be blamed accordingly. Moreover, (b) before some audiences not even the possession of the exactest knowledge will make it easy for what we say to produce conviction. For argument based on knowledge implies instruction, and there are people whom one cannot instruct. Here, then, we must use, as our modes of persuasion and argument, notions possessed by everybody, as we observed in the Topics when dealing with the way to handle a popular audience. Further, (c) we must be able to employ persuasion, just as strict reasoning can be employed, on opposite sides of a question, not in order that we may in practice employ it in both ways (for we must not make people believe what is wrong), but in order that we may see clearly what the facts are, and that, if another man argues unfairly, we on our part may be able to confute him. No other of the arts draws opposite conclusions: dialectic and rhetoric alone do this. Both these arts draw opposite conclusions impartially. Nevertheless, the underlying facts do not lend themselves equally well to the contrary views. No; things that are true and things that are better are, by their nature, practically always easier to prove and easier to believe in. Again, (d) it is absurd to hold that a man ought to be ashamed of being unable to defend himself with his limbs, but not of being unable to defend himself with speech and reason, when the use of rational speech is more distinctive of a human being than the use of his limbs. (10) And if it be objected that one who uses such power of speech unjustly again do great harm, that is a charge which may be made in common against all good things except virtue, and above all against the things that are most useful, as strength, health, wealth, generalship. A man can confer the greatest of benefits by a right use of these, and inflict the greatest of injuries by using them wrongly. It is clear, then, that rhetoric is not bound up with a single definite class of subjects, but is as universal as dialectic; it is clear, also, that it is useful.

(11) It is clear, further, that its function is not simply to succeed in persuading, but rather to discover the means of coming as near such success as the circumstances of each particular case allow. In this it resembles all other arts. For example, it is not the function of medicine simply to make a man quite healthy, but to put him as far as may be on the road to health; it is possible to give excellent treatment even to those who can never enjoy sound health. (12) Furthermore, it is plain that it is the function of one and the same art to discern the real and the apparent means of persuasion, just as it is the function of dialectic to discern the real and the apparent syllogism. What makes a man a "sophist" is not his faculty, but his moral purpose. In rhetoric, however, the

term 'rhetorician' may describe either the speaker's knowledge of the art, or his moral purpose. In dialectic it is different: a man is a "sophist" because he has a certain kind of moral purpose, a "dialectician" in respect, not of his moral purpose, but of his faculty. Let us now try to give some account of the systematic principles of Rhetoric itself-of the right method and means of succeeding in the object we set before us. We must make as it were a fresh start, and before going further define what rhetoric is.

Chapter 2

(1) Rhetoric may be defined as the faculty of observing in any given case the available means of persuasion. This is not a function of any other art. Every other art can instruct or persuade about its own particular subject-matter . . . (2) Of the modes of persuasion some belong strictly to the art of rhetoric and some do not. By the latter I mean such things as are not supplied by the speaker but are there at the outset-witnesses, evidence given under torture, written contracts, and so on. By the former I mean such as we can ourselves construct by means of the principles of rhetoric. The one kind has merely to be used, the other has to be invented. (3) Of the modes of persuasion furnished by the spoken word there are three kinds. The first kind depends on the personal character of the speaker; the second on putting the audience into a certain frame of mind; the third on the proof, or apparent proof, provided by the words of the speech itself. Persuasion is achieved by the speaker's personal character when the speech is so spoken as to make us think him credible. We believe good men more fully and more readily than others: this is true generally whatever the question is, and absolutely true where exact certainty is impossible and opinions are divided. This kind of persuasion, like the others, should be achieved by what the speaker says, not by what people think of his character before he begins to speak. It is not true, as some writers assume in their treatises on rhetoric, that the personal goodness revealed by the speaker contributes nothing to his power of persuasion; on the contrary, character may almost be called the most effective means of persuasion he possesses. Secondly, persuasion may come through the hearers, when the speech stirs their emotions. Our judgements when we are pleased and friendly are not the same as when we are pained and hostile. It is towards producing these effects, as we maintain, that present-day writers on rhetoric direct the whole of their efforts. This subject shall be treated in detail when we come to speak of the emotions. Thirdly, persuasion is effected through the speech itself when we have proved a truth or an apparent truth by means of the persuasive arguments suitable to the case in question. There are, then, these three means of effecting persuasion. The man who is to be in command of them must, it is clear, be able (a) to reason logically, (b) to understand

human character and goodness in their various forms, and (c) to understand the emotions-that is, to name them and describe them, to know their causes and the way in which they are excited. . . .

(4) The duty of rhetoric is to deal with such matters as we deliberate upon without arts or systems to guide us, in the hearing of persons who cannot take in at a glance a complicated argument, or follow a long chain of reasoning. The subjects of our deliberation are such as seem to present us with alternative possibilities: about things that could not have been, and cannot now or in the future be, other than they are, nobody who takes them to be of this nature wastes his time in deliberation. . . . Most of the things about which we make decisions, and into which therefore we inquire, present us with alternative possibilities. For it is about our actions that we deliberate and inquire, and all our actions have a contingent character; hardly any of them are determined by necessity. Again, conclusions that state what is merely usual or possible must be drawn from premises that do the same, just as "necessary" conclusions must be drawn from "necessary" premises; this too is clear to us from [Aristotle's treatise on logic]. It is evident, therefore, that the propositions forming the basis of enthymemes, though some of them may be "necessary," will most of them be only usually true.

Chapter 3

(1) Rhetoric falls into three divisions, determined by the three classes of listeners to speeches. For of the three elements in speech-making—speaker, subject, and person addressed—it is the last one, the hearer, that determines the speech's end and object. The hearer must be either a judge, with a decision to make about things past or future, or an observer. A member of the assembly decides about future events, a juryman about past events: while those who merely decide on the orator's skill are observers. From this it follows that there are three divisions of oratory—(a) political, (b) forensic, and (c) the demonstrative oratory of display. (2) Political speaking urges us either to do or not to do something: one of these two courses is always taken by private counsellors, as well as by people who address public assemblies. Forensic speaking either attacks or defends somebody: one or other of these two things must always be done by the parties in a case. The demonstrative oratory of display either praises or censures somebody. These three kinds of rhetoric refer to three different kinds of time. The political orator is concerned with the future: it is about things to be done hereafter that he advises, for or against. The party in a case at law is concerned with the past; one person accuses the other, and the other defends himself, with reference to things already done. The demonstrative orator is, properly speaking, concerned with the present, since everyone praises or blames in view of the state of things existing at the time, though they often find it useful also to recall

the past and to make guesses at the future. (3) Rhetoric has three distinct ends in view, one for each of its three kinds. The political orator aims at establishing the expediency or the harmfulness of a proposed course of action; if he urges its acceptance, he does so on the ground that it will do good; if he urges its rejection, he does so on the ground that it will do harm; and all other points, such as whether the proposal is just or unjust, honorable or dishonorable, he brings in as subsidiary and relative to this main consideration. Parties in a law-case aim at establishing the justice or injustice of some action, and they too bring in all other points as subsidiary and relative to this one. Those who praise or attack a man aim at proving him worthy of honor or the reverse, and they too treat all other considerations with reference to this one. That the three kinds of rhetoric do aim respectively at the three ends we have mentioned is shown by the fact that speakers will sometimes not try to establish anything else. Thus, the litigant will sometimes not deny that a thing has happened or that he has done harm. But that he is guilty of injustice he will never admit; otherwise there would be no need of a trial. So too, political orators often make any concession short of admitting that they are recommending their hearers to take an inexpedient course or not to take an expedient one. The question whether it is not unjust for a city to enslave its innocent neighbors often does not trouble them at all. In like manner those who praise or censure someone do not consider whether his acts have been expedient or not, but often make it a ground of actual praise that he has neglected his own interest to do what was honorable. Thus, they praise Achilles because he championed his fallen friend Patroclus, though he knew that this meant death, and that otherwise he need not die: yet while to die thus was the nobler thing for him to do, the expedient thing was to live on. It is evident from what has been said that it is these three subjects, more than any others, about which the orator must be able to have propositions at his command.

SCHENCK V. UNITED STATES, 249 U.S. 47 (1919)

Garver Note: We will compare Justice Holmes's majority opinion in *Schenck*, upholding the conviction of persons under the Espionage Act for seeking to persuade men not to submit to being drafted to fight in World War I, with his dissenting opinion in *Abrams* the following year in which he adopts the opposite view and refuses to uphold a conviction for sedition during wartime. The excerpt begins with the syllabus of the court.[2]

Syllabus of the Court.

While the United States was at war, defendants circulated leaflets that urged men to refuse to submit to the draft into military service. For attempting to obstruct military recruitment, defendants were convicted of crimes pursuant to the Espionage Act, 40 Stat. 217, 219. Defendants contended that the distribution of the leaflets was activity protected by the First Amendment. The Court admitted that in many places and in ordinary times, the distribution of the leaflets would have been within defendants' constitutional rights. The Court explained, however, that the character of protected speech depended upon the circumstances in which it was expressed. For example, the most stringent protection of free speech would not protect a man in falsely shouting fire in a theatre and causing a panic. The question in every case was whether the words were used in such circumstances and were of such nature as to create a clear and present danger that they would bring about the substantive evils that Congress had a right to prevent. Because Congress was within its power to punish activity intended to obstruct the draft, the conviction of defendants did not violate the First Amendment.

Mr. Justice HOLMES delivered the opinion of the Court.

This is an indictment in three counts. The first charges a conspiracy to violate the Espionage Act of June 15, 1917, . . . by causing and attempting to cause insubordination, &c., in the military and naval forces of the United States, and to obstruct the recruiting and enlistment service of the United States, when the United States was at war with the German Empire, to-wit, that the defendant willfully conspired to have printed and circulated to men who had been called and accepted for military service under the Act of May 18, 1917, a document set forth and alleged to be calculated to cause such insubordination and obstruction. The count alleges overt acts in pursuance of the conspiracy, ending in the distribution of the document set forth. The second count alleges a conspiracy to commit an offense against the United States, to-wit, to use the mails for the transmission of matter declared to be non-mailable, to-wit, the above mentioned document, with an averment of the same overt acts. The third count charges an unlawful use of the mails for the transmission of the same matter and otherwise as above. The defendants were found guilty on all the counts. They set up the First Amendment to the Constitution forbidding Congress to make any law abridging the freedom of speech, or of the press, and bringing the case here on that ground have argued some other points also of which we must dispose.

Of course the document would not have been sent unless it had been intended to have some effect, and we do not see what effect it could be expected to have upon persons subject to the draft except to influence them to obstruct the carrying of it out. The defendants do not deny that the jury might find against them on this point. . . .

But it is said, suppose that that was the tendency of this circular, it is protected by the First Amendment to the Constitution. Two of the strongest expressions are said to be quoted respectively from well-known public men. It well may be that the prohibition of laws abridging the freedom of speech is not confined to previous restraints, although to prevent them may have been the main purpose. . . . We admit that in many places and in ordinary times the defendants in saying all that was said in the circular would have been within their constitutional rights. But the character of every act depends upon the circumstances in which it is done. The most stringent protection of free speech would not protect a man in falsely shouting fire in a theatre and causing a panic. It does not even protect a man from an injunction against uttering words that may have all the effect of force. . . . The question in every case is whether the words used are used in such circumstances and are of such a nature as to create a clear and present danger that they will bring about the substantive evils that Congress has a right to prevent. It is a question of proximity and degree. When a nation is at war many things that might be said in time of peace are such a hindrance to its effort that their utterance will not be endured so long as men fight and that no Court could regard them as protected by any constitutional right. It seems to be admitted that if an actual obstruction of the recruiting service were proved, liability for words that produced that effect might be enforced. The statute of 1917 punishes conspiracies to obstruct as well as actual obstruction. If the act, (speaking, or circulating a paper,) its tendency and the intent with which it is done are the same, we perceive no ground for saying that success alone warrants making the act a crime. . . . Indeed that case might be said to dispose of the present contention if the precedent covers all media concludendi. But as the right to free speech was not referred to specially, we have thought fit to add a few words.

It was not argued that a conspiracy to obstruct the draft was not within the words of the Act of 1917. The words are "obstruct the recruiting or enlistment service," and it might be suggested that they refer only to making it hard to get volunteers. Recruiting heretofore usually having been accomplished by getting volunteers the word is apt to call up that method only in our minds. But recruiting is gaining fresh supplies for the forces, as well by draft as otherwise. It is put as an alternative to enlistment or voluntary enrollment in this act.

Judgments affirmed.

ABRAMS ET. AL. V. U.S., 250 U.S. 616 (1919)

Garver Note: In his opinion in *Abrams* Justice Holmes seemingly reverses course, dissenting from a decision upholding convictions under the Sedition Act because the defendants wrote and circulated a pair of leaflets condemning President Wilson for sending troops to intervene in the civil war in Russia against the Soviets. The Sedition Act was enacted to prevent interference with the war against Germany; it made it a crime to "willfully urge, incite, or advocate any curtailment of production [of materials] . . . necessary or essential to the prosecution of the war."

This indictment is founded wholly upon the publication of two leaflets which I shall describe in a moment.

No argument seems to be necessary to show that these pronuncamentos in no way attack the form of government of the United States, or that they do not support either of the first two counts. . . . It seems too plain to be denied that the suggestion to workers in the ammunition factories that they are producing bullets to murder their dearest, and the further advocacy of a general strike, both in the second leaflet, do urge curtailment of production of things necessary to the prosecution of the war within the meaning of the Act of May 16, 1918. But to make the conduct criminal that statute requires that it should be 'with intent by such curtailment to cripple or hinder the United States in the prosecution of the war.' It seems to me that no such intent is proved.

I am aware of course that the word "intent" as vaguely used in ordinary legal discussion means no more than knowledge at the time of the act that the consequences said to be intended will ensue. Even less than that will satisfy the general principle of civil and criminal liability. A man may have to pay damages, may be sent to prison, at common law might be hanged, if at the time of his act he knew facts from which common experience showed that the consequences would follow, whether he individually could foresee them or not. But, when words are used exactly, a deed is not done with intent to produce a consequence unless that consequence is the aim of the deed. It may be obvious, and obvious to the actor, that the consequence will follow, and he may be liable for it even if he regrets it, but he does not do the act with intent to produce it unless the aim to produce it is the proximate motive of the specific act, although there may be some deeper motive behind.

It seems to me that this statute must be taken to use its words in a strict and accurate sense. They would be absurd in any other. A patriot might think that we were wasting money on aeroplanes, or making more cannon of a certain kind than we needed, and might advocate curtailment with success, yet even if it turned out that the curtailment hindered and was thought by other minds to have been obviously likely to hinder the United States in the prosecution of the war, no one would hold such conduct a crime. I admit that my illustration does not answer all that might be said but it is enough to show what I think and to let me pass to a more important aspect of the case. I refer to the First Amendment to the Constitution that Congress shall make no law abridging the freedom of speech.

I never have seen any reason to doubt that the questions of law that alone were before this Court in the cases of *Schenck*, *Frohwerk*, and *Debs*, were rightly decided. I do not doubt for a moment that by the same reasoning that would justify punishing persuasion to murder, the United States constitutionally may punish speech that produces or is intended to produce a clear and imminent danger that it will bring about forthwith certain substantive evils that the United States constitutionally may seek to prevent. The power undoubtedly is greater in time of war than in time of peace because war opens dangers that do not exist at other times.

But as against dangers peculiar to war, as against others, the principle of the right to free speech is always the same. It is only the present danger of immediate evil or an intent to bring it about that warrants Congress in setting a limit to the expression of opinion where private rights are not concerned. Congress certainly cannot forbid all effort to change the mind of the country. Now nobody can suppose that the surreptitious publishing of a silly leaflet by an unknown man, without more, would present any immediate danger that its opinions would hinder the success of the government arms or have any appreciable tendency to do so. Publishing those opinions for the very purpose of obstructing, however, might indicate a greater danger and at any rate would have the quality of an attempt. So I assume that the second leaflet if published for the purposes alleged in the fourth count might be punishable. But it seems pretty clear to me that nothing less than that would bring these papers within the scope of this law. . . .

Even if I am technically wrong and enough can be squeezed from these poor and puny anonymities to turn the color of legal litmus paper; I will add, even if what I think the necessary intent were shown; the most nominal punishment seems to me all that possible could be inflicted, unless the defendants are to be made to suffer not for what the indictment alleges but for the creed that they avow—a creed that I believe to be the creed of ignorance and immaturity when honestly held, as I see no reason to doubt that it was held here but which, although made the subject of examination at the trial, no one has a right even to consider in dealing with the charges before the Court.

Persecution for the expression of opinions seems to me perfectly logical. If you have no doubt of your premises or your power and want a certain result with all your heart you naturally express your wishes in law and sweep away all opposition. To allow opposition by speech seems to indicate that you think the speech impotent, as when a man says that he has squared the circle, or that you do not care whole heartedly for the result, or that you doubt either your power or your premises. But when men have realized that time has upset many fighting faiths, they may come to believe even more than they believe the very foundations of their own conduct that the ultimate good desired is better reached

> by free trade in ideas—that the best test of truth is the power of the thought to get itself accepted in the competition of the market, and that truth is the only ground upon which their wishes safely can be carried out. That at any rate is the theory of our Constitution. It is an experiment, as all life is an experiment. Every year if not every day we have to wager our salvation upon some prophecy based upon imperfect knowledge. While that experiment is part of our system I think that we should be eternally vigilant against attempts to check the expression of opinions that we loathe and believe to be fraught with death, unless they so imminently threaten immediate interference with the lawful and pressing purposes of the law that an immediate check is required to save the country. I wholly disagree with the argument of the Government that the First Amendment left the common law as to seditious libel in force. History seems to me against the notion. I had conceived that the United States through many years had shown its repentance for the Sedition Act of 1798, by repaying fines that it imposed. Only the emergency that makes it immediately dangerous to leave the correction of evil counsels to time warrants making any exception to the sweeping command, "Congress shall make no law abridging the freedom of speech." Of course I am speaking only of expressions of opinion and exhortations, which were all that were uttered here, but I regret that I cannot put into more impressive words my belief that in their conviction upon this indictment the defendants were deprived of their rights under the Constitution of the United States.

CRITICAL ASSESSMENT

Recall Aristotle's definition of rhetoric at the end of chapter 1 and the start of chapter 2 in *Rhetoric*, as excerpted in this chapter. Rhetoric is the art of finding in any case the available means of persuasion. He denies that successful persuading is its definition, comparing the art of rhetoric to medicine, where a doctor can successfully exercise her art even though she fails to heal some particular patient. That is, there are values of argument distinct from the value of winning. Holmes's image of the marketplace of ideas in *Abrams* denies such internal values; the only good of an idea is its ability to win customers. Both of these can be arguments in favor of a place for persuasion in a democracy, but they are very different appeals.

Recall, too, Aristotle's three kinds of rhetoric in chapter 3 in this book. While legislatures make decisions about what they think will be useful in the future, and demonstrative or epideictic rhetoric celebrates the community's values and praises acts that exhibit those values and blames actions that violate them, law courts use judicial or forensic rhetoric to make judgments about the justice or injustice of past acts, deciding whether they violating a law.

In his final paragraph in *Abrams*, Holmes turns from judicial to demonstrative or epideictic rhetoric, which presents constitutive American values, connected to the Constitutions. He says that the constitution is an experiment. Under his interpretation, advocacy is itself an experiment to be tested against competing hypotheses. The speakers, whether poor and puny anonymities or Supreme Court justices, don't present their arguments as hypotheses but as true assertions, to be accepted and not tested. Holmes invites his readers, and eventually the American community, to interpret those assertions as hypotheses. (Think too of his opinion in *Lochner* (at 546): a "constitution is not intended to embody a particular economic theory. [I]t is made for people of fundamentally differing views.")

Changing the kind of persuasive argument from judicial to demonstrative rhetoric can be a distracting tactic: if you can't prove your innocence, wave the American flag. Holmes's epideictic argument is more worth considering because in saying that their speech should be protected, he doesn't invite the audience to think any more highly of the speakers or the value of their speech; their speech should be protected not because it's good speech but because permitting it is an American value.

DISCUSSION QUESTIONS

Discussion Question 1: Holmes's dissent in *Abrams*, with the famous paragraph about not suppressing other people's fighting faiths, can be read in at least two ways. Either there is a truth, a right answer to the question of "the ultimate good," and free debate is the best way of uncovering that truth. Or, the truth is, by definition, what wins the debate. Truth, then, is the outcome of a human process. Might makes right. Competition in the market either uncovers the best product, or simply the most popular.

In a similar vein Aristotle says that rhetoric "draws opposite conclusions. Nevertheless, the underlying facts do not lend themselves equally well to the contrary views. Things that are true and things that are better are, by their nature, practically always easier to prove and easier to believe in." This might be a dictum independent of the idea of rhetorical argument, or it says something about how persuasive argument works.

What difference does it make for constructing and interpreting legal argument whether you think that truths are out there to be discovered or need to be constructed through argument itself?

See whether this quotation from Mill's *On Liberty* helps you to think about the question:

> The dictum that truth always triumphs over persecution is one of those pleasant falsehoods which men repeat after one another till they pass into commonplaces, but which all experience refutes. History teems with instances of truth put down by persecution. If not suppressed forever, it may be thrown back for centuries.[3]

There is a difference between seeing rhetoric as a necessary part of political decision-making and judgment through an analogy to a marketplace and an analogy to the progress of science through testing hypotheses through experiment. Aristotle doesn't offer either analogy in his exposition of why rhetoric is useful (see chapter 1, (9), above). But it's worth comparing both Aristotle and Holmes on this point with the analogy between free political debate and the scientific method. For a refutation of that idea, consider the following:

> Some people fancy that bias and counter-bias are favorable to the extraction of truth—that hot and cold partisan debate is the way to investigate. This is the theory of our atrocious legal procedure. But logic puts its heel upon this suggestion. It irrefragably demonstrates that knowledge can only be furthered by the real desire for it, and that the methods of obstinacy, of authority, and every mode of trying to reach a foregone conclusion, are absolutely of no value.[4]

Peirce denies that the adversary system, and the marketplace of ideas, has anything to do with the methods of science. It implies that the winner in that marketplace has nothing to do with its truth, that there is no reason to think that marketplace of ideas will lead to truth. Does Holmes, and does the American legal system, have any resources to defend the marketplace of ideas against the criticisms from Mill and Peirce?

Discussion Question 2: Consider the "marketplace" side of Holmes's image. Markets are rarely free. Costs of entry make it easier for some people to sell their products than others. The defendants, with no power to get their message across, aren't likely to have their product adopted by the marketplace of ideas, while the powerful, as in *Citizens United* elsewhere in this volume. There are other factors that the marketplace image doesn't take into account: a product can produce and not just satisfy desires. Given such considerations, does a triumph in the marketplace of ideas mean a that the successful argument is the one that wins a popularity contest, a contest that isn't one between equals? What would it take for the competition between ideas to be more than a popularity contest? The question of regulating markets is important enough to receive two clauses in Article I of the Constitution which authorizes Congress the power to regulate economic activity in at least two ways, by "fix[ing] the standard of weights and measurement," and "to promote the Progress of Science and useful Arts, by securing for limited Times to Authors and Inventors the exclusive Right to their respective Writings and Discoveries." The state has to be able to prevent, or punish, fraud, and do many other things—and refrain from doing others—to make sure that "competition of the market" really is competitive. Does Holmes's dictum give any ideas of what regulations could be parallel for the competition of the market of ideas?

We asked earlier of Aristotle what are the conditions in which the most persuasive argument is one that leads to truth and the exercise of practical reason. The parallel question for Holmes in *Abrams* is: What are the conditions under which a market, whether for goods or ideas, is a system that leads to the success of not only the cheapest way of satisfying desires but truths we can live by? Consider how your answer would have consequences for the adversary system in law, whether in a court in front of a judge or jury, or in a decision to go to trial, or other places where rhetorical competition is at work.

Discussion Question 3: What is the disagreement between the Holmes who wrote *Schenck* and the one who wrote the *Abrams* dissent? I'm not asking about what factors made Holmes change his mind, if he did, but the difference in legal analysis. The facts in *Schenck* and in *Abrams* don't seem different enough to explain the different outcomes. He says that he regards *Schenck*, which he wrote, as good law. If the facts and the law haven't changed, is one argument simply right and the other wrong?

Discussion Question 4: Should we think differently depending on how powerful the speakers are? The pamphlet may be silly, and its authors "poor and puny anonymities," but incendiary language is a weapon of the weak. One could say that if the leaflets actually might succeed in their purpose, the case should be treated differently. But that's different from saying that the language of someone in a position to say something that could succeed has to be stylistically different.

Or, to look at the question from the point of view of the speakers, does one's power limit the possible modes of arguing—what is an appropriate (or at least protected) appeal for a poor and pure anonymity might be incitement or count as an attempt when made by someone more powerful?

Does this defense of free speech reduce to saying that political speech should be free when it doesn't matter?

Discussion Question 5: Holmes says that "when men have realized that time has upset many fighting faiths, they *may* come to believe even more than they believe the very foundations of their own conduct that the ultimate good desired is better reached by free trade in ideas." The emphasis on "*may*" asks what it takes for people to have this even stronger belief in the free trade in ideas. What if one were to emphasize *the ultimate good desired*." What would this mean?

Holmes does not say that people should give up their fighting faiths. They add to those fighting faiths a faith in the democratic experiment. Advocates shouldn't stop being advocates. So how does this realization that Holmes identifies with the American experiment affect the way lawyers should argue? This new belief that people may come to have changes their ēthos as arguers. Character or *ēthos* was one of Aristotle's modes of persuasion, and the one he picks out as most powerful. Is the change that Holmes advocates toleration as an ethical virtue of how we treat one another, or is it an ethical value concerning how the state and society are organized?

ADDITIONAL READINGS

Aristotle, *Rhetoric*. Translated by W. Rhys Roberts. New York: Modern Library, 1954.

Foucault, Michel. *Discourse and Truth and Parrēsia*. Edited by Henri-Paul Fruchaud and Daniele Lorenzini. English edition established by Nancy Luxon. Chicago: University of Chicago Press, 2019.

Garver, Eugene. *Aristotle's Rhetoric: An Art of Character*. Chicago: University of Chicago Press, 1995.

———. *For the Sake of Argument: Practical Reasoning, Character and the Ethics of Belief*. Chicago: University of Chicago Press, 2004.

Healy, Thomas. *The Great Dissent: How Oliver Wendell Holmes Changed His Mind—and Changed the History of Free Speech in America*. New York: Metropolitan Books, 2013.

Levy, Leonard W. *Origins of the Bill of Rights*. New Haven, CT: Yale University Press, 2008.

McKeon, Richard. "Rhetoric and Poetic in the Philosophy of Aristotle." In Elder Olson, *Aristotle's Poetics and English Literature; A Collection of Critical Essays*, 201–36. Chicago: University of Chicago Press, 1965.

10

Aristotle

Aristotle's Topics and U.S. v. Lopez

CATHERINE L. LANGFORD

INTRODUCTION

Around 600 BCE in ancient Greece, following the overthrow of tyrants and the establishment of a democratic system of governance, people needed the ability to generate persuasive arguments. Teachers of rhetoric taught public speaking, focusing on the question of how to persuade an audience within the legislative assembly and courts of law. At issue was what types of arguments might effectively persuade an audience. One of the most significant teachers of rhetoric was Aristotle, whose ideas became the foundation of public speaking as it is taught today. According to Aristotle, speakers can use commonplace topics to invent or to discover persuasive arguments.

A scholar of rhetoric, philosophy, metaphysics, ethics, politics, logic, and more, Aristotle wrote many influential treatises on a variety of subjects during the last decade of his life. One influential subject is his concept of commonplace topics, also known as "topoi." The singular form of the word, "topos," translates from Greek to English to mean "place" or "location." The spatial metaphor of "place" relates back to the classical tradition of memorizing information by connecting it to a physical location—what some have called a "memory palace" in contemporary parlance. The topics provide a quick and easy shorthand approach to argumentation. Commonplace topics help with the invention process in argumentation, as topoi can be discovered or invented. For subjects about which commonplaces already exist, one merely needs to access the topics that exist about that subject. For subjects about which commonplaces do not already exist, they can be invented. Invention, or the coming up with arguments and reasoning, is the first of five canons of classical rhetoric (the others being arrangement, style, memory, and delivery; see chapter 2).

Although other scholars in the classical era also discussed the use of topoi in argumentation, Aristotle's treatment of the subject in his books titled *Topics* and *Rhetoric* offer the most throughout accounting of topoi in antiquity, enabling advocates to construct arguments regarding a wide variety of topics. According to the *Rhetoric*, a topos is selected based upon a claim we want either to defend or to refute. The *Rhetoric* then discusses general topics and specific topics. General topics can apply to almost any topic and include, among others, accidents, what is better or worse, genus, property, and definitions. Specific topics are relevant to a particular subject matter. Aristotle focuses his discussion on specific topics related to the three genres of rhetoric: deliberative, epideictic, and forensic. Deliberative rhetoric attempts to persuade the audience to take an action in the future. Epideictic rhetoric is a speech of praise or blame. Forensic rhetoric focuses on convincing someone that something is just or unjust, right or wrong. Aristotle tells us that the law can use both general and specific topics. Once a conclusion has been established, the topos allows an advocate to construct an argument in support of the chosen conclusion.

Topics, therefore, are heuristic devices that aid lawyers in interpretive processes. Topics also can be used to analyze the legal decision-making by judges. When bringing the case before a court, lawyers should evaluate the types of arguments judges use in their judicial opinions and craft arguments that will be persuasive to the judges before whom they appear based on their evaluation.

Aristotle's topoi teach us that advocates do not always produce fresh and unique arguments each time they approach a legal quandary. Rather, lawyers deploy arguments that fall predictably within certain typologies or topics. Using and looking for topics in legal arguments enables lawyers and judges to determine which legal doctrines apply to cases and ascertain how best to develop and present their side within acceptable legal frameworks.

The subsequent excerpt is from Aristotle's discussion of topics in *Rhetoric*, where he organizes topoi by subject matter, including (1) the three branches of rhetoric: deliberative (political), epideictic (ceremonial), and forensic (judicial), and (2) a general category. Aristotle is followed by an excerpt from the 1995 US Supreme Court case *United States v. Lopez*. In that case, the court considered the question of whether, under the US Constitution's commerce clause, the federal government could regulate the possession of guns on school premises. *Lopez* provides an opportunity to look for topoi in a court opinion.

ARISTOTLE, *ON RHETORIC*

Editors' Note: The following are excerpts from John Henry Freese's (1852–1930) translation of Aristotle's *Rhetoric*, books 1 and 2. This version is available in the public domain at the Perseus Digital Library hosted by Tufts University's website.

Internal page references and footnotes have been removed. Some minor grammatical changes have been made to improve readability. Ellipses indicate omissions. Numbers in brackets around a colon indicate books and chapters (e.g., "[1:2]" is book 1, chapter 2), and those around a single numeral indicate individual sections within those chapters, all according to the conventional division used in the Perseus edition.

[1:2] Rhetoric then may be defined as the faculty of discovering the possible means of persuasion in reference to any subject whatever. . . . [2] As for proofs, some are artificial, others inartificial. By the latter I understand all those which have not been furnished by ourselves but were already in existence, such as witnesses, tortures, contracts, and the like; by the former, all that can be constructed by system and by our own efforts. Thus we have only to make use of the latter, whereas we must invent the former. . . .

Langford Note: Aristotle discusses inartistic proofs of forensic oratory.

[1:15] [2] These proofs are five in number: laws, witnesses, contracts, torture, oaths. [3] Let us first then speak of the laws, and state what use should be made of them when exhorting or dissuading, accusing or defending. [4] For it is evident that, if the written law is counter to our case, we must have recourse to the general law and equity, as more in accordance with justice; [5] and we must argue that, when the dicast takes an oath to decide to the best of his judgement, he means that he will not abide rigorously by the written laws; [6] that equity is ever constant and never changes, even as the general law, which is based on nature, whereas the written laws often vary. . . .

[13] Witnesses are of two kinds, ancient and recent; of the latter some share the risk of the trial, others are outside it. . . . [14] One should appeal to such witnesses for the past, but also to interpreters of oracles for the future. . . . [15] By recent witnesses I mean all well-known persons who have given a decision on any point, for their decisions are useful to those who are arguing about similar cases. . . . [16] And those who share the risk of the trial, if they are thought to be perjurers. Such witnesses only serve to establish whether an act has taken place or not, whether it is or is not the case; but if it is a question of the quality of the act, for instance, whether it is just or unjust, expedient or inexpedient, [17] they are not competent witnesses; but witnesses from a distance are very

trustworthy even in regard to this. But ancient witnesses are the most trustworthy of all, for they cannot be corrupted. In regard to the confirmation of evidence, when a man has no witnesses, he can say that the decision should be given in accordance with probabilities, and that this is the meaning of the oath "according to the best of one's judgement"; that probabilities cannot be bribed to deceive, and that they cannot be convicted of bearing false witness. But if a man has witnesses and his adversary has none, he can say that probabilities incur no responsibility, and that there would have been no need of evidence, if an investigation according to the arguments were sufficient. [18] Evidence partly concerns ourselves, partly our adversary, as to the fact itself or moral character; so that it is evident that one never need lack useful evidence. For, if we have no evidence as to the fact itself, neither in confirmation of our own case nor against our opponent, it will always be possible to obtain some evidence as to character that will establish either our own respectability or the worthlessness of our opponent. [19] As for all the other questions relative to a witness, whether he is a friend, an enemy, or neutral, of good or bad or middling reputation, and for all other differences of this kind, we must have recourse to the same topics as those from which we derive our enthymemes.

[20] As for contracts, argument may be used to the extent of magnifying or minimizing their importance, of proving that they do or do not deserve credit. If we have them on our side, we must try to prove them worthy of credit and authoritative; but if they are on the side of our opponent, we must do the opposite. . . . [27] As to oaths four divisions may be made; for either we tender an oath and accept it, or we do neither, or one without the other, and in the last case we either tender but do not accept, or accept but do not tender. Besides this, one may consider whether the oath has already been taken by us or by the other party. . . .

[1:2] [21] I mean by dialectical and rhetorical syllogisms those which are concerned with what we call "topics," which may be applied alike to Law, Physics, Politics, and many other sciences that differ in kind, such as the topic of the more or less, which will furnish syllogisms and enthymemes equally well for Law, Physics, or any other science whatever, although these subjects differ in kind.

Langford note: A syllogism is formal reasoning that reaches a conclusion from two premises. An enthymeme is a syllogism that is missing one of its premises.

Specific topics on the other hand are derived from propositions which are peculiar to each species or genus of things; there are, for example, propositions about Physics which can furnish neither enthymemes nor syllogisms about Ethics, and there are propositions concerned with Ethics which will be useless for furnishing conclusions about Physics; and the same holds good in all cases. The first kind of topics will not make a man practically wise about any particular class of things, because they do not deal with any particular subject matter; but as to the specific topics, the happier a man is in his choice of propositions, the more he will unconsciously produce a science quite different from Dialectic and Rhetoric. For if once he hits upon first principles, it will no longer be Dialectic or Rhetoric, but that science whose principles he has arrived at. [22] Most enthymemes are constructed from these specific topics, which are called particular and special, fewer from those that are common or universal. . . .

Langford Note: Aristotle discusses the specific topics of deliberative rhetoric.

[1:4] . . . [7] Now, we may say that the most important subjects about which all men deliberate and deliberative orators harangue, are five in number, to wit: ways and means, war and peace, the defense of the country, imports and exports, legislation.

[8] Accordingly, the orator who is going to give advice on ways and means should be acquainted with the nature and extent of the State resources, so that if any is omitted it may be added, and if any is insufficient, it may be increased. Further, he should know all the expenses of the State, that if any is superfluous, it may be removed, or, if too great, may be curtailed. . . . [9] In regard to war and peace, the orator should be acquainted with the power of the State, how great it is already and how great it may possibly become; of what kind it is already and what additions may possibly be made to it; further, what wars it has waged and its conduct of them. . . . [10] Again, in regard to the defense of the country, he should not be ignorant how it is carried on; he should know both the strength of the guard, its character, and the positions of the guard-houses (which is impossible for one who is unacquainted with the country), so that if any guard is insufficient it may be increased, or if any is superfluous it may be disbanded, and greater attention devoted to suitable positions. [11] Again, in regard to food, he should know what amount of expenditure is sufficient to support the State; what kind of food is produced at home or can be imported; and what exports and imports are necessary, in order that contracts and agreements may be made with those who can furnish them; for it is necessary to keep the citizens free from reproach in their relations with two classes of people—those who are stronger and those who are useful for commercial purposes. [12] With a view to the safety of the State, it is necessary that the orator should be able to judge of all these questions, but an understanding of legislation is of special importance, for it is on the laws that the safety of the State is based. Wherefore he must know how many forms of government there are; what is expedient for

each; and the natural causes of its downfall, whether they are peculiar to the particular form of government or opposed to it. . . . [13] Moreover, with reference to acts of legislation, it is useful not only to understand what form of government is expedient by judging in the light of the past, but also to become acquainted with those in existence in other nations, and to learn what kinds of government are suitable to what kinds of people. . . .

Langford Note: Aristotle discusses the specific topics of epideictic rhetoric.

[1:9] [1] We will next speak of virtue and vice, of the noble and the disgraceful, since they constitute the aim of one who praises and of one who blames; for, when speaking of these, we shall incidentally bring to light the means of making us appear of such and such a character, which, as we have said, is a second method of proof; for it is by the same means that we shall be able to inspire confidence in ourselves or others in regard to virtue. . . .

[5] The components of virtue are justice, courage, self-control, magnificence, magnanimity, liberality, gentleness, practical and speculative wisdom. [6] The greatest virtues are necessarily those which are most useful to others, if virtue is the faculty of conferring benefits. For this reason, justice and courage are the most esteemed, the latter being useful to others in war, the former in peace as well. Next is liberality, for the liberal spend freely and do not dispute the possession of wealth, which is the chief object of other men's desire. [7] Justice is a virtue which assigns to each man his due in conformity with the law; injustice claims what belongs to others, in opposition to the law. [8] Courage makes men perform noble acts in the midst of dangers according to the dictates of the law and in submission to it; the contrary is cowardice. [9] Self-control is a virtue which disposes men in regard to the pleasures of the body as the law prescribes; the contrary is licentiousness. [10] Liberality does good in many matters; the contrary is avarice. [11] Magnanimity is a virtue productive of great benefits; the contrary is little-mindedness. [12] Magnificence is a virtue which produces greatness in matters of expenditure; the contraries are little-mindedness and meanness. [13] Practical wisdom is a virtue of reason, which enables men to come to a wise decision in regard to good and evil things, which have been mentioned as connected with happiness. . . .

Langford Note: Aristotle discusses the specific topics of forensic rhetoric.

[1:10] [1] We have next to speak of the number and quality of the propositions of which those syllogisms are constructed which have for their object accusation and defense. [2] Three things have to be considered; first, the nature and the number of the motives which lead men to act unjustly; secondly, what is the state of mind of those who so act; thirdly, the character and dispositions of those who are exposed to injustice. [3] We will discuss these questions in order, after we have first defined acting unjustly. Let injustice, then, be defined as voluntarily causing injury contrary to the law. Now, the law is particular or general. By particular, I mean the written law in accordance with which a state is administered; by general, the unwritten regulations which appear to be universally recognized. . . .

Langford Note: Aristotle next discusses general topics.

[2:22] . . . [17] Let us now endeavor to find topics about enthymemes in general in another way, noting in passing those which are refutative and those which are demonstrative, and those of apparent enthymemes, which are not really enthymemes, since they are not syllogisms. After this has been made clear, we will settle the question of solutions and objections, and whence they must be derived to refute enthymemes. . . .

[2:23] [1] One topic of demonstrative enthymemes is derived from opposites; for it is necessary to consider whether one opposite is predicable of the other, as a means of destroying an argument, if it is not, as a means of constructing one, if it is. . . . [2] Another topic is derived from similar inflections, for in like manner the derivatives must either be predicable of the subject or not; for instance, that the just is not entirely good, for in that case good would be predicable of anything that happens justly; but to be justly put to death is not desirable. [3] Another topic is derived from relative terms. . . . [4] Another topic is derived from the more and less. . . . [6] Another topic is derived from the consideration of time. . . . [7] Another topic consists in turning upon the opponent what has been said against ourselves. . . . [8] Another topic is derived from definition. . . . [9] Another topic is derived from the different significations of a word, as explained in the *Topics*, where the correct use of these terms has been discussed. . . . [10] Another, from division. . . . [11] Another, from induction. . . . [12] Another topic is that from a previous judgement in regard to the same or a similar or contrary matter, if possible when the judgement was unanimous or the same at all times; if not, when it was at least that of the majority, or of the wise, either all or most, or of the good; or of the judges themselves or of those whose judgement they accept, or of those whose judgement it is not possible to contradict, for instance, those in authority, or of those whose judgement it is unseemly to contradict, for instance, the gods, a father, or instructors. . . . [13] Another topic is that from enumerating the parts. . . . [14] Again, since in most human affairs the same thing is accompanied by some bad or good result, another topic consists in employing the consequence to exhort or dissuade, accuse or defend, praise or blame. . . . [15] Another topic may be employed when it is necessary to exhort or dissuade in regard to two opposites, and one has to employ the method previously stated in the case of both. . . . [16] Again, since men do not praise the same things in public and in secret, but in public chiefly praise what is just and beautiful, and in secret rather wish for what is expedient, another topic consists in endeavoring to infer its opposite from one or other of these statements. . . . [17] Another topic is derived from analogy in things. . . . [18] Another topic consists in concluding the identity of antecedents from the identity of results. . . . [19] Another topic is derived from the fact that the same men do not always choose the same thing before and after, but the contrary. . . . [20] Another topic consists in maintaining that the cause of something which is or has been is something which would generally, or possibly might, be the cause of it; for example, if one were to make a present of something to another, in order to cause him pain by depriving him of it. . . . [21] Another topic common to forensic and deliberative rhetoric consists in examining what is hortatory and dissuasive, and the reasons which make men act or not. . . . [22] Another topic is derived from things which are thought to happen but are incredible, because it would never have been thought so, if they had not happened or almost happened. . . . [23] Another topic, appropriate to refutation, consists in examining contradictories, whether in dates, actions, or words, first, separately in the case of the adversary, for instance, "he says that he loves you, and yet he conspired with the Thirty;" next, separately in your own case, "he says that I am litigious, but he cannot prove that I have ever brought an action against anyone"; lastly, separately in the case of your adversary and yourself together: "he has never yet lent anything, but I have ransomed many of you." [24] Another topic, when men or things have been attacked by slander, in reality or in appearance, consists in stating the reason for the false opinion; for there must be a reason for the supposition of guilt. . . . [25] Another topic is derived from the cause. . . . [26] Another topic consists in examining whether there was or is another better course than that which is advised, or is being, or has been, carried out. . . . [27] Another topic, when something contrary to what has already been done is on the point of being done, consists in examining them together. . . . [28] Another topic consists in making use of errors committed, for purposes of accusation or defense. . . . [29] Another topic is derived from the meaning of a name. . . .

UNITED STATES V. LOPEZ, 514 U.S. 549 (1995)

Langford Note: Aristotle tells us that rhetoric is the ability to discover persuasive arguments in any given situation. As such, his theory about general and specific topics applies to the judicial opinions judges hand down to decide questions of law, where the courts make arguments in their opinions to persuade their readers about what the law is and what it commands. The landmark Supreme Court majority, concurring, and dissenting opinions in *United States v. Lopez* make arguments that can be analyzed using Aristotle's topoi. They are excerpted subsequently.

In *Lopez*, a high school student was charged with violating the 1990 Gun-Free School Zones Act for bringing a handgun to school. The question was whether the federal government could regulate the possession of guns on school property under the power given to it under the commerce clause. Justice William H. Rehnquist wrote the majority opinion, joined by Justices Sandra Day O'Connor, Antonin Scalia, Anthony Kennedy, and Clarence Thomas. The case also had a number of concurrences and dissents. The majority of the Supreme Court held that the Gun-Free Schools Zones Act was a criminal statute that had nothing to do with "commerce" or any sort of economic activity and that the possession of a gun in a school zone was not an economic activity that has a substantial effect on interstate commerce. Therefore, the federal government had no power under the commerce clause to regulate guns on school premises.

Editors' Note: Internal citations have either been shortened to the name and year or removed without indication. Unless otherwise indicated, ellipses have been added by the chapter author, not the court.

Chief Justice Rehnquist [writing for the majority].

The Constitution delegates to Congress the power "[t]o regulate Commerce with foreign Nations, and among the several States, and with the Indian Tribes." The Court, through Chief Justice Marshall, first defined the nature of Congress' commerce power in *Gibbons v. Ogden* (1824): "Commerce, undoubtedly, is traffic, but it is something more: it is intercourse. It describes the commercial intercourse between nations, and parts of nations, in all its branches, and is regulated by prescribing rules for carrying on that intercourse."

The commerce power "is the power to regulate; that is, to prescribe the rule by which commerce is to be governed. This power, like all others vested in Congress, is complete in itself, may be exercised to its utmost extent, and acknowledges no limitations, other than are prescribed in the constitution." The *Gibbons* Court, however, acknowledged that limitations on the commerce power are inherent in the very language of the Commerce Clause. . . .

For nearly a century thereafter, the Court's Commerce Clause decisions dealt but rarely with the extent of Congress' power, and almost entirely with the Commerce Clause as a limit on state legislation that discriminated against interstate commerce. See, *e.g.*, *Veazie v. Moor* (1853) (upholding a state created steamboat monopoly because it involved regulation of wholly internal commerce); *Kidd v. Pearson* (1888) (upholding a state prohibition on the manufacture of intoxicating liquor because the commerce power "does not comprehend the purely domestic commerce of a State which is carried on between man and man within a State or between different parts of the same State").... See *Wickard v. Filburn* (1942) (describing development of Commerce Clause jurisprudence).

In 1887, Congress enacted the Interstate Commerce Act, and in 1890, Congress enacted the Sherman Antitrust Act. These laws ushered in a new era of federal regulation under the commerce power. When cases involving these laws first reached this Court, we imported from our negative Commerce Clause cases the approach that Congress could not regulate activities such as "production," "manufacturing," and "mining." See, *e.g.*, *United States v. E. C. Knight Co.* (1895) ("Commerce succeeds to manufacture, and is not part of it"); *Carter v. Carter Coal Co.* (1936) ("Mining brings the subject matter of commerce into existence. Commerce disposes of it"). Simultaneously, however, the Court held that, where the interstate and intrastate aspects of commerce were so mingled together that full regulation of interstate commerce required incidental regulation of intrastate commerce, the Commerce Clause authorized such regulation.

In *A.L.A. Schechter Poultry Corp. v. United States* (1935), the Court struck down regulations that fixed the hours and wages of individuals employed by an intrastate business because the activity being regulated related to interstate commerce only indirectly. In doing so, the Court characterized the distinction between direct and indirect effects of intrastate transactions upon interstate commerce as "a fundamental one, essential to the maintenance of our constitutional system." Activities that affected interstate commerce directly were within Congress' power; activities that affected interstate commerce indirectly were beyond Congress' reach. The justification for this formal distinction was rooted in the fear that otherwise "there would be virtually no limit to the federal power and for all practical purposes we should have a completely centralized government."

Two years later, in the watershed case of *NLRB v. Jones & Laughlin Steel Corp.* (1937), the Court upheld the National Labor Relations Act against a Commerce Clause challenge, and in the process, departed from the distinction between "direct" and "indirect" effects on interstate commerce ("The question [of the scope of Congress' power] is necessarily one of degree"). The Court held that intrastate activities that "have such a close and substantial relation to interstate commerce that their control is essential or appropriate to protect that commerce from burdens and obstructions" are within Congress' power to regulate.

In *United States v. Darby* (1941), the Court upheld the Fair Labor Standards Act, stating:

> "The power of Congress over interstate commerce is not confined to the regulation of commerce among the states. It extends to those activities intrastate which so affect interstate commerce or the exercise of the power of Congress over it as to make regulation of them appropriate means to the attainment of a legitimate end, the exercise of the granted power of Congress to regulate interstate commerce." . . .

In *Wickard v. Filburn* (1942), the Court upheld the application of amendments to the Agricultural Adjustment Act of 1938 to the production and consumption of homegrown wheat. The *Wickard* Court explicitly rejected earlier distinctions between direct and indirect effects on interstate commerce, stating:

> "[E]ven if appellee's activity be local and though it may not be regarded as commerce, it may still, whatever its nature, be reached by Congress if it exerts a substantial economic effect on interstate commerce, and this irrespective of whether such effect is what might at some earlier time have been defined as 'direct' or 'indirect.'"

The *Wickard* Court emphasized that although Filburn's own contribution to the demand for wheat may have been trivial by itself, that was not "enough to remove him from the scope of federal regulation where, as here, his contribution, taken together with that of many others similarly situated, is far from trivial."

Jones & Laughlin Steel, *Darby*, and *Wickard* ushered in an era of Commerce Clause jurisprudence that greatly expanded the previously defined authority of Congress under that Clause. In part, this was a recognition of the great changes that had occurred in the way business was carried on in this country. Enterprises that had once been local or at most regional in nature had become national in scope. But the doctrinal change also reflected a view that earlier Commerce Clause cases artificially had constrained the authority of Congress to regulate interstate commerce.

But even these modern-era precedents which have expanded congressional power under the Commerce Clause confirm that this power is subject to outer limits. In *Jones & Laughlin Steel*, the Court warned that the scope of the interstate commerce power "must be considered in the light of our dual system of government and may not be extended so as to embrace effects upon interstate commerce so indirect and remote that to embrace them, in view of our complex society, would effectually obliterate the distinction between what is national and what is local and create a completely centralized government" . . . see also *Darby*, (Congress may regulate intrastate activity that has a "substantial effect" on interstate commerce); *Wickard*, (Congress may regulate activity that "exerts a substantial economic effect on interstate commerce"). Since that time, the Court has heeded that warning and undertaken to decide whether a rational basis existed for concluding that a regulated activity sufficiently affected interstate commerce. . . .

Similarly, in *Maryland v. Wirtz* (1968), the Court reaffirmed that "the power to regulate commerce, though broad indeed, has limits" that "[t]he Court has ample power" to enforce. In response to the dissent's warnings that the Court was powerless to enforce the limitations on Congress' commerce powers because "[a]ll activities affecting commerce, even in the minutest degree, [*Wickard*], may be regulated and controlled by Congress," (Douglas, J., dissenting), the *Wirtz* Court replied that the dissent had misread precedent as "[n]either here nor in *Wickard* has the Court declared that Congress may use a relatively trivial impact on commerce as an excuse for broad general regulation of state or private activities." Rather, "[t]he Court has said only that where *a general regulatory statute bears a substantial relation to commerce*, the *de minimis* character of individual instances arising under that statute is of no consequence." (First emphasis added.) . . .

These are not precise formulations, and in the nature of things they cannot be. But we think they point the way to a correct decision of this case. The possession of a gun in a local school zone is in no sense an economic activity that might, through repetition elsewhere, substantially affect any sort of interstate commerce. Respondent was a local student at a local school; there is no indication that he had recently moved in interstate commerce, and there is no requirement that his possession of the firearm have any concrete tie to interstate commerce.

To uphold the Government's contentions here, we would have to pile inference upon inference in a manner that would bid fair to convert congressional authority under the Commerce Clause to a general police power of the sort retained by the States. Admittedly, some of our prior cases have taken long steps down that road, giving great deference to congressional action. The broad language in these opinions has suggested the possibility of additional expansion, but we decline here to proceed any further. To do so would require us to conclude that the Constitution's enumeration of powers does not presuppose something not enumerated, and that there never will be a distinction between what is truly national and what is truly local. This we are unwilling to do.

For the foregoing reasons the judgment of the Court of Appeals is

Affirmed.

Justice Kennedy, with whom Justice O'Connor joins, concurring.

Of the various structural elements in the Constitution, separation of powers, checks and balances, judicial review, and federalism, only concerning the last does there seem to be much uncertainty respecting the existence, and the content, of standards that allow the judiciary to play a significant role in maintaining the design contemplated by the Framers. Although the resolution of specific cases has proved difficult, we have derived from the Constitution workable standards to assist in preserving separation of powers and checks and balances. . . . These standards are by now well accepted. Judicial review is also established beyond question, *Marbury v. Madison* (1803), and though we may differ when applying its principles, *Planned Parenthood v. Casey* (1992), its legitimacy is undoubted. Our role in preserving the federal balance seems more tenuous. . . .

The theory that two governments accord more liberty than one requires for its realization two distinct and discernable lines of political accountability: one between the citizens and the Federal Government; the second between the citizens and the States. If, as Madison expected, the federal and state governments are to control each other, see The Federalist No. 51, and hold each other in check by competing for the affections of the people, see The Federalist No. 46, those citizens must have some means of knowing which of the two governments to hold accountable for the failure to perform a given function. "Federalism serves to assign political responsibility, not to obscure it." Were the Federal Government to take over the regulation of entire areas of traditional state concern, areas having nothing to do with the regulation of commercial activities, the boundaries between the spheres of federal and state authority would blur and political responsibility would become illusory. The resultant inability to hold either branch of the government answerable to the citizens is more dangerous even than devolving too much authority to the remote central power. . . .

For these reasons, it would be mistaken and mischievous for the political branches to forget that the sworn obligation to preserve and protect the Constitution in maintaining the federal balance is their own in the first and primary instance. . . . [S]ome Congresses have accepted responsibility to confront the great questions of the proper federal balance in terms of lasting consequences for the constitutional design. The political branches of the Government must fulfill this grave constitutional obligation if democratic liberty and the federalism that secures it are to endure. . . .

While it is doubtful that any State, or indeed any reasonable person, would argue that it is wise policy to allow students to carry guns on school premises, considerable disagreement exists about how best to accomplish that goal. In this circumstance, the theory and utility of our federalism are revealed, for the States may perform their role as laboratories for experimentation to devise various solutions where the best solution is far from clear.

If a State or municipality determines that harsh criminal sanctions are necessary and wise to deter students from carrying guns on school premises, the reserved powers of the States are sufficient to enact those measures. Indeed, over 40 States already have criminal laws outlawing the possession of firearms on or near school grounds. . . .

For these reasons, I join in the opinion and judgment of the Court.

Justice Thomas, concurring.

While the principal dissent concedes that there are limits to federal power, the sweeping nature of our current test enables the dissent to argue that Congress can regulate gun possession. But it seems to me that the power to regulate "commerce" can by no means encompass authority over mere gun possession, any more than it empowers the Federal Government to regulate marriage, littering, or cruelty to animals, throughout the 50 States. Our Constitution quite properly leaves such matters to the individual States, notwithstanding these activities' effects on interstate commerce. Any interpretation of the Commerce Clause that even suggests that Congress could regulate such matters is in need of reexamination. . . .

Early Americans understood that commerce, manufacturing, and agriculture, while distinct activities, were intimately related and dependent on each other—that each "substantially affected" the others. After all, items produced by farmers and manufacturers were the primary articles of commerce at the time. If commerce was more robust as a result of federal superintendence, farmers and manufacturers could benefit. . . . Yet, despite being well aware that agriculture, manufacturing, and other matters substantially affected commerce, the founding generation did not cede authority over all these activities to Congress. . . .

Justice Stevens, dissenting.

Guns are both articles of commerce and articles that can be used to restrain commerce. Their possession is the consequence, either directly or indirectly, of commercial activity. In my judgment, Congress' power to regulate commerce in firearms includes the power to prohibit possession of guns at any location because of their potentially harmful use; it necessarily follows that Congress may also prohibit their possession in particular markets. The market for the possession of handguns by school age children is, distressingly, substantial. Whether or not the national interest in eliminating that market would have justified federal legislation in 1789, it surely does today.

Justice Souter, dissenting.

The question for the courts, as all agree, is not whether as a predicate to legislation Congress in fact found that a particular activity substantially affects interstate commerce. The legislation implies such a finding, and there is no reason to entertain claims that Congress acted ultra vires intentionally. Nor is the question whether Congress was correct in so finding. The only question is whether the legislative judgment is within the realm of reason. . . . Congressional findings do not, however, directly address the question of reasonableness; they tell us what Congress actually has found, not what it could rationally find. If, indeed, the Court were to make the existence of explicit congressional findings dispositive in some close or difficult cases something other than rationality review would be afoot. The resulting congressional obligation to justify its policy choices on the merits would imply either a judicial authority to review the justification (and, hence, the wisdom) of those choices, or authority to require Congress to act with some high degree of deliberateness, of which express findings would be evidence. But review for congressional wisdom would just be the old judicial pretension discredited and abandoned in 1937, and review for deliberateness would be as patently unconstitutional as an Act of Congress mandating long opinions from this Court. Such a legislative process requirement would function merely as an excuse for covert review of the merits of legislation under standards never expressed and more or less arbitrarily applied. Under such a regime, in any case, the rationality standard of review would be a thing of the past. . . .

I respectfully dissent.

Justice Breyer, with whom Justice Stevens, Justice Souter, and Justice Ginsburg join, dissenting.

In my view, the statute falls well within the scope of the commerce power as this Court has understood that power over the last half century.

In reaching this conclusion, I apply three basic principles of Commerce Clause interpretation. First, the power to "regulate Commerce . . . among the several States" [ellipsis in original] encompasses the power to regulate local activities insofar as they significantly affect interstate commerce. . . .

Second, in determining whether a local activity will likely have a significant effect upon interstate commerce, a court must consider, not the effect of an individual act (a single instance of gun possession), but rather the cumulative effect of all similar instances (*i.e.*, the effect of all guns possessed in or near schools). As this Court put the matter almost 50 years ago: "it is enough that the individual activity when multiplied into a general practice . . . contains a threat to the interstate economy that requires preventative regulation." [Ellipsis in original.]

Third, the Constitution requires us to judge the connection between a regulated activity and interstate commerce, not directly, but at one remove. Courts must give Congress a degree of leeway in determining the existence of a significant factual connection between the regulated activity and interstate commerce—both because the Constitution delegates the commerce power directly to Congress and because the determination requires an empirical judgment of a kind that a legislature is more likely than a court to make with accuracy. The traditional words "rational basis" capture this leeway. Thus, the specific question before us, as the Court recognizes, is not whether the "regulated activity sufficiently affected interstate commerce," but, rather, whether Congress could have had "*a rational basis*" for so concluding. *Ante*, at 8 (emphasis added). . . .

Applying these principles to the case at hand, we must ask whether Congress could have had a *rational basis* for finding a significant (or substantial) connection between gun related school violence and interstate commerce. Or, to put the question in the language of the *explicit* finding that Congress made when it amended this law in 1994: Could Congress rationally have found that "violent crime in school zones," through its effect on the "quality of education," significantly (or substantially) affects "interstate" or "foreign commerce"? . . . As long as one views the commerce connection, not as a "technical legal conception," but as "a practical one," the answer to this question must be yes. Numerous reports and studies—generated both inside and outside government—make clear that Congress could reasonably have found the empirical connection that its law, implicitly or explicitly, asserts.

Specifically, Congress could have found that gun-related violence near the classroom poses a serious economic threat (1) to consequently inadequately educated workers who must endure low paying jobs, and (2) to communities and businesses that might (in today's "information society") otherwise gain, from a well-educated work force, an important commercial advantage . . . of a kind that location near a railhead or harbor provided in the past. Congress might also have found these threats to be no different in kind from other threats that this Court has found within the commerce power, such as the threat that loan sharking poses to the "funds" of "numerous localities," and that unfair labor practices pose to instrumentalities of commerce. As I have pointed out, Congress has written that "the occurrence of violent crime in school zones" has brought about a "decline in the quality of education" that "has an adverse impact on interstate commerce and the foreign commerce of the United States." The violence-related facts, the educational facts, and the economic facts, taken together, make this conclusion rational. And, because under our case law the sufficiency of the constitutionally necessary Commerce Clause link between a crime of violence and interstate commerce turns simply upon size or degree, those same facts make the statute constitutional. . . .

Respectfully, I dissent.

CRITICAL ASSESSMENT

In formulating legal argument, lawyers can use both general and specific topics. Aristotle tells us general topics would ask about the definition of a thing (the issue to be discussed), its division (amplifying or clarifying parts or a whole), its comparison to other laws, its relationships to other things (such as cause/effect, antecedent/consequence, contraries, or contradictions), its circumstances (what the law makes possible or what happened in the past or will happen in the future), and testimony (what Aristotle refers to as "proofs") about the thing (from authorities, witnesses, documents, precedent, etcetera). General topics are used to confirm (what he refers to as a "demonstrative" argument) or to refute (what he refers to as a "refutative" argument) the validity of a claim. Aristotle tells us that specific topics would result in arguments that consider what is just or unjust, right or wrong; to these topics we also could add what is constitutional or unconstitutional.

For example, rhetorical critics can identify several of Aristotle's general topics in the arguments used by Chief Justice William Rehnquist in his majority opinion to declare the act regulating guns on school grounds unconstitutional. His analysis of the reasoning established by previous opinions (which themselves are a form of testimony from which Rehnquist argues) leads Rehnquist to draw three conclusions: (1) the act dealt with a criminal activity that had nothing to do with commerce and had no substantial economic impact upon interstate commerce, (2) the act did not identify any "jurisdictional element" of how possession of handguns in schools particularly pertains to interstate commerce, and (3) Congress did not report how firearms in schools places an undue burden upon or hindrance of interstate commerce.

Rehnquist's first claim that the act involved a criminal and not a civil issue is an argument from definition. Arguments from definition claim that an entity belongs to a particular class because its qualities meet the definition of that class. A definitional discussion allows a rhetor to discuss how things are similar to, or different from, that class. In this case, to fall within the scope of the commerce clause, a legislative act would need to have an economic impact upon interstate commerce. Since prohibiting guns in schools does not have an economic impact upon interstate commerce, it is not an economic activity and thus does not fall within the class of activities regulated by the commerce clause.

Rehnquist's second claim that the act does not identify any jurisdictional element regarding how the act applies falls within the argument from division.

An argument from division amplifies or clarifies the whole by considering its constituent parts. The commerce clause gives Congress the power to regulate (1) the channels of interstate commerce, (2) the instrumentalities of interstate commerce, and (3) local activities that have a substantial economic effect on interstate commerce. If the act had clarified that the banned gun "had traveled in interstate commerce," the act would have included jurisdictional language—but it did not make this clarification, so the gun does not fall within the purview of the act. It is important to note that arguments from definition and division are similar. Arguments from definition discuss the class as a whole; for example, a criminal or a civil act, whereas arguments from division focus on its constituent parts, such as a jurisdictional element.

Rehnquist's third claim that Congress did not explain how firearms in school places an undue burden or hindrance on interstate commerce is also an argument from definition. This argument is similar to Rehnquist's first claim. If firearms in schools are an undue burden on interstate commerce, then the act is a constitutional deployment of congressional power. If they are not an undue burden, then the act is unconstitutional. Since Congress is silent on the matter, we can conclude guns in schools do not constitute an undue burden.

All of Rehnquist's arguments are refutative; they are used to challenge the validity of the congressional act at issue in *Lopez*. Because of these three refutative reasons, Rehnquist held in his majority opinion that Congress's statute violated the Constitution by usurping a traditional police power held by the state and fundamentally blurring the distinction between local and national authority.

DISCUSSION QUESTIONS

Discussion Question 1: You have seen an analysis of how Chief Justice Rehnquist used rhetorical topoi in his opinion. Which topoi are used in the concurring and dissenting opinions?

Discussion Question 2: Did the court miss any arguments you can think of that are inspired by Aristotle's topoi? For instance, Aristotle mentions in the general topics that arguments can be made from "different significations of a word." Are there different significations for the word "commerce" that the dissents might have mentioned? Why might they have chosen not to do so?

Discussion Question 3: The critical assessment suggests that argument from precedent or authority is a special type of "testimony." What do you think that means? What is special about it?

Discussion Question 4: Looking back to Aristotle's nonforensic topoi (deliberative and epideictic), are there any that appear in any of the *Lopez* opinions? Why do you think a justice might include arguments from these topics if they are not forensic topics?

One might question whether it is effective to use nonlegal arguments in judicial opinions. But might an epideictic appeal combined with a forensic appeal be persuasive? For instance, Justice Kennedy writes in his concurrence that "it would be mistaken and mischievous for the political branches to forget that the sworn obligation to preserve and protect the Constitution in maintaining the federal balance is their own in the first and primary instance . . . [S]ome Congresses have accepted responsibility to confront the great questions of the proper federal balance in terms of lasting consequences for the constitutional design. The political branches of the Government must fulfill this grave constitutional obligation if democratic liberty and the federalism that secures it are to endure." Is Kennedy appealing to virtue in this quote? Courage? Practical wisdom? Nobility?

ADDITIONAL READINGS

Balkin, Jack M. "A Night in the Topics: The Reason of Legal Rhetoric and the Rhetoric of Legal Reason." In *Law's Stories: Narrative and Rhetoric in the Law*, edited by Peter Brooks and Paul Gerwitz, 211–24. New Haven, CT: Yale University Press, 1996.

Balkin, Jack M., and Sanford Levinson. "Constitutional Grammar." *Texas Law Review* 72 (June 1994): 1771–803.

Bobbitt, Philip. *Constitutional Fate: Theory of the Constitution*. Oxford: Oxford University Press, 1982.

Harris, William F., III. *The Interpretable Constitution*. Baltimore: John Hopkins University Press, 1993.

Langford, Catherine L. *Scalia v. Scalia: Opportunistic Textualism in Constitutional Interpretation*. Tuscaloosa: Alabama University Press, 2017.

Saunders, Kurt M. "Law as Rhetoric, Rhetoric as Argument." *Journal of Legal Education* 44, no. 4 (December 1994): 566–78.

Sloane, Thomas O. *On the Contrary: The Protocol of Traditional Rhetoric*. Washington, DC: Catholic University of America Press, 1997.

11

Demosthenes

Founding Principles—The Role of Tradition in Persuasive Argument

Vasileios Adamidis and Laura A. Webb

INTRODUCTION

The theme of tradition links ancient and contemporary legal rhetoric. Advocates refer to traditional values as a way to create shared identity with their audience and marginalize the opposing view. Speakers artfully select the relevant tradition that suits their narrative—often by reference to corresponding founding principles of the community—and demonstrate how their position adheres to those principles. Using tradition as an example, this chapter demonstrates how a theme can be used in rhetorical practice as the undercurrent of an orator's strategy, providing the thread that permeates and binds together various parts of an argument.

In both classical and contemporary rhetoric, advocates rely on tradition to persuade through ethos, pathos, and logos (see chapter 2). Advocates align themselves with historical figures to establish credibility through their projected character (ethos); they remind the audience of important cultural values to evoke emotions (pathos); and they attempt to persuade through appeals to reason by the construction of coherent and logical rhetorical arguments (logos) that, in a common-law system, include references to how the system has handled similar problems before (precedent). In this chapter, comparing and contrasting the use of tradition in a classical and a contemporary persuasive argument gives us insight into the three modes of persuasion as well as a commonly used type (topos) of argument.

Demosthenes (384–22 BCE) was a Greek statesman and one of the most famous orators of ancient Athens. According to Plutarch, Demosthenes had physical challenges that hindered his rhetorical performance, as he had a weak voice, spoke with a peculiar hesitation, and was plagued by shortness of breath. His outstanding speechwriting and oratorical skills were not the result of nature but of tireless effort, rigorous training, and thorough preparation, which, according to legend, included practicing speaking with a mouth full of pebbles to improve his enunciation; practicing gestures in front of a mirror; building a subterranean study (into which he would descend every day, without exception, in order to practice his performative skills and cultivate his voice); and practicing declaiming while running and climbing stairs to improve his breath control.

Demosthenes's speech *In Defense of Ctesiphon on the Crown* (330 BCE) has been considered a masterpiece of judicial oration since antiquity. Ctesiphon had proposed that Demosthenes should be awarded a golden crown by Athens because Demosthenes had always acted and spoken in the best interests of the city. Demosthenes's long-time political rival, Aeschines, opposed Ctesiphon's proposal. Aware that his entire political career and his legacy were at stake, Demosthenes responded to Aeschines in this speech.

Demosthenes and Aeschines had disagreed fiercely since at least 347 BCE over the question of the policy of the Athenian city-state toward the threat of the rising power of the rival Kingdom of Macedon. On this topic, the two statesmen delivered five orations in court and numerous political orations in the assembly. Demosthenes took a hard line against Macedonian expansion and orchestrated the formation of an alliance of Greek cities against the growing power of King Philip II, a policy that eventually led to defeat of the Greeks in the Battle of Chaeronea in 338 BCE. After Philip's assassination in 336 BCE and the proclamation of his son Alexander as the new king of Macedon, Demosthenes saw an opportunity for Athens to regain its full independence. This attempt was also unsuccessful, and these failed ventures were fiercely criticized by his political rivals, including Aeschines. Nonetheless, Demosthenes remained popular with Athenians who wished to restore their independence. Against this background, the orator Ctesiphon in 336 BCE proposed that Athens honor Demosthenes for his services to the city by presenting him, according to custom, with a golden crown.

Masterfully showcasing persuasive rhetoric in action, Demosthenes defends his policies and motives by reference to a historical sense of the destiny of Athens and offers a moral lesson about the values of freedom, patriotism, and self-sacrifice to contemporary and future generations alike. Throughout the speech, Demosthenes demonstrates why he (and the audience) stand on the right side of the historical narrative by choosing to actively lead an alliance with other Greek cities in the defense of their freedom against the expansion of Macedon. Demosthenes artfully portrays himself as a loyal yet humble patriot, whose entire political career and most recent decision to stand against Macedon were guided by the principles and values stemming from the noblest Athenian traditions. Against this portrait of a statesman who embodies the traditional aims and aspirations of the Athenian people, Demosthenes contrasts his opponent, Aeschines, as a malevolent and unworthy citizen whose objections are only voiced after the unfortunate outcome of the Athenian noble struggle for independence.

The speech was delivered as a response to Aeschines's accusation speech (*Against Ctesiphon*), before a panel of not less than five hundred Athenian judges and an audience consisting of Athenians and foreigners who flocked, probably in the thousands, to witness a forceful oratorical contest between Demosthenes and Aeschines, two of the most celebrated orators of the Greek world. Demosthenes defeated Aeschines by an overwhelming majority of votes; Aeschines was fined and forced into exile.

To better understand rhetoric in action, compare and contrast Demosthenes's use of tradition in his speech to the contemporary legal argument posed in the 2015 case *Obergefell v. Hodges*. There the Commonwealth of Virginia, like Demosthenes, creates an argument that incorporates traditional values while carefully identifying what traditions are relevant. *Obergefell* required the US Supreme Court to decide whether same-sex marriage is protected by the US Constitution. In interpreting the Fourteenth Amendment's protection of due process, the court has often looked to a "backdrop of history, tradition, and practice" to decide whether a "fundamental right . . . deeply rooted in this Nation's history and tradition" exists.[1] Opponents of same-sex marriage noted that there was no traditional recognition of a right for same-sex couples to marry.

In an amicus curiae ("friend of the court") brief supporting the same-sex petitioners in this case, Virginia cleverly uses a broad interpretation of tradition as a persuasive argument to support its position.[2] Superficially, a reliance on tradition should have hurt this position, because there was no long-standing traditional custom supporting same-sex marriage. Knowing the importance of tradition in persuasive argument, and noting that a narrow focus on tradition in the sense of a specific, long-standing custom could result in a bad outcome for its side, Virginia identifies a more general, overarching principle (equality) that could still be identified as traditional within an evolving historical narrative. Virginia first notes that this principle is enshrined in the country's founding documents. Virginia then criticizes the Founders, prior members of the court, and Virginia itself, noting that all these actors had "failed [at times] to appreciate the full majesty of the equality-of-right principle that they otherwise regarded as sacred." Virginia aligns the broad traditional principle with the current position of the petitioners by pointing to the court's evolving views about equality, demonstrated by its repudiation of prior positions on issues such as racial segregation, prohibition of interracial marriage, and the exclusion of students on the basis of sex. It argues that the honorable political traditions of the country include an evolving tradition: equality that disfavors discrimination against minorities. This evolving tradition would then support protecting same-sex marriage. Virginia also defines the appropriate tradition more broadly, as a right to marry generally rather than a right for same-sex couples to marry. Virginia thus interprets and reclaims tradition to support its position.

Much of Virginia's brief focuses on telling a story of America (through court decisions) becoming more receptive to groups that it had traditionally discriminated against (including racial minorities and women). This allows Virginia to make the case that same-sex couples, although historically discriminated against, should have their rights recognized here. Identifying the broad right (right to marry) rather than the narrow right (same-sex right to marry) then fits in with the narrative of increasing rights over time and allows Virginia to reconcile traditional values with the right asserted here. Just as Demosthenes argues that he was on the right side of the historical narrative, Virginia argues that the court should identify with the right side of a historical narrative that shows the country moving towards equality-of-right principles. In a historic 5–4 decision, the court found for the same-sex petitioners, ruling that they had a right to marry.

DEMOSTHENES 18 (*IN DEFENSE OF CTESIPHON ON THE CROWN*)

Editors' Note: The excerpt is drawn from Demosthenes, "In Defense of Ctesiphon on the Crown," *Demosthenes, Speeches 18 and 19*, trans. Harvey Yunis (Austin: University of Texas Press, 2005), 23-113, and is used with permission. Numbers in brackets indicate section numbers in the text in this translation.

Adamidis and Webb Note: In sections 62-72, Demosthenes seeks to persuade the audience to accept his decision to actively resist Philip as the only honorable option. Demosthenes vituperates and marginalizes Aeschines by linking him inextricably to the other, less noble and, thus, less "Athenian" alternatives that would erase "the just achievements of our forebears."

> [62] Since all Greeks were in this situation, still ignorant of the gathering, growing evil, you need to consider, Athenians, what were the policies and actions that the city ought to have chosen, and you need to hear an explanation of these matters from me. For I am the one who took up that post in the city. [63] Ought the city, Aeschines, to have dispensed with its pride and the esteem in which it is held and to have taken up its post alongside Thessalians and Dolopians, thereby helping Philip acquire his empire over Greece and erasing the noble and just achievements of our forebears?[3] Or was the city right not to have

done that—it would have been truly horrible—and should we instead merely have watched events develop even though we perceived them, it seems, in advance and saw they would take place if no one prevented them? [64] Even now I would gladly put the question to the severest critic of our policy: Which side does he wish the city had joined? Those who share the blame for the evil, disgraceful outcome that befell the Greeks, among whom one could mention the Thessalians and their allies? Or those who looked on as events transpired in the hope of some profit for themselves, in which group I would put the Arcadians, the Messenians, and the Argives?[4] [65] But many of these cities, indeed all of them, fared worse than we did! For if after his victory Philip straightaway up and left and then kept to himself, bringing grief neither to any of his allies nor to any other Greeks, then one could blame and disparage those who opposed his actions. But since he stripped from all alike their reputation, their power, and their freedom, and, from as many as he could, even their very form of government, how is it that your decision to follow my advice was not absolutely commendable?

[66] But I return to my previous point. What, Aeschines, should the city have done when it saw Philip building towards empire and tyranny over the Greeks? And what was an adviser in Athens—for that makes all the difference—obliged to say and propose? During all my time until the day I myself stepped onto the speaker's platform, I knew that our country always fought for the first prize in honor and glory and had expended more money and men in pursuit of honor and the common good than all the other Greeks had expended on their own behalf. [67] Yet I also saw that in pursuit of power and domination, Philip, our opponent in the struggle, had his eye knocked out, his collarbone broken, his hand and leg maimed, in fact that he readily sacrificed any part of his body that fortune might take so that afterwards he might live in honor and glory. [68] Indeed, no one would have dared assert that a man raised in Pella, a small, obscure place at the time, would become so bold as to desire rule over the Greeks and to make that his purpose, or that you—Athenians!—who every day behold reminders of the valor of your forebears in all manner of speeches and monuments, would be so cowardly as to surrender your freedom to Philip voluntarily.[5] No one would say that. [69] Surely the only remaining course of action, indeed the necessary course, was to oppose on the side of right everything that he did to wrong you. That is what you did from the beginning, reasonably and appropriately, while I moved the decrees and argued the case for as long as I have been active as a politician. I admit it. What should I have done? I ask you [Aeschines] that now, putting aside all other matters. . . .

[72] For if that was not necessary, but it had to be revealed that Greece was "Mysian plunder," as the saying goes, even though Athens was still alive and

well, then my labor in speaking about these matters has been wasted, and your labor in heeding my advice has been wasted too.[6] Let everything the city has done count as my crimes and my mistakes. But if there was a need for someone to step forward to stop these things, who should have done it but the Athenian people? That, in fact, was my policy, and when I saw him enslaving all mankind I opposed him, and I constantly proclaimed and advised that people should not surrender. . . .

Adamidis and Webb Note: In sections 95–101, to identify the noble values that guided the deeds of their forefathers and associate them with his own policies, Demosthenes employs examples from Athenian history stretching back to the early fourth century BCE. The precedents of Athenian practice offered here build upon and anticipate the one great precedent—the Persian Wars—which is the culmination of Demosthenes's forceful argument (sections 199–208). Demosthenes periodically revisits the core question of his case: what would the honorable course of action be?

[95] Next, I intend to show that when Aeschines slandered the Euboeans and Byzantians by recalling whether they had ever mistreated you, he was trying to cause mischief.[7] Not only were his claims false, as I think you already know, but even if they were entirely true, it was to our advantage to handle the situation as I handled it. To that end, I wish to discuss briefly one or two of the noble acts done by the city during your lifetime. Both individual citizens and the city as a whole must ever strive to act in accord with the noblest standards of our tradition. [96] When the Spartans ruled sea and land, Athenians, and held the territories round Attica with garrisons and military governors—Euboea, Tanagra, all Boeotia, Megara, Aegina, Ceos, the other islands—when the city still possessed no ships and no walls, you marched out to Haliartus and then again not many days later to Corinth, even though the Athenians of that day could well have borne a grudge against the Corinthians and Thebans for their actions during the Decelean War.[8] But they did not come close to doing that.

[97] It was not that they performed these two actions in aid of benefactors, Aeschines, or failed to see the dangers. But that was not reason for them to abandon those who sought help from them. Rather, they were ready to submit to mortal danger for the sake of glory and honor, which was the right and noble decision. Indeed, since all men find the limit of life in death—even one who has shut himself in a closet and watches—good men must always venture all noble acts with good hope as their shield and worthily endure whatever god gives them. [98] That is how your ancestors acted, and that is how you older men acted when the Thebans defeated the Spartans at Leuctra and tried to destroy them.[9] You prevented it, though the Spartans were neither friends nor

benefactors and had inflicted many grievous injuries on our city. You did not fear the power and reputation of the Thebans at that time, nor did you stop to consider how the people for whose sake you were about to risk your lives had behaved. [99] So in this case too you showed all Greeks that when someone wrongs you in any way, though you generally get angry, you neither bear a grudge nor let it affect your judgment when their safety or freedom is somehow endangered. That was your disposition not only then but also when the Thebans were trying to take over Euboea. You did not sit by idly or recall the injuries that Themison and Theodorus inflicted on you for the sake of Oropus, but you sent help even to them. That was the first occasion on which the city used volunteer trierarchs, of which I was one; but more about that later.[10] [100] You performed a noble act just to save the island, yet it was still nobler, while holding power over the cities and their inhabitants, to give them back, as fairness required, to the people who had wronged you and to allow none of the wrongs you had suffered to influence the trust that they placed in you. I pass over countless other examples I might mention, engagements at sea and on land, both long ago and during our own day, all of which the city undertook for the freedom and safety of the rest of Greece. [101] Since I had seen so many instances of this kind where the city was ready to fight for the interests of others, what was I to urge the city to do, what was I to advise, when the question essentially concerned its own interests? That we should bear a grudge, by Zeus, against those who wished to be saved and that we should seek excuses for giving up completely. Who would not have been right to kill me had I endeavored to shame the city's noble tradition just by making a proposal to that effect? That you would not actually have done it, I know perfectly well. For had you wanted to, what prevented it? Was it not possible? Were not these men on hand advising you to do it?[11] . . .

Adamidis and Webb Note: In sections 199–208, Demosthenes argues that despite the unfortunate outcome of the specific action here, Athenians should always follow (as they did in the past) the very core of their identity, which is informed by the noble values bequeathed to them by their ancestors. This is what Demosthenes advocated, this is what the Athenian people chose to endorse, this is why they deserve to be praised on a par with their forefathers for their selfless and honorable deeds. Therefore, there is only one acceptable outcome to the case at hand: they should vote for Demosthenes and against Aeschines; if Demosthenes were stripped of the honor to be crowned, this would also mean that the Athenians have regretted the policy that brought them eternal glory.

[199] Since Aeschines insists vehemently on how things have turned out, I wish to say something rather paradoxical. No one, by Zeus and the gods, should

be astonished if my argument is extreme; rather, it should be examined sympathetically. If what was going to happen was clear to all in advance, and all knew in advance, and if you, Aeschines, spoke out in advance and shouted and shrieked in protest, you who uttered not even a sound, not even in those circumstances should the city have abandoned its policy, if indeed it valued its reputation or its forebears or future ages. [200] True, the city seems to have failed in its objectives, which is the common lot of all mankind when god so decides. But if it claimed to be the leader of the rest of Greece and then abandoned that claim to Philip, it would have been guilty of betraying all Greeks. For if the city chose to surrender without a fight the position that our forefathers faced every danger to acquire, who would not have spat on—you? Not, indeed, on the city, nor on me!

[201] With what expression, by Zeus, would we look upon visitors to the city if events turned out as they have, and Philip was elected leader and master of all, but others, without us, had undertaken the struggle to prevent that outcome, even though up to that time the city had never yet chosen inconspicuous safety in preference to the risk of fighting for a noble cause? [202] What Greek, what barbarian does not know that the Thebans, the Spartans (who dominated before the Thebans), and the Persian King too would have graciously and gladly allowed the city to take what it wanted and retain what it had so long as it followed orders and surrendered to another the leadership of Greece? [203] But that was not part of the Athenians' heritage; it was intolerable and not in their nature. Since the beginning of time, no one has ever been able to persuade the city to side with the powerful but unjust and to find safety in servitude. Rather, in every age, despite the danger, the city constantly fought for the first prize in honor and glory. [204] You consider that principle so important and intrinsic to your character that you praise most those ancestors who demonstrated it in action. With good reason, for who could fail to admire the courage of those citizens who, to avoid having to follow orders, dared to leave land and city behind and took to the ships? Themistocles, who proposed that course, they elected general, while Cyrsilus, who advised submission, they stoned to death, and not only him, but your wives did the same to his wife. [205] Those Athenians did not look for a politician or general to lead them into a prosperous slavery; they thought life not worth living unless they could do it in freedom. Each one of them saw himself as the child not only of his father and mother but of his country as well. What does that matter? He who considers himself born to his parents alone awaits the natural death allotted him by fate, but he who considers himself born to his country too will prefer to die than to see it enslaved. He will regard the insults and humiliations that one must bear when his city is enslaved as more terrible than death.

[206] Were it my intention to argue that I moved you to aspire to the standards of your forebears, everyone would chastise me with good reason. But my point, in fact, is that you made that choice yourselves, and I have been demonstrating that the city aspired to those standards even before my time; I do claim, however, to have been of service in bringing about particular achievements. [207] This man, on the other hand, denounces the whole enterprise and urges you to despise me for putting the city in terrible danger, and though he yearns to deprive me of an honor for the present, he is trying to steal from you the praises of all future time. For if you convict Ctesiphon because my policy was not the best one, you will make it appear that you were wrong, not that subsequent events befell you by fortune's cruelty. [208] But you were not wrong, no, you were not, Athenians, to take on danger for the sake of the freedom and safety of all—I swear by your forefathers who led the fight at Marathon, by those who stood in the ranks at Plataea, by those who fought aboard ship at Salamis and Artemisium, and by the many other brave men who lie in the public tombs, all of whom the city buried, deeming them all equally worthy of the same honor, Aeschines, not just those among them who were successful or victorious. Rightly so, for they all performed the task required of brave men, and they each met with the fortune conferred on them by god.

BRIEF OF THE COMMONWEALTH OF VIRGINIA AS AMICUS CURIAE IN SUPPORT OF PETITIONERS, *OBERGEFELL V. HODGES*, 576 U.S. 644 (2015)

Adamidis and Webb Note: In *Obergefell*, a group of same-sex couples challenged laws in Michigan, Ohio, Kentucky, and Tennessee that barred the performance or recognition of same-sex marriages. Prior to this case, federal courts in some jurisdictions had found bans on same-sex marriages unconstitutional, while other federal courts found the opposite. The Supreme Court took this case to resolve the "circuit split" between federal circuit courts. Virginia was not a party to the case but choose to file an amicus curiae[12] brief urging the Court to rule in favor of the same-sex couples. The court ultimately did so, thus requiring all fifty states to perform and recognize same-sex marriages.

Editors' Note: In the following excerpt, original footnotes and internal citations are omitted.

VIRGINIA'S INTEREST AS AMICUS CURIAE

Virginia is proud to be "the home of many of the Founding Fathers." We revere James Madison as the "father of the Constitution" and the "drafter" of the Bill of Rights. The Bill of Rights included the Fifth Amendment's guarantee of "due process of law," a protection that implicitly prohibits the Federal Government from "denying to any person the equal protection of the laws." The Bill of Rights followed in the tradition of the Virginia Declaration of Rights, in which George Mason wrote that "all men are by nature equally free and independent and have certain inherent rights . . . namely, the enjoyment of life and liberty, with the means of acquiring and possessing property, and pursuing and obtaining happiness and safety." And Thomas Jefferson's Declaration of Independence proclaimed the new nation's commitment to the "self-evident" truth that "all men are created equal."

We are proud of our Commonwealth's contributions to America's exceptional form of democracy, yet it is also self-evident that the scope of the equality-of-right principle that these Virginians shared with the world and helped enshrine in our Constitution was not fully recognized in their day. Slavery was not abolished until 1865, after a bitter civil war that nearly split our country in two. Women were not guaranteed the right to vote until 1920. And State-sponsored segregation was not declared unconstitutional until 1954, when *Brown v. Board of Education* overruled the 1896 decision in *Plessy v. Ferguson*. The Founders and the majority in *Plessy* were not the only ones who failed in their own era to appreciate the full majesty of the equality-of-right principle that they otherwise regarded as sacred. Virginia's government fell short of fidelity to that principle in defending:

- the segregation of public school students in the companion case to *Brown v. Board;*
- the prohibition of interracial marriage in *Loving v. Virginia;* and
- the exclusion of female cadets from the Virginia Military Institute in *United States v. Virginia.*

Yet the arguments offered to defend those unjust laws are the same arguments offered by marriage-equality opponents today. Virginia invoked federalism, arguing that education policy and marriage regulation are quintessentially State prerogatives that federal courts should leave alone. Virginia also invoked history and tradition to justify segregation and anti-miscegenation laws, arguing that such laws were acceptable to the Founders because they were commonplace when the Bill of Rights and the Fourteenth Amendment were ratified. But Virginia's government was wrong then, and the four States that reprise modern-day versions of those failed arguments are wrong here.

"Every state legislator and executive and judicial officer is solemnly committed by oath taken pursuant to Art. VI, cl. 3, 'to support this Constitution.'" The purpose of that oath is to "preserve [the Federal Constitution] in full force, in all its powers, and to guard against resistance to or evasion of its authority, on the part of a State. . . ."

In fidelity to that oath, and to a comparable oath under the Virginia Constitution, the Attorney General of Virginia changed the Commonwealth's legal position in *Bostic v. Rainey*, acknowledging that Virginia's ban on same-sex marriage violated the Fourteenth Amendment. After full adversarial proceedings in which Virginia's marriage ban was vigorously defended by two circuit court clerks, the Attorney General's conclusion was vindicated by the district court and the Fourth Circuit. . . .

Adamidis and Webb Note: Virginia then describes how the state has implemented *Bostic*, so that same-sex marriage as well as adoptions by same-sex couples are now permitted.

Virginia's same-sex spouses and their children can now travel to the thirty-seven other States in which marriage equality is recognized without fear that those States will treat them as legal strangers to each other. But the Sixth Circuit's ruling below leaves them at risk of that consequence when they travel to or through Kentucky, Michigan, Ohio and Tennessee.

Virginia submits this amicus brief in support of reversal because its experience on the wrong side of *Brown* and *Loving*, and on the right side of this issue, has taught us the truth of what the Court recognized in *Lawrence v. Texas*: "those who drew and ratified . . . the Fourteenth Amendment" chose not to specify the full measure of freedom that it protected because they "knew [that] times can blind us to certain truths and later generations can see that laws once thought necessary and proper in fact serve only to oppress." . . .

ARGUMENT

I. The fundamental right of marriage is protected by the Due Process Clause and cannot be restricted to the narrowest context in which it was historically practiced.

To defeat the fundamental right to marry at issue in this case, the respondent States seek to define the right so narrowly that it disappears. They would define it as the right of same-sex couples to marry, not the right of two people to marry. But two interrelated reasons show why respondents' cramped definition is untenable.

A. The Court's marriage cases do not limit the right of marriage to the narrowest context in which it was historically practiced.

First, this Court's marriage cases teach that the fundamental right of marriage is not limited to the historical context in which it was practiced. Until Virginia's interracial-marriage ban was struck down in *Loving*, such laws had been in effect "since the colonial period." Yet that history could not save them. As *Casey* explained, the Fourteenth Amendment bars States from prohibiting interracial marriage *despite* that "interracial marriage was illegal in most States in the 19th century. . . ." There was likewise no historical precedent to support the right of prisoners or dead-beat parents to marry. Yet the Court in *Turner v. Safley* held that prisoners are entitled to wed. And it held in *Zablocki v. Redhail* that States could not deny marriage to persons who were behind in their child-support obligations. Thus, most courts have correctly read *Loving*, *Zablocki*, and *Turner* as requiring the freedom to marry to be defined at a *broad* level of generality, even if the context in question, as here, was not one in which marriage rights had been traditionally recognized or historically practiced.

Those cases cannot be distinguished, as the panel tried below, on the ground that they all involved different-sex couples. No case before *Loving* involved interracial marriage; no case before *Zablocki* involved betrotheds behind in their child-support obligations; and no case before *Turner* involved marriage to a prisoner. But the Court nonetheless described each case as involving the right to marry, a right "of fundamental importance for *all* individuals."

Nor can those cases be restricted by sectarian notions that marriage exists only for procreative couples or purposes. *Turner* granted prisoners the right to marry despite that incarceration prevented consummation. The "important attributes of marriage" that remained included "expressions of emotional support and public commitment," "spiritual significance," and considerable economic and non-economic benefits. Although the Court noted that most inmates expect to be released someday and so may wed anticipating that the marriage "ultimately will be fully consummated," nothing in *Turner* suggested that consummation, let alone procreation, was indispensable, or that inmates serving life-terms could be prohibited from marrying.

But if there were any doubt whether a State could make procreation a condition of marriage, *Griswold* dispelled it. *Griswold* upheld the right of married couples *not* to procreate. The Court described marriage in poetic terms that apply with equal force to same-sex and different-sex marriages:

> Marriage is a coming together for better or for worse, hopefully enduring, and intimate to the degree of being sacred. It is an association that promotes a way of life, not causes; a harmony in living, not political faiths; a bilateral loyalty, not commercial or social projects. Yet it is an association for as noble a purpose as any involved in our prior decisions.

Justice Scalia put the point more bluntly in his dissent in *Lawrence*: "what justification could there possibly be for denying the benefits of marriage to homosexual couples . . . ? Surely not the encouragement of procreation, since the sterile and the elderly are allowed to marry."

B. *Casey* and *Lawrence* rejected the narrowest-historical-context approach to restricting established fundamental rights.

A second basis requires rejecting the respondents' effort to define the fundamental right here as the narrow right of same-sex marriage, rather than the broader right of two people to marry. This Court in *Casey* squarely rejected the narrowest-historical-context approach, previously urged by Justice Scalia, that would limit established fundamental rights to the most specific level at which they were historically practiced.

In footnote 6 of the plurality opinion in *Michael H. v. Gerald D.*, Justice Scalia proposed that fundamental rights under the Due Process Clause be defined at "the most specific level at which a relevant tradition protecting, or denying protection to, the asserted right can be identified." For that proposition he relied on *Bowers v. Hardwick*, where this Court upheld Georgia's "sodomy" law as applied to consenting male adults in the privacy of their own home.[13] To demonstrate the historical basis for *Bowers*, Justice Scalia noted that when "the Fourteenth Amendment was ratified all but 5 of the 37 States had criminal sodomy laws, that all 50 of the States had such laws prior to 1961, and that 24 States and the District of Columbia continued to have them" in 1986, when *Bowers* was decided. Thus, he argued, there was no "relevant tradition" and no fundamental right protecting two adult men who wished to engage in sexually intimate conduct in the privacy of their own home.

But only Chief Justice Rehnquist joined footnote 6. The theory was rejected by Justice O'Connor, in a concurring opinion joined by Justice Kennedy, who explained that it "sketche[d] a mode of historical analysis . . . that may be somewhat inconsistent with our past decisions in this area." "On occasion," she continued, "the Court has characterized relevant traditions protecting asserted rights at levels of generality that might not be 'the most specific level' available." She gave *Loving* and *Turner* as examples. Justice O'Connor therefore rejected "the prior imposition of a single mode of historical analysis."

Justices O'Connor and Kennedy were not alone; the three dissenting justices in *Michael H.* likewise rejected footnote 6, explaining that limiting rights to those "traditionally protected by our society" would limit substantive-due-process protection to only those interests "already protected by a majority of the States," a position that would "mock[] those who, with care and purpose, wrote the Fourteenth Amendment."

The separate views rejecting footnote 6 in *Michael H.* coalesced in *Casey*, where a full majority of the Court explicitly rejected the narrowest-historical-context theory. In a joint opinion by Justices O'Connor, Kennedy and Souter, in which Justices Blackmun and Stevens joined, the Court explained:

> It is . . . tempting . . . to suppose that the Due Process Clause protects only those practices, defined at the most specific level, that were protected against government interference . . . when the Fourteenth Amendment was ratified. . . . *But such a view would be inconsistent with our law.* . . . Marriage is mentioned nowhere in the Bill of Rights and interracial marriage was illegal in most States in the 19th century, but the Court was no doubt correct in finding it to be an aspect of liberty protected against state interference by the substantive component of the Due Process Clause in *Loving*. . . .

Justice Scalia himself later acknowledged that his narrowest-historical-context theory had not gained traction. In dissenting from the Court's holding that Virginia could not exclude women from VMI, he wrote, it "is my position that the term 'fundamental rights' should be limited to 'interest[s] traditionally protected by our society,' . . .; *but the Court has not accepted that view*. . . ."

The epilogue in the story of the demise of footnote 6 then came in 2003, when *Lawrence* overruled *Bowers*, the primary authority on which Justice Scalia had based the narrowest-historical-context theory. Writing for the majority in *Lawrence*, Justice Kennedy explained that the Court had erred when it framed the question in *Bowers* too narrowly as "whether the Federal Constitution confers a fundamental right upon homosexuals to engage in sodomy. . . ." "That statement, we now conclude, discloses the Court's own failure to appreciate the extent of the liberty at stake." Those who define the right at issue here as the right to same-sex marriage make the same mistake.

Nothing in *Washington v. Glucksberg* revivified the narrowest-historical-context theory that had been interred by *Casey*. *Glucksberg* declined to recognize a fundamental right to assisted suicide, finding no such right anywhere in "700 years [of] Anglo-American" history. . . .

Adamidis and Webb Note: In omitted text, Virginia then discusses the *Glucksberg* decision.

Notably, the handful of judges who have invoked *Glucksberg* to define marriage narrowly have uniformly ignored that this Court has not applied the narrowest-historical-context approach to restrict established rights—like the right to marry—that had *already been recognized* as fundamental.

> Applying the correct legal doctrine is crucial to getting the right answer. Virginia mistakenly applied the narrowest historical context approach when it defended segregation in *Brown*, anti-miscegenation laws in *Loving*, and the exclusion of women from VMI, all practices with a long tradition and historical pedigree. Kentucky, Michigan, Ohio and Tennessee are simply repeating that mistake here. . . .
>
> A decisive ruling here also will help mute the siren song calling some individuals to think that States' rights can somehow justify disobeying this Court when it protects fundamental rights. . . . [H]istory teaches that adherence "to the command of the Constitution [is] *indispensable* for the protection of the freedoms guaranteed by our fundamental charter for all of us."
>
> We have learned that lesson in Virginia. Those who drafted and ratified the Fourteenth Amendment might not have thought that it prohibited a State from practicing segregation or from barring interracial marriage, even though we take for granted today that it does. Hypothesizing what the drafters might have thought about same-sex marriage likewise asks the wrong question. The scope of that Amendment is not governed by what its draftsmen might have thought, but by what they wrote, and by how their words have been authoritatively construed by this Court.[14] We revere the Founders because their words and ideals are timeless, even if they failed to practice the full meaning of those words and ideals in their own day.
>
> "The Constitution created a government dedicated to equal justice under law." That principle is not new. What is new is *this generation's* recognition that that principle cannot be reconciled with governmental discrimination against gay people. Selecting a life-partner of the same gender is a "choice [ ] the Constitution protects." So too, the principle of equal justice under law prohibits States from denying to gay couples and their children "the most important relation in life."

CRITICAL ASSESSMENT

Both Demosthenes and Virginia rely on appeals to tradition in their work. Both ask the audiences to identify with revered traditions of the country and then use shared identity between rhetor and audience to further their persuasive arguments.

Demosthenes advances his argument with the theme that a state should be guided by its most noble traditions. As he builds on a fundamentally repetitive argument that unfolds progressively throughout the speech, the oration reaches its climax in sections 199–208 in an emotive outburst. Demosthenes touches upon the most important query—what it means to be an Athenian—and suggests that adherence to traditional principles provides an answer. He asks the audience to decide the question of "who we (Athenians) really are," what are the constants that determine the right course of action, and what is the testament of contemporaries to the future generations.

Virginia creatively frames the relevant right and the historical narrative so it can claim tradition supports its position. Its rhetorical strategies place it (and the petitioning parties supported by the brief) on the right side of what it means to be American and committed to the foundational principle of equality. The brief first establishes shared identity with the reader by noting agreement on matters that are currently uncontroversial, such as a rejection of segregated schools and an acceptance of interracial marriage. It then connects those uncontroversial positions to an evolving understanding of what equality means. Finally, it addresses the current, more controversial question of same-sex marriage, in an effort to (1) demonstrate similarities in terms of equal treatment of minority groups and (2) show that previously rejected stances may become commonplace over time as we reach a better understanding of what our traditional commitment to equality encompasses. This creative approach to defining "tradition," along with a broader framing of the right, allows Virginia to argue that tradition compels a rejection of the opposing position, which itself claimed to rely on tradition (in the sense of a long-standing custom narrowly defining marriage).

DISCUSSION QUESTIONS

Discussion Question 1: Both Demosthenes and Virginia refer to history and tradition, in the sense of the acts and policies of founders, as they frame their arguments. How does each advocate integrate revered historical figures? How does each establish ethos by aligning the proposed outcome here with the views or policies previously accepted as correct? Are their approaches similar, or different?

Examine sections 95–101 in Demosthenes's speech, where he relies on the use of examples from Athenian history to develop his maxim that the public conduct of a state, like the private conduct of a man, should always be guided by its most honorable traditions. Why did Demosthenes choose these particular examples, what are their common features, and how did he use them?

Now look closely at the first four paragraphs of Virginia's brief. Can you compare or contrast Demosthenes's examples to the examples that Virginia chose as it framed the issue? How did Virginia's examples support its framing of the relevant tradition and its assertion that prior cases "teach that the right to marry cannot be restricted to the narrowest context in which it was historically practiced"? Do those examples support the underlying principle of Virginia's argument, namely, that a narrow view of traditionally acceptable practice does not support America's foundational dedication to equality?

Discussion Question 2: Both advocates suggest that their position is consistent with the society's traditional values and principles. How do Demosthenes's attempts to define what it means to be Athenian compare to Virginia's attempts to define what it means to be American?

Review sections 199–208 of Demosthenes's speech and see if you can identify how he managed to reach an emotional climax in his oration. What techniques did Demosthenes employ to arouse the emotions of the audience (pathos)? What is the core of Athenian identity and what values inform it?

Now examine the penultimate paragraph of Virginia's brief. How does Virginia align the values of America's founders, and the text they wrote, with its current position?

Advocates often claim adherence to traditional values to create a shared identity between the orator and the audience and thus marginalize the adversary or opposing view. You can see this approach in sections 63–69 of Demosthenes's oration. Do these advocates portray those with different views as ethical outsiders who should be excluded from the group? If yes, is that problematic?[15]

Finally, look at the last paragraph in the section of Virginia's brief titled "Virginia's Interest as Amicus Curiae." Virginia positions itself as an actor who has previously behaved badly but now sees the error of its ways; does this establish its credibility (ethos)? Does it matter that Virginia is not a party to the case but is writing as a "friend of the court" to help the court make a decision?

Discussion Question 3: Storytelling, or using narrative to evoke an emotional reaction in audiences, is a common rhetorical strategy. The use of tradition as a persuasive argument invites the reader to consider historical narratives. What narratives can you identify in each of these arguments?

Does tradition evolve over time, or is it fixed? How does Virginia construct a historical narrative supporting its position? Is Virginia's view of tradition similar to or different from Demosthenes's view?

ADDITIONAL READINGS

Adamidis, V. "Populist Rhetorical Strategies in the Courts of Classical Athens." *Athens Journal of History* 7, no. 1 (January 2021): 21–40.

Forde-Mazrui, Kim. "Tradition as Justification: The Case of Opposite-Sex Marriage." *University of Chicago Law Review* 78, no. 1 (2011): 281–344.
Harris, Edward. s.v. "Demosthenes (2), Athenian Orator." *Oxford Classical Dictionary*, March 25, 2021.
MacDowell, D. M. *Demosthenes the Orator*. Oxford: Oxford University Press, 2009.
Murphy, J. J., ed. *Demosthenes' "On the Crown": Rhetorical Perspectives*. Landmarks in Rhetoric and Public Address. Carbondale: Southern Illinois University Press, 2016.
Turner, Ronald. "Marriage Equality and Obergefell's Generational (Not Glucksberg's Traditional) Due Process Clause." *Duke Journal of Gender Law and Policy* 23, no. 2 (2016): 145–62.
Yunis, Harvey, trans. *Demosthenes: On the Crown*. Cambridge Greek and Latin Classics. Cambridge, UK: Cambridge University Press, 2001.

12

Cicero

Legal Stases and the Supreme Court

Brian N. Larson and Susan E. Provenzano

INTRODUCTION

During his confirmation hearings in 2005, soon-to-be Chief Justice of the United States John Roberts asserted that Supreme Court justices interpreting laws should behave as metaphorical umpires, not players: "Umpires don't make the rules; they apply them. . . . And I will remember that it's my job to call balls and strikes and not to pitch or bat." Chief Justice Roberts's claimed stance is one of judicial restraint—that judges should apply the law as the legislature wrote it, not make the law. But judicial decisions regarding the interpretation of statutes—including the Supreme Court's—lie somewhere between this "apply" and "make" polarity. To interpret a law is to discern meaning that the law itself has not made explicit. When judges are cast in an interpretive role, it can be hard to tell whether they are "players" contributing to the law's meaning or umpires who simply "call" meaning as the legislature wrote it.

Some judges take very active roles in discerning statutory meaning. Just before his retirement from the bench, US Seventh Circuit Court of Appeals Judge Richard Posner endorsed "judicial interpretive updating" as a method of statutory interpretation in a landmark case holding that sexual orientation discrimination is a form of illegal sex discrimination. Using this interpretive method, judges "update" older laws by giving "fresh meaning" to statutory text that "infuses [it] with vitality and significance today."[1] In contrast, Chief Justice Roberts and others see the proper judicial role as simply to apply the written text.

This dichotomy did not concern the Roman orator Cicero, whose rhetorical writings extensively addressed argumentation about written texts. Unconstrained by stock interpretive methods or philosophical debates about judging roles, Cicero's approach turned on dialogic persuasion. He urged orators arguing written texts to appeal to judges sometimes as umpires, sometimes as players, and often as both. A consummate player himself, Cicero was always ready to switch up his arguments to favor the side he was on.

Born Marcus Tullius Cicero (106–43 BCE), Cicero, sometimes called "Tully," was a leading jurist, orator, senator, politician, rhetorical theorist, and philosopher during the later Roman Republic. Rising from relative obscurity in an "equestrian" family from Arpinum, some seventy miles from Rome, he officially began his career as orator by pleading in a case in 81 or 80 BCE; his final contribution to classical oratory came in the final year of his life with his *Philippics*. Between his first oration and the last, Cicero rose to extraordinary heights of power in Rome, becoming a quaestor (a financial officer) in 76 BCE; aedile (an administrative officer) in 69; praetor (an officer responsible for supervision of criminal courts, among other things) in 66; and consul, the highest administrative position in the Republic, in 63. He achieved each of these offices having barely attained the minimum required age.

Cicero wrote about rhetoric both near the beginning and near the end of his career. Late in his teens or early in his twenties, he wrote *On Invention* (*De Inventione*), excerpted in this chapter, an extended treatment of the first canon of rhetoric. In 46 BCE he wrote *Brutus* and *Orator*, his final works on the subject. *On Invention* provided a detailed outline of the *stases* (Gk.) or *status* (Lat.), the issues on which a case could turn. The stases gave orators a roadmap for identifying the argumentative positions available in any legal dispute. In turn, the stases gave judges a method of figuring out the real decision points in a case. Theoretically, the orator who identified these decision points and supported them with the best arguments would win the dispute. Probably first organized by Greek rhetorician Hermagoras of Temnos in the second century BCE (in works now lost to us), the stases went through a variety of forms over the next three hundred years. (See the select bibliography at the end of this chapter for details.)

In *On Invention*, Cicero identified four *rational stases* that could be raised in a given legal dispute: conjecture (What happened?), definition (By what name or label do we call it?), quality (Was the act good or bad?), and translation (Is there a procedural problem?). A separate set of interpretive stases addressed *legal questions* focused on disputes over writings, identifying the main points of argumentative departure over textual meaning.[2] These interpretive stases, devised in ancient times, remarkably capture the essence of modern legal interpretation.

This excerpt shows how Cicero approached two of these legal questions—the interpretive stases of *ambiguity* and *letter and intent*—in *On Invention*. The excerpt from the US Supreme Court case *Chickasaw Nation v. United States*

(2001) shows how at least one contemporary court used these very stases to settle a statutory meaning debate. In the context of a federal taxing law, the majority and dissenting opinions in *Chickasaw* echo Cicero's rhetorical strategies, using ordinary meaning, surrounding language, and ever-widening forms of context in the quest to resolve ambiguous language and to square the law's text with congressional intent. *Chickasaw* offers a poignant example of how classical rhetoric speaks to contemporary legal problems.

MARCUS TULLIUS CICERO, *ON INVENTION* (*DE INVENTIONE*) (CA. 89 BCE)

Editors' Note: This translation is that of H. M. Hubbell from the Harvard University Press Loeb Classical Library, originally published 1949. This version is in the public domain. We have made minor spelling edits with notation and other changes that are enclosed in square brackets. Numbers in square brackets indicate sections of the text as follows: the first one-digit number (always "2" here) refers to the volume of the text, which has been divided since ancient times in two volumes; the three-digit numbers refer to manuscript pages in the text from which Hubbell's translation derives and are commonly used by scholars across many editions and translations of Cicero. Thus, referring to "Cicero, *De Inventione* 2.116" is a fairly unambiguous way to refer to the first paragraph of this excerpt, regardless of a reader's edition.

> [2.116] A controversy turns upon written documents when some doubt arises from the nature of writing. This comes about from ambiguity, from the letter and intent, from conflict of laws, from reasoning by analogy, from definition.
>
> A controversy arises from ambiguity when there is doubt as to what the writer meant, because the written statement has two or more meanings, after this fashion: A father, in making his son his principal heir bequeathed to his wife a hundred pounds of silver plate in the following terms: "Let my heir give to my wife a hundred pounds of silver plate as desired." After his death the mother asks her son for some magnificent examples of plate with costly chasing. He says that he is obligated to give her only what *he* desires.

Larson and Provenzano Note: Cicero now discusses the interpretive stasis of ambiguity.

> In the first place it should be shown, if possible, that there is no ambiguity in the statement, because in ordinary conversation everyone is accustomed to use this single word or phrase in the sense in which the speaker will prove that it should be taken. [2.117] In the second place it must be shown that from what precedes or follows in the document the doubtful point becomes plain. Therefore, if words are to be considered separately by themselves, every word, or at

least many words, would seem ambiguous; but it is not right to regard as ambiguous what becomes plain on consideration of the whole context.

In the next place, one ought to estimate what the writer meant from his other writings, acts, words, disposition and in fact his whole life, and to examine the whole document which contains the ambiguity in question in all its parts, to see if anything is apposite to our interpretation or opposed to the sense in which our opponent understands it. . . .

[2.119] Another point which will deserve careful attention is whether it will not appear if we accept the interpretation proposed by our opponent, that the writer neglected something more expedient, more honorable or more necessary. This can be brought about by saying that the interpretation which we make is honorable, expedient and necessary, and that of the opposition by no means of such a nature. Then if the controversy arises over an ambiguity in a law, we must try to make it appear that the interpretation which our opponent offers is dealt with [2.120] in another law. It will help greatly to show how he would have written if he had wished the opponent's interpretation to be carried out or adopted. For instance, in this case which deals with the silver plate, the woman could say that there was no point in adding the words "as desired" if the testator was leaving the choice to his heir. For with these words omitted there is no doubt that the heir was to give what he himself wished. It was therefore stark madness, if he wished to provide for the interest of his heir, to add the words the omission of which would not prejudice the heir's interest. [2.121] Therefore in such cases it will be necessary to make use of this kind of argument: "He would have written it in this way," "He would not have used that word," "He would not have put that word in that place." For these considerations particularly reveal the intention of the writer. Then one might ask when it was written, so that it may be known what he was likely to write at such a time. Finally . . . we must show what was more expedient and more honorable both for the testator to write and for our opponents to sanction. . . .

Larson and Provenzano Note: Cicero now takes up the interpretive stasis of letter and intent.

A controversy over the letter and the intent occurs when one party follows the exact words that are written, and the other directs his whole pleading [2.122] to what he says the writer meant. The one who bases his defense on the intent will sometimes show that the intent of the writer always had the same end in view and desired the same result, at other times he will show that the writer's purpose has to be modified to fit the occasion as a result of some act or event. He may be proved to have always had the same end in view in the following way:

A head of a family, having a wife but no children, drew his will as follows: "If one or more sons are born to me, he or they are to inherit my estate. . . ." Then comes, "If my son dies before coming of age, then So-and-So is to be my heir." No son was born. The [man's other family members] dispute with the man who was to be the reversionary [2.123] heir in case the son died before coming of age. In this kind of case it cannot be said that the intent of the writer ought to be made to fit some time or some event, because the only possible meaning is shown to be that on which the litigant who opposes the literal interpretation of the will defends his own right to inherit. But there is another kind of argument brought forward by advocates of the intent in which the wish of the writer is shown not to be absolute, i.e. having the same weight for every occasion and for every action, but it is argued that his wishes ought to be interpreted to fit the occasion in the light of some act or some event . . . as in the case of the man who, though the law forbade opening the gates at night, opened them in a certain war and let certain auxiliary forces into the town in order that they might not be wiped out by the enemy if left outside, for the enemy was encamped near the walls. [2.124] To sum up, intent will be presented so as to show that the writer desired one definite thing, or to prove that he desired this in such circumstances and at such a time.

[2.125] An advocate who will defend the letter will be able to use all of the following topics most of the time, and the greater part of them on every occasion; first, high praise of the writer, and a common topic that the judges should regard nothing except what is written; and this may be made more emphatic if some statutory document is offered, i.e. either a whole law or some part of it; after that one may use the most effective argument, a comparison of the action and purpose of the opponents with the letter of the law, showing what was written, what was done, what the judge has sworn to do. And it will be well to vary this topic in many ways, first expressing wonder in his own mind as to what can possibly be said on the other side, then turning to the judge's duty and asking what more he can think it necessary to hear or expect. Then one may bring in the opponent himself like a witness, that is ask him whether he denies that the law is so written, or denies that he has acted contrary to it or endeavored so to do, and offer to stop speaking if he dares deny either. [2.126] But if he denies neither statement and still continues to dispute, say that there is no reason why anyone should think that he will ever see a more shameless man. It will be wise to linger over this point as if it were unnecessary and impossible to say anything more, often reading the document, often comparing the act of the opponent with the letter of the law, and often turning sharply to the judge. In this connection one should point out to the judge what oath he has taken, and what course he is bound to follow, saying that there are two reasons why a judge should hesitate: if the document is obscurely drawn, or if the accused denies [2.127] any allegation.

That when the document is plain and the accused confesses everything, then the judge ought to comply with the law and not interpret it.

When this point has been established it will be time to attack the arguments which can be made on the other side. Arguments will be made in reply to either of two positions, that is, if it is shown definitely that the writer meant one thing and wrote another, as in the controversy which we have cited about the will, or if an . . . argument is introduced to show why it was impossible or undesirable to comply with the written word.

[2.128] If the writer is alleged to have meant one thing and written another, the advocate who follows the letter will say: It is not right for us to argue about the intent of one who left us a clear indication of his intent in order that we might not be able to dispute it; that much inconvenience would result if it should be established as a principle that we may depart from the written word. For those who draw up a written document will not feel that what they have written will be fixed and unalterable, and judges will have no sure guide to follow if once they become accustomed to depart from the written word. Therefore if the object is to carry out the wish of the writer, counsel will urge that it is he rather than the opponents who adhere to the writer's wishes; for one gets much closer to a writer's intent if one interprets it from the writer's own words than one who does not learn the writer's intention from his own written document which he has left as a picture, one might say, of his own desires, but makes one's own inferences.

[2.130] . . . The first topic will be supported by arguments like these: the author of the law did not lack the intelligence, diligence or opportunity to write plainly what he intended; it was not hard or difficult to make an exception of the excuse which the opposing advocates offer, if he had thought that any exception ought to be made. The lawmakers are accustomed to make [2.131] exceptions. Then it will be in point to read laws that include exceptions and in particular to see if there is any exception in any chapter of the law in question or in laws by the same law-maker, in order that it may be better established that he would have made an exception if he had thought one ought to be made. Furthermore, one should show that accepting an excuse is nothing more than repealing the law, because when once an excuse is taken into consideration there is no point in weighing it with reference to the law, seeing that it is not written in the law. . . . [J]udges will have no rule to follow if they depart from the letter of the law, nor will they have any means of winning the approval of others to their decision which has been made contrary to the law, and other citizens will not know what to do if everyone regulates all his affairs according to his own ideas or any whim that strikes his mind or fancy, and not according to the ordinances common to the whole state. And then he may make an appeal to the judges' own interest, asking them why they spend their time over other people's business; why they let public duties prevent them from serving their own interest and advantage; why they swear a precise and definite oath; why they assemble at a fixed time and leave at a fixed time, and no one offers any excuse for not serving the state frequently except such excuse as is particularly stated in the law. Do they think it fair that they should be bound by law in so many annoying details, and [2.133] allow our opponents to violate the laws? . . . [2.134] . . . Then it may be urged that it is improper to repeal a law in part or in whole or to change any provision when the people have no opportunity to examine the matter and approve or disapprove; that such conduct is certain to bring the judges into ill repute; that this is not the place nor the time to correct the laws; such action should be taken before the people and by the people; that if they are trying to do that now, he would like to know who is proposing the amendment, and what body is going to accept it; that he sees party strife arising and wishes to resist it. . . . By these and similar arguments it is shown that an excuse ought not to be accepted contrary to the letter of the law.

[2.135] The second head is that under which it is made plain that departure from the letter of the law though permissible under other laws, is not permissible in this case. This may be done if it is made to appear that the law has to do with matters of the highest importance, advantage, honor and sanctity; that it is inexpedient, or base or criminal not to follow the law most exactly in such a case. Or it may be shown that the law was so carefully framed, that such provision was made for every situation and proper exceptions made, that it is not at all fitting to think that anything was omitted from a document drawn up with such care.

The third head is highly important for one who is speaking in favor of the letter; in this he should show that, if it is proper to accept an excuse contrary to the letter of the law, the excuse offered by the opponents should by no means be admitted. [2.136] This topic is indispensable for him because one who is speaking against the letter ought always to adduce some principle of equity. For it would be the height of impudence for one who wishes to gain approval for some act contrary to the letter of the law, not to attempt to gain his point with the help of equity. If, then, the prosecutor can weaken this argument at all, his accusation would seem in every way more just and plausible. For all the earlier part of his speech was devoted to making conviction necessary even if the judges were unwilling: but this, to making them willing to convict even if it [2.137] is unnecessary. . . .

[2.138] On the other hand the speaker who is attacking the letter will first of all present the argument to prove the equity of making an excuse; or he will show with what intention or design he did what he did, and for what reason; and whatever excuse he adopts he will make his defense with the . . . arguments which we have discussed above. When he has spent some time on this topic and put a fair front on the reason for his act and the justice of his excuse, he will then use the following arguments against his opponents to prove that excuses ought to be accepted. He will point out that there is no law which requires the performance of any inexpedient or unjust act; that all penalties provided by law were established to punish wickedness and [2.139] vice; that the author of the law himself, if he should rise from the dead, would approve this act, and would have done the same if he had been in a similar situation; that the reason why the author of the law provided for judges from a certain class and of a certain age was that there might be a judicial body able not only to read his law, which any child could do, but to comprehend it with the mind and interpret his intentions; again, that if the law-maker had been giving his law to ignorant men and barbarous judges, he would have written everything out in precise detail; but as he knew the quality of the men who were to judge the cases, he did not add what he saw was perfectly plain. . . .

[2.140] After that he will ask his opponents: "Suppose that I had done so and so; suppose that so and so had happened—mentioning any of those acts for which there is a most honorable excuse or a certain plea of necessity—would you still accuse me?" But the law makes no exception. Therefore all cases are not covered by exceptions expressed in writing, but some that are self-evident are covered by exceptions understood but not expressed. Then it may be urged that nothing at all could be done either with laws or with any instrument in writing, or even about our everyday conversation and the orders issued in our own homes, if everyone wished to consider only the literal meaning of the words and not to follow the intentions of the speaker.

[2.141] Then from the principles of advantage and honor he may show how inexpedient and base is the course of conduct which the opponents say we were or are bound to follow, and how advantageous and honorable is our act or request. Then, that we value the laws not because of the words, which are but faint and feeble indications of intention, but because of the advantage of the principles which they embody, and the wisdom and care of the law-makers. Next he may set forth the true nature of law, that it may be shown to consist of meanings, not of words, and that the judge who follows the meaning may seem to comply with law more than one who follows the letter. Again, how harsh it is to visit the same punishment on one who from criminal audacity has violated the laws, and on one who from some honorable and necessary cause has departed from the letter but not from the intent of the law. . . .

[2.142] And just as we said that the speaker who is upholding the letter of the law would find it most useful to lessen in some degree the justice or equity which supports his opponent's claim, so the speaker who opposes the letter will profit greatly by converting something in the written document to his own case or by showing that it contains some ambiguity; then on the basis of that ambiguity he may defend the passage which helps his case, or introduce a definition of some word and interpret the meaning of the word which seems to bear hard upon him, so as to support his own case, or develop from the written word something that is not expressed; this is the method of reasoning from [2.143] analogy, which we shall discuss below. In a word, in whatever way, however slightly plausible it may be, he can defend himself by appealing to the letter of the law, when his case is amply supported by abstract justice, he will profit greatly, because if he can remove the foundation on which his opponents' case rests, he will lessen and mitigate all its force and effectiveness.

Common topics from the other parts of the . . . issue will suit both sides. In addition, however, the speaker who defends the letter of the law may use the following: laws ought to be judged with reference to their own intrinsic merits and not to the advantage of the transgressor; and that nothing should be esteemed more highly than the laws. Against the letter of the law: the value of law depends on the intention of the legislator and on the common weal, not on words: how unfair it is that justice and equity, which it is the intention of the legislator to protect, should be hindered by words.

CHICKASAW NATION V. UNITED STATES, 534 U.S. 84 (2001)

Larson and Provenzano Note: This case ended two Native American tribes' challenges to the federal government's taxation of tribal gaming operations. It raises the legal-interpretive question whether the Indian Gaming Regulatory Act put tribes' gaming operations on equal taxation footing with state and local gaming operations. The litigation also raises larger questions about equity in US-tribal versus US-state relationships.

Justice Stephen Breyer wrote this majority opinion, in which six of the eight other justices joined (though Justices Scalia and Thomas did not join in Part II.B., much of which is omitted here). Justice O'Connor wrote a dissent—an opinion that explains why she did not vote with the majority—in which Justice Souter joined. The dissent does not appear in this excerpt, though the critical assessment at the end of this chapter raises some of its arguments. Omissions in this excerpt are generally indicated by ellipses, except that some citations are omitted without notice and some quotations by Justice Breyer of the court's previous opinions are not indicated with quotation marks here.

In these cases we must decide whether a particular subsection in the Indian Gaming Regulatory Act . . . exempts tribes from paying the gambling-related taxes that chapter 35 of the Internal Revenue Code imposes—taxes that States need not pay. We hold that it does not create such an exemption.

I.

The relevant Indian Gaming Regulatory Act (Gaming Act) subsection . . . reads as follows:

> The provisions of [the Internal Revenue Code of 1986] (including sections 1441, 3402(q), 6041, and 6050I, and chapter 35 of such [Code]) concerning the reporting and withholding of taxes with respect to the winnings from gaming or wagering operations shall apply to Indian gaming operations . . . in the same manner as such provisions apply to State gaming and wagering operations.

The subsection says that Internal Revenue Code provisions that "concer[n] the reporting and withholding of taxes" with respect to gambling operations shall apply to Indian tribes in the same way as they apply to States. The subsection also says in its parenthetical that those provisions "includ[e]" Internal Revenue Code "chapter 35." Chapter 35, however, says nothing about the *reporting* or the *withholding* of taxes. Rather, that chapter simply *imposes* taxes—excise taxes and occupational taxes related to gambling—from which it exempts certain state-controlled gambling activities. . . .

In this lawsuit two Native American Indian Tribes, the Choctaw and Chickasaw Nations, claim that the Gaming Act subsection exempts them from paying those chapter 35 taxes from which States are exempt. . . . The Tenth Circuit rejected their claim on the ground that the subsection, despite its parenthetical reference, applies only to Code provisions that concern the "reporting and withholding of taxes." . . .

We agree with the Tenth Circuit.

II.

The Tribes' basic argument rests upon the subsection's explicit reference to "chapter 35"—contained in a parenthetical that refers to four other Internal Revenue Code provisions as well. The subsection's language outside the parenthetical says that the subsection applies to those Internal Revenue Code provisions that concern "reporting and withholding." The other four parenthetical references are to provisions that concern, or at least arguably concern, reporting and withholding. *See* 26 U.S.C. § 1441 (1994 ed. and Supp. V) (withholding of taxes for nonresident alien); § 3402(q) (withholding of taxes from certain gambling winnings); § 6041 (reporting by businesses of payments, including payments of gambling winnings, to others); § 6050I (reporting by businesses of large cash receipts, arguably applicable to certain gambling winnings or receipts).

But what about chapter 35? The Tribes correctly point out that chapter 35 has nothing to do with "reporting and withholding." They add that the reference must serve some purpose, and the only purpose that the Tribes can find is that of expanding the scope of the Gaming Act's subsection beyond reporting and withholding provisions—to the tax-imposing provisions that chapter 35 does contain. The Gaming Act therefore must exempt them (like States) from those tax payment requirements. The Tribes add that at least the reference to chapter 35 makes the subsection ambiguous. And they ask us to resolve the ambiguity by applying a special Indian-related interpretative canon, namely, "statutes are to be construed liberally in favor of the Indians with ambiguous provisions interpreted to their benefit."

We cannot accept the Tribes' claim. We agree with the Tribes that rejecting their argument reduces the phrase "(including . . . chapter 35)" to surplusage. Nonetheless, we can find no other reasonable reading of the statute.

A.

The language of the statute is too strong to bend as the Tribes would wish—i.e., so that it gives the chapter 35 reference independent operative effect. For one thing, the language outside the parenthetical is unambiguous. It says without qualification that the subsection applies to "provisions . . . concerning the reporting and withholding of taxes." And the language inside the parenthetical, prefaced with the word "including," literally says the same. To "include" is to "contain" or "comprise as part of a whole." *Webster's Ninth New Collegiate Dictionary* 609 (1985). In this instance that which "contains" the parenthetical references—the "whole" of which the references are "parts"—is the phrase "provisions . . . concerning the reporting and withholding of taxes." The use of parentheses emphasizes the fact that that which is within is meant simply to be illustrative, hence redundant—a circumstance underscored by the lack of any suggestion that Congress intended the illustrative list to be complete.

Nor can one give the chapter 35 reference independent operative effect without seriously rewriting the language of the rest of the statute. One would have to read the word "including" to mean what it does not mean, namely, "including . . . and." One would have to read the statute as if, for example, it placed "chapter 35" outside the parenthetical and said "provisions of the . . . Code *including chapter 35 and also provisions* . . . concerning the reporting and withholding of taxes." Or, one would have to read the language as if it said "provisions of the . . . Code . . . concerning *the taxation and* the reporting and withholding of taxes."

We mention this latter possibility because the congressional bill that became the law before us once did read that way. But when the bill left committee, it contained not the emphasized words ("the taxation and") but the cross-reference to chapter 35.

We recognize the Tribes' claim . . . that one could avoid rewriting the statute by reading the language outside the parenthetical as if it referred to two kinds of "provisions of the . . . Code": first, those "concerning the reporting and withholding of taxes with respect to the winnings from gaming," and, second, those "concerning . . . wagering operations." The subsection's grammar literally permits this reading. But that reading, even if ultimately comprehensible, is far too convoluted to believe Congress intended it. Nor is there any reason to think Congress intended to sweep within the subsection's scope every Internal Revenue Code provision concerning wagering—a result that this unnatural reading would accomplish.

The subject matter at issue also counsels against accepting the Tribes' interpretation. That subject matter is tax exemption. When Congress enacts a tax exemption, it ordinarily does so explicitly. We can find no comparable instance in which Congress legislated an exemption through an inexplicit numerical cross-reference—especially a cross-reference that might easily escape notice.

As we have said, the more plausible role for the parenthetical to play in this subsection is that of providing an illustrative list of examples. So considered, "chapter 35" is simply a bad example—an example that Congress included inadvertently. The presence of a bad example in a statute does not warrant rewriting the remainder of the statute's language. Nor does it necessarily mean that the statute is ambiguous, *i.e.*, "capable of being understood in two or more possible senses or ways." *Webster's Ninth New Collegiate Dictionary* 77 (1985). Indeed, in ordinary life, we would understand an analogous instruction—say, "Test drive some cars, including Plymouth, Nissan, Chevrolet, Ford, and Kitchenaid"—not as creating ambiguity, but as reflecting a mistake. Here too, in context, common sense suggests that the cross-reference is simply a drafting mistake, a failure to delete an inappropriate cross-reference in the bill that Congress later enacted into law.

B.

The Gaming Act's legislative history on balance supports our conclusion. The subsection as it appeared in the original Senate bill applied both to taxation and to reporting and withholding. It read as follows:

> Provisions of the Internal Revenue Code . . . concerning *the taxation and* the reporting and withholding of taxes with respect to gambling or

wagering operations shall apply to Indian gaming operations . . . the same as they apply to State operations." S. 555, 100th Cong., 1st Sess., 37 (1987).

With the "taxation" language present, it would have made sense to include chapter 35, which concerns taxation, in a parenthetical that included other provisions that concern reporting and withholding. But the Senate committee deleted the taxation language. Why did it permit the cross-reference to chapter 35 to remain? Committee documents do not say. . . .

In sum, to adopt the Tribes' interpretation would read back into the Act the very word "taxation" that the Senate committee deleted. We ordinarily will not assume that Congress intended to enact statutory language that it has earlier discarded in favor of other language.

C.

The Tribes point to canons of interpretation that favor their position. The Court has often said that every clause and word of a statute should, if possible, be given effect. The Tribes point out that our interpretation deprives the words "chapter 35" of any effect. The Court has also said that statutes are to be construed liberally in favor of the Indians with ambiguous provisions interpreted to their benefit. The Tribes point out that our interpretation is not to the Indians' benefit.

Nonetheless, these canons do not determine how to read this statute. For one thing, canons are not mandatory rules. They are guides that need not be conclusive. They are designed to help judges determine the Legislature's intent as embodied in particular statutory language. And other circumstances evidencing congressional intent can overcome their force. In this instance, to accept as conclusive the canons on which the Tribes rely would produce an interpretation that we conclude would conflict with the intent embodied in the statute Congress wrote. In light of the considerations discussed earlier, we cannot say that the statute is "fairly capable" of two interpretations, nor that the Tribes' interpretation is fairly "possible."

Specific canons are often countered . . . by some maxim pointing in a different direction. The canon requiring a court to give effect to each word "*if possible*" is sometimes offset by the canon that permits a court to reject words "as surplusage" if "inadvertently inserted or if repugnant to the rest of the statute." K. Llewellyn, *The Common Law Tradition* 525 (1960). And the latter canon has particular force here where the surplus words consist simply of a numerical cross-reference in a parenthetical. Cf. *Cabell Huntington Hospital, Inc. v. Shalala*, 101 F. 3d 984, 990 (CA4 1996) ("A parenthetical is, after all, a parenthetical, and it cannot be used to overcome the operative terms of the statute").

Moreover, the canon that assumes Congress intends its statutes to benefit the tribes is offset by the canon that warns us against interpreting federal statutes as providing tax exemptions unless those exemptions are clearly expressed. *See United States v. Wells Fargo Bank*, 485 U.S. 351, 354 (1988) ("[E]xemptions from taxation . . . must be unambiguously proved"); *Squire v. Capoeman*, 351 U.S. 1, 6 (1956) ("[T]o be valid, exemptions to tax laws should be clearly expressed"); *United States Trust Co. v. Helvering*, 307 U.S. 57, 60 (1939) ("Exemptions from taxation do not rest upon implication"). Nor can one say that the pro-Indian canon is inevitably stronger—particularly where the interpretation of a congressional statute rather than an Indian treaty is at issue. This Court's earlier cases are too individualized, involving too many different kinds of legal circumstances, to warrant any such assessment about the two canons' relative strength. *Compare, e.g., Choate v. Trapp*, 224 U.S. 665, 675–76 (1912) (interpreting statement in treaty-related Indian land patents that land is "nontaxable" as creating property right invalidating later congressional effort to tax); *Squire v. Capoeman*, 351 U. S. 1, 3 (1956) (Indian canon offsetting tax canon when related statutory provision and history make clear that language freeing Indian land "'of all charge or incumbrance whatsoever'" includes tax); *McClanahan v. Arizona Tax Comm'n*, 411 U.S. 164, 174 (1973) (state tax violates principle of Indian sovereignty embodied in treaty), with *Mescalero Apache Tribe v. Jones*, 411 U. S. 145 (1973) (relying on tax canon to find Indians taxable); *Choteau v. Burnet*, 283 U. S. 691 (1931) (language makes clear no exemption); *Superintendent of Five Civilized Tribes v. Commissioner*, 295 U. S. 418 (1935).

Consequently, the canons here cannot make the difference for which the Tribes argue. We conclude that the judgments of the Tenth Circuit must be affirmed.

It is so ordered.

CRITICAL ASSESSMENT

The *Chickasaw* excerpt treats two of the five interpretive stases that the Cicero excerpt identifies as major points of dispute about textual meaning—ambiguity and letter and intent. Cicero gives fairly brief attention to ambiguity, addressing it only in 2.116–2.121, while he considers letter and intent from 2.121 to 2.143. For the stasis of ambiguity, Cicero describes the interpretive method of using ever-widening contexts to argue meaning (2.117). He also suggests identifying what the author might have said instead to achieve the outcome that is "more expedient, more honorable or more necessary."

Justice Breyer's majority opinion rejects the contention that the Indian Gaming Regulatory Act is ambiguous, focusing primarily on letter and intent. Nevertheless, just as Cicero advises, in analyzing letter and intent, the opinion employs some ambiguity-resolving methods. At the end of the day, for Breyer and the majority, both the letter and the intent of this act reveal that its reference to chapter 35 is a simple drafting mistake—nothing more.

Justice O'Connor's dissent takes the majority opinion to task on both points. Like the majority, she notes that when the bill emerged from revisions in committee, one reference to "taxation" in the text had been removed, but the other reference to chapter 35, in the parenthetical, had not. Why, she wondered, would the majority assume that retaining "chapter 35" was erroneous and that deleting "taxation" was not? Interpreting the text either way, she argued, required "rewriting the statute," something the majority claimed to want to avoid. As she said, "The importance of statutory language depends not on its punctuation, but on its meaning." She concluded that the ambiguity could not be resolved without reference to context, including the "unique trust relationship between the United States and the Indians," a move presaged by Cicero's emphasis on context as a means of resolving ambiguity in one's favor.[3] Under the stasis of letter and intent, Cicero frames one response to a strict reading of the letter—now referred to as "textualism"—as an appeal to judicial expertise and intellectual capacity. The argument is that judges should not blindly follow text, which "any child could do," but instead should "comprehend it with the mind and interpret [the writer's] intentions." Cicero points out that "laws consist of meanings, not of words" and that words are "but faint and feeble indications of intention."

DISCUSSION QUESTIONS

Discussion Question 1: What do you think Cicero sees as the difference between "meanings" and "words"? In addressing the act's letter and intent, does the court accept this view of the judicial role in statutory interpretation? Is the court acting as umpire, player, or a bit of both?

In contemporary legal interpretation, textual ambiguity is seen as a prerequisite for addressing intent. Even though Breyer refuses to view the act as ambiguous, he still gives a nod to congressional intent. For example, section C's premise for rejecting the tribe's canons of construction is that those canons would "produce an interpretation that we conclude would conflict with the intent embodied in the statute Congress wrote."

Discussion Question 2: Does the court explain to your satisfaction what that congressional intent is? Should the court have used additional methods of discerning congressional intent, taking pages from Cicero's playbook? Do the court and Cicero agree on what it means to discern a writer's intent?

Likewise, as Justice Breyer points out, contemporary legal interpretation resorts to canons of construction as aids to meaning only when the statutory text is ambiguous. (Justice O'Connor does so in her dissent, too.) Still, Breyer spends considerable time addressing those canons. The canons of construction loom large in American law courtesy of Professor Karl Llewellyn, an important figure in twentieth-century American jurisprudence. In a well-known article, he listed twenty-seven canons and their countercanons, the rhetorical consequence of which was to diminish their force, but not their use.

Many of these same canons are identified by Cicero, though he would not limit their use to the stasis of ambiguity. Cicero sees the canons' utility in arguing the stasis of letter and intent—in fact, he notes that a challenge for these arguments is that they may come up against the plain meaning of the text (2.125, 2.128). Fundamentally, Cicero believes that "nothing at all could be done either with laws or with any instrument in writing, or even about our everyday conversation and the orders issued in our own homes, if everyone wished to consider only the literal meaning of the words and not to follow the intentions of the speaker" (2.140).

Discussion Question 3: Despite Cicero's willingness to set the intent of the law against its letter, he offers several arguments for why the letter should be preferred. Do these arguments justify the Supreme Court's view that intent matters only when the text is ambiguous? Do other arguments justify that view?

For Cicero, the canons correspond to the "topics" or common arguments that a litigator on one side or the other might address. In contemporary law, canons can be thought of as rules of thumb for interpreting texts.

Discussion Question 4: Identify as many rules of thumb and their opposing rules in the Cicero text and in *Choctaw* as you can. What sense do you make of them?

In arguing an ambiguous writing's meaning, Cicero advises advocates to persuade the judge that "the interpretation which we make is honorable, expedient, and necessary, and that of the opposition by no means of such a nature." In legal parlance, this kind of appeal is variously called a "policy" argument, a "practical results" argument, or a "consequentialist" argument. Typically, such arguments anticipate the real-world consequences of taking one interpretation over another.

Discussion Question 5: Given its selective use of intent-discerning methods, should the court have added this one to the mix? What are the real-world consequences of rejecting the tribe's statutory interpretation?

In Cicero's time, legal disputes were presented and resolved orally in a system with very different procedural constraints than the contemporary

US legal system. In addition, although Cicero was known for emphasizing the moral character of an orator, this quality did not necessarily translate to ethical constraints on legal argument. Because the ancients' aim was to win at all costs, arguments went beyond contemporary notions of rationality and restraint, with orators appealing, for example, to bald assumptions, class and sex stereotypes, and the desire for retribution.

Discussion Question 6: Can you find in *De Inventione* examples of appeals that would be unacceptable to contemporary judges? Can you find in the court's opinion examples of statutory interpretation reasoning that would not find purchase with the *De Inventione* audience? Do any of these differences reflect the fact that Cicero's writings applied to both private, single-author documents and the public enactments of legislative bodies, while the contemporary exercise of statutory construction is limited to the latter?

ADDITIONAL READINGS

Calboli Montefusco, Lucia. *La dottrina degli "status" nella retorica greca e romana*. Hildesheim, Germany: Olms-Weidmann, 1986.

Camper, Martin. *Arguing over Texts: The Rhetoric of Interpretation*. Oxford: Oxford University Press, 2018.

Cicero. *De Inventione, De Optimo Genere Oratorum, Topica*. Translated by H. M. Hubbell. Cambridge, MA: Harvard University Press, 1949.

Eskridge, William N., Jr. "The New Textualism." *UCLA Law Review* 37 (1990): 621–92.

Eskridge, William N., Jr., and Phillip P. Frickey. "Statutory Interpretation as Practical Reasoning." *Stanford Law Review* 42 (1990): 321–84.

Eskridge, William N., Jr., Phillip P. Frickey, and Elizabeth Garrett. *Cases and Materials on Legislation: Statutes and the Creation of Public Policy*. 5th ed. St. Paul, MN: West Academic Publishing, 2014.

Hubbell, H. M. and Cicero. "Introduction." In *De Inventione, de Optimo Genere Oraturm, Topica*. Cambridge, MA: Harvard University Press, 1949.

Llewellyn, Karl N. "Remarks on the Theory of Appellate Decision and the Rules or Canons about How Statutes Are to Be Construed." *Vanderbilt Law Review* 3 (1950): 395–406.

May, James M., Jakob Wisse, and Cicero. "Introduction." In *On the Ideal Orator [De Oratore]*. Oxford: Oxford University Press, 2001.

Nadeau, Ray. "Classical Systems of Stases in Greek: Hermagoras to Hermogenes." *Greek, Roman, and Byzantine Studies* 2 (1959): 53–71.

Provenzano, Susan E., and Brian N. Larson. "Civil Procedure as a Critical Discussion." *Nevada Law Journal* 20 (2020): 967–1036.

Provenzano, Susan E., Sarah O. Schrup, Carter G. Phillips, and Jeffrey T. Green. *Advanced Appellate Advocacy*. Frederick, MD: Aspen Publishing, 2016.

13

Quintilian

The Lawyer, Speaking—The Lawyer as "Perfect Orator"

KIRSTEN K. DAVIS

INTRODUCTION

Investigation into the ethos or character of orators, including lawyers, dates back to Ancient Greece and Rome. During the first century CE, Quintilian, a Roman lawyer, defined the "perfect orator" in terms of not only effective speaking but also, and necessarily, good moral character. The question of the character of lawyers when they speak in public is one that persists today. That is, what do we think are (or should be) the qualities of a lawyer who is both a public speaker providing the public information about the workings of the justice system and an officer of the court responsible for fair trials? The US Supreme Court struggled with this identity question in a 1991 case about a lawyer who decided to plead his client's case to the public in the form of a press conference rather than wait for the jury trial. The court was split on the question of the lawyer's character as a public speaker, an issue Quintilian addressed millennia ago.

Marcus Fabius Quintilianus (ca. 35–100 CE) was a well-known Roman lawyer and rhetoric scholar, teaching rhetoric and practicing as a legal advocate during the more repressive era of the Roman Empire that followed the fall of the Roman Republic. During this era, the practice of rhetoric was largely confined to legal arguments in Rome's law courts. In Quintilian's Rome, corruption pervaded society and government and there "was no longer any safe public position in Rome for the outspoken citizen of the type that Cicero represented in the days of the Roman Republic."[1] It was in this context that Quintilian was challenged to think deeply about the ethos of the "perfect" or "ideal" orator,[2] one who was not only effective but also moral or ethical. In some ways, Quintilian's assertion that an orator did not exist without morality was an act of subtle resistance during a time of tyrannical leadership.

Quintilian wrote his opus on the teaching of rhetoric, *Institutio Oratoria*, sometime around 95 CE, near the end of his life and career. The purpose of the book, he said, was to explore how to "form, then, the perfect orator, who cannot exist unless he is above all a good [person]" (well-known by the Latin phrase *vir bonus*).[3] In other words, Quintilian set out to define what made a perfect citizen-orator, not only practically but also morally or ethically. In book 12, the last in *Institutio Oratoria* and excerpted here, Quintilian discusses the orator's necessary moral foundations. Quintilian argues in book 12 that rhetoric is necessarily a morally good act and requires that a speaker be morally good as well. Rhetoric scholars James Murphy, Richard Katula, and Michael Hoppman note that Quintilian's view represented "a revolutionary doctrine in the development of rhetoric,"[4] transforming rhetoric from the value-neutral handmaiden of philosophy into a motivated, positively valenced act.

This excerpt introduces Quintilian's thoughts about the ideal orator. It is followed by an excerpt from the 1991 US Supreme Court case *Gentile v. State Bar of Nevada*, which demonstrates the court's contemporary struggle with lawyers as ideal orators.

MARCUS FABIUS QUINTILIAN, *INSTITUTES OF ORATORY (INSTITUTIO ORATORIA)*, BOOK 12 (CA. 95 CE)

Editors' Note: This translation of Quintilian's *Institutes of Oratory* is that of Harold Edgeworth Butler from the Harvard University Press, originally published in 1922. Book 12 is divided into a Preface (Pr.) plus eleven numbered chapters. Numbers (or Pr.) in brackets indicate the number of the book, the number of the chapter, and the number of the section from which the text comes. This is consistent with the numbering system in the Perseus Digital Library hosted by Tufts University, where this version is found in the public domain under a Creative Commons License.

Internal page references and footnotes have been removed. Ellipses were added by the author to indicate omissions from the original text. Brackets indicate alterations. To avoid the gendered language of the translation, the word "man" is changed to "person" throughout and, where needed, singular "they" and "their" have been used as a gender-neutral substitution for "he" or "his," and verbs have been changed to agree without indication. Minor spelling and punctuation edits have been made without indication.

> [12.Pr. 4] I [write] to form my orator's character and to teach them their duties. . . .
>
> [12.1.1] The orator then, whom I am concerned to form, shall be [defined

as] "a good person skilled in speaking." [12.1.3] For I do not merely assert that the ideal orator should be a good person, but I affirm that no person can be an orator unless he is a good person. [12.1.4] [I]t is as impossible for one and the same mind to harbor good and evil thoughts as it is for one person to be at once both good and evil. [12.1.7] There is nothing so preoccupied, so distracted, so rent and torn by so many and such varied passions as an evil mind. [12.1.8] Surely every one of my readers must by now have realized that oratory is in the main concerned with the treatment of what is just and honorable? Can a bad and unjust person speak on such themes as the dignity of the subject demands? [12.1.9] Nay, even if we exclude the most important aspects of the question now before us, and make the impossible concession that the best and worst of [people] may have the same talent, industry and learning, we are still confronted by the question as to which of the two is entitled to be called the better orator. The answer is surely clear enough: it will be [the one] who is the better person.

[12.1.11] There is one point at any rate which no one will question, namely, that the aim of every speech is to convince the judge that the case which it puts forward is true and honorable. Well then, which will do this best, the good person or the bad? The good person will without doubt more often say what is true and honorable. [12.1.12] But even supposing that his duty should, as I shall show may sometimes happen, lead them to make statements which are false, their words are still certain to carry greater weight with their audience. On the other hand bad persons, in their contempt for public opinion and their ignorance of what is right, sometimes drop their mask unawares, and are impudent in the statement of their case and shameless in their assertions. [12.1.13] Further, in their attempt to achieve the impossible they display an unseemly persistency and unavailing energy. For in lawsuits no less than in ordinary paths of life, they cherish depraved expectations. . . .

[12.1.23] [T]rue courage cannot be conceived of without the accompaniment of virtue. [12.1.24] Surely the advocate who is called to defend the accused requires to be a person of honor, honor which greed cannot corrupt, influence seduce, or fear dismay. . . . [I]f the quality which is termed goodness is to be found even in quite ordinary advocates, why should not the orator, who has not yet existed, but may still be born, be no less perfect in character than in excellence of speech?

[12.1.28] [W]ill not this same person, whom we are striving to form, if in time of war they be called upon to inspire their soldiers with courage for the fray, draw for his eloquence on the innermost precepts of philosophy? . . . [12.1.29] And assuredly the person who will best inspire such feelings in others are they who have first inspired them in themself. For however we strive to conceal it, insincerity will always betray itself, and there was never in any person so great eloquence as would not begin to stumble and hesitate so soon as his words ran counter to their inmost thoughts. [12.1.30] Now: a bad person cannot help speaking things other than they feel. On the other [h]and, the good will never be at a loss for honorable words or fail to find matter full of virtue for utterance, since among his virtues practical wisdom will be one. . . . [12.1.32] At any rate let us banish from our hearts the delusion that eloquence, the fairest of all things, can be combined with vice. The power of speaking is even to be accounted an evil when it is found in evil [people]; for it makes its possessors yet worse than they were before. . . .

[12.1.36] But it is even true, although at first sight it seems hard to believe, that there may be sound reason why at times a good person who is appearing for the defense should attempt to conceal the truth from the judge. If any of my readers is surprised at my making such a statement (although this opinion is not of my own invention, but is derived from those whom antiquity regarded as the greatest teachers of wisdom), I would have them reflect that there are many things which are made honorable or the reverse not by the nature of the facts, but by the causes from which they spring. . . . [12.1.38] [T]he good person will sometimes tell a lie, and further that they will sometimes do so for comparatively trivial reasons; for example we tell countless lies to sick children for their good and make many promises to them which we do not intend to perform. [12.1.39] And there is clearly far more justification for lying when it is a question of diverting an assassin from his victim or deceiving an enemy to save our country. Consequently a practice which is at times reprehensible . . . , may on other occasions be praiseworthy even in a wise person.

[12.1.42] [N]o one will hesitate for a moment to hold the view that it is in the interests of the commonwealth that guilty persons should be acquitted rather than punished, if it be possible thereby to convert them to a better state of mind, a possibility which is generally conceded. If then it is clear to an orator that a person who is guilty of the offenses laid to his charge will become a good person, will they not strive to secure their acquittal? . . . [12.1.44] . . . For my purpose is not to assert that such tasks will often be incumbent on the orator whom I desire to form, but merely to show that, in the event of their being compelled to take such action, it will not invalidate our definition of an orator as a "good person, skilled in speaking." [12.45] And it is necessary also both to teach and learn how to establish difficult cases by proof. For often even the best cases have a resemblance to bad and, the charges which tell heavily against an innocent person frequently have a strong resemblance to the truth. Consequently, the same methods of defense have to be employed that would be used if they were guilty. . . . Therefore, while maintaining their integrity of purpose, the orator will modify their pleading to suit the circumstances.

[12.2.1] The orator must above all things . . . acquire a complete knowledge of all that is just and honorable. For without this knowledge no one can be either a good person or skilled in speaking.[12.2.2] [C]an the person who does not know what [justice] is claim to be truly [just] . . . [12.2.3] if they ha[ve] never . . . in language approaching that of philosophy, discussed the nature of virtue and justice, or of the laws that have been given to [hu]mankind by nature or established among individual peoples and nations? . . .

[12.2.7] . . . I desire that they, whose character I am seeking to mold, should be a "wise person" in the Roman sense, that is, one who reveals themselves as a true statesperson, not in the discussions of the study, but in the actual practice and experience of life.

[12.2.11] For oratory is like a river: the current is stronger when it flows within deep banks and with a mighty flood, than when the waters are shallow and broken by the pebbles that bar their way.

[12.3.8] Now I regard the orator above all as being a person of virtue and good sense. [12.3.11] [W]e are familiar with many who, because they were weary of the toil entailed on those who seek to scale the heights of eloquence, . . . study of law as a refuge . . . and have preferred to become specialists in formulae, or legalists, . . . on the pretext of preferring a more useful branch of study, whereas their real motive was its comparative easiness.

[12.3.17] [T]he orator will assuredly have much to say on such topics as justice, fortitude, abstinence, self-control and piety. But the good person, who has come to the knowledge of these things not by mere hearsay, as though they were just words and names for their tongue to employ, but has grasped the meaning of virtue and acquired a true feeling for it, will never be perplexed when they ha[ve] to think out a problem, but will speak out truly what they know. [12.3.19] [D]oes not every question of law turn either on the precise meaning of words, the discussion of equity, or conjecture as to the intention—subjects which in part encroach on the domain of dialectic and in part on that of ethics? [12.3.21] How can we conceive of any real eloquence at all proceeding from a person who is ignorant of all that is best in the world?

[12.3.31] . . . No person will ever be the consummate orator . . . unless they have both the knowledge and the courage to speak in accordance with the promptings of honor. . . .

[12.5.2] [M]odesty (which, though a fault in itself, is an amiable failing which may easily be the mother of virtues) is on occasion an impediment and has frequently caused the fruits of genius and study to consume away in the mildew of obscurity merely because they have never been displayed to the public day. [12.5.3] [What I mean to say is that is an] excess of modesty . . . is really a form of fear deterring the soul from doing what is its duty to do. . . . [12.5.4] On the other hand, I am not unwilling that the person who has got to make a speech should show signs of nervousness when they rise to their feet, should change color and make it clear that they feel the risks of their position. . . . [T]he feeling that stirs us should be due to the realization of the magnitude of our task and not to fear: we should be moved, but not to the extent of collapsing. But the best remedy for such excess of modesty is confidence. . . .

[12.7.1] A good person [should carefully choose the cases he will take] and will undoubtedly prefer defense to prosecution, but he will not have such a rooted objection to the task of accuser as to disregard his duty towards the state or towards individuals. . . . [12.7.2] Therefore, our orator will not suffer the complaints of our allies, the death of friends or kinsmen, or conspiracies that threaten the common weal to go unavenged, while their conduct will be governed not by a passion to secure the punishment of the guilty, but by the desire to correct vice and reform morals. [12.7.3] [Prosecution, on the other hand,] to rid one's country of the pests that gnaw its vitals is conduct worthy of comparison with that of heroes, who champion their country's cause in the field of battle.

[12.7.4] [The] orator of ours will not defend all and sundry: that haven of safety which their eloquence provides will never be opened to pirates as it is to others, and they will be led to undertake cases mainly by consideration of their nature. [12.7.6] [A] case is not rendered either just or the reverse by the social position of the parties engaged. Nor, again, will a sense of shame deter them from throwing over a case which they have undertaken in the belief that it had justice on its side, but which their study of the facts has shown to be unjust, although before doing so they should give their client their true opinion on the case. [12.7.7] For, if we judge aright, there is no greater benefit that we can confer on our clients than this, that we should not cheat them by giving them empty hopes of success. On the other hand, no client that does not take their advocate into their counsel deserves that advocate's assistance, and it is certainly unworthy of our ideal orator that they should wittingly defend injustice. For if they are led to defend what is false by any of the motives which I mentioned above, their own action will still be honorable. . . .

OVERVIEW OF *GENTILE V. STATE BAR OF NEVADA*

In *Gentile v. State Bar of Nevada*, the US Supreme Court addressed what it meant for a lawyer to ethically advocate in public on behalf of a client. In other words, the court considered what it meant for a lawyer to act as a "good person skilled in speaking," to be Quintilian's ideal orator. What follows are the important background facts of the case as well as excerpts from Justice Anthony Kennedy's and Chief Justice William Rehnquist's opinions.

Background

In the late 1980s Nevada attorney Dominic Gentile held a press conference the day after his client Grady Sanders was criminally indicted for theft of money and other items from Western Vault Corporation, a Las Vegas safety deposit vault that Sanders owned and operated. A large amount of cocaine and travelers' checks had gone missing from a vault that the Las Vegas Police Department had been using in an undercover investigation, and a subsequent investigation suggested that property was missing from other vaults as well. Leading up to the indictment, the police had focused their investigation on Western Vault and Sanders, but news reports had suggested that the FBI suspected Las Vegas police officers were responsible for the theft. Prior to Sanders's indictment, media coverage of the theft and investigation had been substantial and, according to Justice Kennedy, "sensational."

At a press conference following the indictment, Gentile gave a prepared statement and responded to questions. In Justice Kennedy's opinion at appendix A, the Supreme Court reproduced Gentile's prepared statement:

> I want to start this off by saying in clear terms that I think that this indictment is a significant event in the history of the evolution of sophistication of the City of Las Vegas, because things of this nature, of exactly this nature have happened in New York with the French connection case and in Miami with cases—at least two cases there—have happened in Chicago as well, but all three of those cities have been honest enough to indict the people who did it; the police department, crooked cops.
>
> When this case goes to trial, and as it develops, you're going to see that the evidence will prove not only that Grady Sanders is an innocent person and had nothing to do with any of the charges that are being leveled against him, but that the person that was in the most direct position to have stolen the drugs and money, the American Express Travelers' checks, is Detective Steve Scholl.
>
> There is far more evidence that will establish that Detective Scholl took these drugs and took these American Express Travelers' checks than any other living human being.
>
> And I have to say that I feel that Grady Sanders is being used as a scapegoat to try to cover up for what has to be obvious to people at Las Vegas Metropolitan Police Department and at the District Attorney's office.
>
> Now, with respect to these other charges that are contained in this indictment, the so-called other victims [of vault thefts], as I sit here today I can tell

you that one, two—four of them are known drug dealers and convicted money launderers and drug dealers; three of whom didn't say a word about anything until after they were approached by Metro and after they were already in trouble and are trying to work themselves out of something.

Now, up until the moment, of course, that they started going along with what detectives from Metro wanted them to say, these people were being held out as being incredible and liars by the very same people who are going to say now that you can believe them.

Another problem that you are going to see develop here is the fact that of these other counts, at least four of them said nothing about any of this, about anything being missing until after the Law Vegas Metropolitan Police Department announced publicly last year their claim that drugs and American Express Travelers' checks were missing.

Many of the contracts that these people had shown on the face of the contract that there is $100,000 in insurance for the contents of the box.

If you look at the indictment very closely, you're going to see that these claims fall under $100,000.

Finally, there were only two claims on the face of the indictment that came to our attention prior to . . . the date that Metro said that there was something missing from their box.

And both of these claims were dealt with by Mr. Sanders and we're dealing here essentially with people that we're not sure if they ever had anything in the box.

That's about all that I have to say.

Six months later, a jury acquitted Sanders of the theft charges against him. However, the Nevada State Bar disciplined Gentile because the bar found that Gentile knew or should have known that his "public communications" at his press conference had a "substantial likelihood of prejudicing" his client's future trial, and, accordingly, Gentile violated Nevada's ethical standards for practicing law. Gentile challenged his discipline as unconstitutional (he asserted a First Amendment "free speech" defense), but the Nevada Supreme Court upheld the bar's decision.

Gentile appealed to the US Supreme Court where, in a 5-to-4 decision, the court rejected Gentile's First Amendment challenge and held that Nevada's prohibition on Gentile's public speech was constitutional because Gentile's speech had a "substantial likelihood of prejudicing" a future trial. The court also held, however, that other language in the Nevada ethics rule was unconstitutional because the language was too vague to give fair notice to Gentile that his press conference would violate the rule.[5] Thus, although the court upheld the "substantial likelihood" language as constitutional,[6] the court reversed Gentile's discipline. The court's resolution of the First Amendment question defined the constitutionally legitimate scope of control a state bar can exercise over a lawyer's free speech.

The Case Excerpt

Although the case is *legally* important for how it treats lawyer free speech, the case is *rhetorically* important for the ways Justice Kennedy, writing in dissent, and Chief Justice Rehnquist writing for both the majority as well as in dissent, describe the oratorical character of Gentile, specifically, and the lawyer, more generally.

Because of how the justices weave together majority and dissenting opinions, the organization of the *Gentile* opinions is confusing even for the most experienced legal reader.[7] For the purposes of the rhetorical analysis in this chapter, however, the nature of the opinions—majority or dissenting—is a minor point. To highlight Justice Kennedy's and Rehnquist's rhetorical conflict about the nature of the lawyer as an advocate, the excerpts here begin with Justice Kennedy's dissent and end with Chief Justice Rehnquist's majority and dissenting opinions.

GENTILE V. STATE BAR OF NEVADA, 501 U.S. 1030 (1991)

Davis Note: Internal citations and some quotation marks showing the justices' quotations of precedent opinions have been removed without indication. Ellipses were added by the author to indicate omitted text. Text in brackets indicates author alterations. For clarity, the word "petitioner" has been replaced with "Gentile" without indication. Justice O'Connor's concurrence is omitted in its entirety.

Justice KENNEDY, writing in dissent in this part of the opinion (joined by Justices Marshall, Blackmun, and Stevens).

[T]his case involves punishment of pure speech in the political forum. Gentile engaged not in solicitation of clients or advertising for his practice. . . . His words were directed at public officials and their conduct in office.

There is no question that speech critical of the exercise of the State's power lies at the very center of the First Amendment. Nevada seeks to punish the dissemination of information relating to alleged governmental misconduct, which . . . we [have] described as speech which has traditionally been recognized as lying at the core of the First Amendment. . . .

It would be difficult to single out any aspect of government of higher concern and importance to the people than the manner in which criminal trials are conducted. Public vigilance serves us well, for the knowledge that every criminal trial is subject to contemporaneous review in the forum of public opinion is an effective restraint on possible abuse of judicial power. Without publicity, all other checks are insufficient; in comparison of publicity, all other checks are of small account. . . . [L]imits upon [lawyers'] public comment about pending cases are likely to fall not only at a crucial time but upon the most important topics of discussion. . . .

Public awareness and criticism have even greater importance where, as here, they concern allegations of police corruption, or where, as is also the present circumstance, the criticism questions the judgment of an elected public prosecutor. Our system grants prosecutors vast discretion at all stages of the criminal process. The public has an interest in its responsible exercise. . . .

The only evidence [of] Gentile [violating the ethics rule] was the videotape of his statement and his own testimony at the disciplinary hearing. The Bar's whole case [that Gentile knew or should reasonably have known that his statements would have a substantial likelihood of materially prejudicing his client's future court proceedings] rests on the fact of the statements, the time they were made, and Gentile's own justifications. . . .

Gentile is a Las Vegas criminal defense attorney, an author of articles about criminal law and procedure, and a former associate dean of the National College for Criminal Defense Lawyers and Public Defenders. Through leaks from the police department, he had some advance notice of the date an indictment would be returned and the nature of the charges against Sanders. Gentile had monitored the publicity surrounding the case, and prior to the indictment, was personally aware of at least 17 articles in the major local newspapers, the Las Vegas Sun and Las Vegas Review-Journal, and numerous local television news stories which reported on the Western Vault theft and ensuing investigation. Gentile determined, for the first time in his career, that he would call a formal press conference. He did not blunder into a press conference, but acted with considerable deliberation. [Gentile's] primary motivation was the concern that, unless some of the weaknesses in the State's case were made public, a potential jury venire would be poisoned by repetition in the press of information being released by the police and prosecutors. . . . Gentile did not indicate he thought he could sway the pool of potential jurors to form an opinion in advance of the trial, nor did he seek to discuss evidence that would be inadmissible at trial. He sought only to counter publicity already deemed prejudicial. . . .

Far from an admission that he sought to materially prejudice an adjudicative proceeding, Gentile sought only to stop a wave of publicity he perceived as prejudicing potential jurors against his client and injuring his client's reputation in the community.

Gentile gave a second reason for holding the press conference, which demonstrates the additional value of his speech. Gentile acted in part because the investigation had taken a serious toll on his client. Sanders was "not a man in good health," having suffered multiple open-heart surgeries prior to these events. And prior to indictment, the mere suspicion of wrongdoing had caused [Sanders's business to close and for him to suffer other business losses].

An attorney's duties do not begin inside the courtroom door. He or she cannot ignore the practical implications of a legal proceeding for the client. Just as an attorney may recommend a plea bargain or civil settlement to avoid the adverse consequences of a possible loss after trial, so too an attorney may take reasonable steps to defend a client's reputation and reduce the adverse consequences of indictment, especially in the face of a prosecution deemed unjust or commenced with improper motives. A defense attorney may pursue lawful strategies to obtain dismissal of an indictment or reduction of charges, including an attempt to demonstrate in the court of public opinion that the client does not deserve to be tried. . . . On the evening before the press conference, Gentile and two colleagues spent several hours researching the extent of an attorney's [ethical] obligations [in making statements to the press]. [Based on this research, he concluded that the timing of his public statement would likely not materially prejudice a jury since that jury would not be empaneled for at least six months.] . . .

Because attorneys participate in the criminal justice system and are trained in its complexities, they hold unique qualifications as a source of information about pending cases. Since lawyers are considered credible in regard to pending litigation in which they are engaged and are in one of the most knowledgeable positions, they are a crucial source of information and opinion. To the extent the press and public rely upon attorneys for information because attorneys are well informed, this may prove the value to the public of speech by members of the bar. If the dangers of their speech arise from its persuasiveness, from their ability to explain judicial proceedings, or from the likelihood the speech will be believed, these are not the sort of dangers that can validate restrictions. The First Amendment does not permit suppression of speech because of its power to command assent.

The vigorous advocacy we demand of the legal profession is accepted because it takes place under the neutral, dispassionate control of the judicial system. . . . [T]he American judicial trial remains one of the purest, most rational forums for the lawful determination of disputes. A profession which takes just pride in these traditions may consider them disserved if lawyers use their skills and insight to make untested allegations in the press instead of in the courtroom. But constraints of professional responsibility and societal disapproval will act as sufficient safeguards in most cases. And in some circumstances press comment is necessary to protect the rights of the client and prevent abuse of the courts. It cannot be said that Gentile's conduct demonstrated any real or specific threat to the legal process, and his statements have the full protection of the First Amendment.

Chief Justice REHNQUIST, writing for the majority in this part of the opinion.

In the United States, the courts have historically regulated admission to the practice of law before them, and exercised the authority to discipline and ultimately to disbar lawyers whose conduct departed from prescribed standards. "Membership in the bar is a privilege burdened with conditions," to use the oft-repeated statement of [Justice] Cardozo. . . .

[T]he outcome of a criminal trial is to be decided by impartial jurors, who know as little as possible of the case, based on material admitted into evidence before them in a court proceeding. Extrajudicial comments on, or discussion of, evidence which might never be admitted at trial and ex parte statements by counsel giving their version of the facts obviously threaten to undermine this basic tenet.

At the same time, however, the criminal justice system exists in a larger context of a government ultimately of the people, who wish to be informed about happenings in the criminal justice system, and, if sufficiently informed about those happenings, might wish to make changes in the system. The way most of them acquire information is from the media. The First Amendment protections of speech and press have been held, in the cases cited above, to require a showing of "clear and present danger" that a malfunction in the criminal justice system will be caused before a State may prohibit media speech or publication about a particular pending trial.

Davis Note: Rehnquist concludes and the majority of the court agrees that lawyers can be disciplined for their public speech on the lesser "substantial likelihood of prejudice" standard rather than a "clear and present danger of prejudice" standard.

It is unquestionable that in the courtroom itself, during a judicial proceeding, whatever right to "free speech" an attorney has is extremely circumscribed. Even outside the courtroom, . . . lawyers in pending cases [are] subject to ethical restrictions on speech to which an ordinary citizen would not be. . . . [A] lawyer can[not] invoke the constitutional right of free speech to immunize himself from evenhanded discipline for proven unethical conduct. . . . [O]bedience to ethical precepts may require abstention from what in other circumstances might be constitutionally protected speech. . . .

Of course, a lawyer is a person and he too has a constitutional freedom of utterance and may exercise it to castigate courts and their administration of justice.

But a lawyer actively participating in a trial, particularly an emotionally charged criminal prosecution, is not merely a person and not even merely a lawyer. . . . He is an intimate and trusted and essential part of the machinery of justice, an "officer of the court" in the most compelling sense. . . .

[A]s officers of the court, court personnel and attorneys have a fiduciary responsibility not to engage in public debate that will redound to the detriment of the accused or that will obstruct the fair administration of justice. Because lawyers have special access to information through discovery and client communications, their extrajudicial statements pose a threat to the fairness of a pending proceeding since lawyers' statements are likely to be received as especially authoritative. [S]tatements by attorneys of record relating to the case "are likely to be considered knowledgeable, reliable and true" because of attorneys' unique access to information [, and] attorneys' role as advocates gives them extraordinary power to undermine or destroy the efficacy of the criminal justice system.

Chief Justice REHNQUIST, writing in dissent on the issues of vagueness and overbreadth (joined by Justices White, Scalia, and Souter).

Gentile's strongest arguments [for not violating the ethics rule] are that the statements were made well in advance of trial, and that the statements did not in fact taint the jury panel. But the Supreme Court of Nevada pointed out that Gentile's statements were not only highly inflammatory—they portrayed prospective government witnesses as drug users and dealers, and as money launderers—but the statements were timed to have maximum impact, when public interest in the case was at its height immediately after Sanders was indicted. Reviewing independently the entire record, we are convinced that Gentile's statements were "substantially likely to cause material prejudice" to the proceedings. While there is evidence pro and con on that point, we find it persuasive that, by his own admission, Gentile called the press conference for the express purpose of influencing the venire. It is difficult to believe that he went to such trouble, and took such a risk, if there was no substantial likelihood that he would succeed.

CRITICAL ASSESSMENT

Applying Quintilian's writings to *Gentile* encourages deeper exploration of the rhetorical tensions in the identities of lawyers. From both a classical and a modern perspective, Quintilian's description of the perfect orator purports to be a description of the perfect lawyer, of a person who represents the interests of others in court. What does the perfect lawyer look like according to Quintilian? That is, who is the lawyer and, more importantly, who *should* that lawyer be?

In Quintilian's view, oratory is not a morally neutral pursuit; oratory and the orator who delivers it have a positive moral valence. Oratory, Quintilian says, is by definition addressed only to what is "just and honorable."

Quintilian says that a person skilled in speaking is an orator not simply because of eloquence but because that person is a *good* person, a person who can speak of the just, the honorable, and the good, but only because that person is equally so. The perfect orator is virtuous, courageous, sincere, modest (but not overly so), confident, practically wise, and moderate in style. The ideal orator is immersed in public life, unlike the legalists who study "law as a refuge," and knowledgeable of the range of human experiences. The perfect orator, says Quintilian, has strength to persist in the face of adversity. The lawyer is careful in the cases she takes but does not turn away the defense of someone because of their social position.

Quintilian's assessment of the ideal orator provides a framework for exploring the choices, points of emphasis, and contradictions that make up the discussion of the lawyer's identity in *Gentile*. Justices Kennedy and Rehnquist, together and separately, explore the idea of the ideal (i.e., ethical) lawyer when speaking to the public in relation to a pending case. The attributes of Quintilian's perfect orator manifest in both Kennedy's and Rehnquist's competing views on the ideal lawyer/orator. Kennedy and Rehnquist are doing more than deciding a case; they are using language to rhetorically constitute competing identities of Quintilian's perfect lawyer.

In *Gentile*, Kennedy and Rehnquist articulate their competing views of the "honorableness" of Gentile's press conference. The justices' constructions of Gentile's character are so at odds that we might wonder if Chief Justice Rehnquist and Justice Kennedy are talking about the same person and course of events. Yet both articulate an argument that, in one version or the other, would make Gentile (and all other lawyers) the rhetorical enactment[8] of Quintilian's "perfect [legal] orator." Yet, that perfect orator looks entirely different, depending on whom one asks.

On one hand, Kennedy sees Gentile as an honorable and just speaker who is perfectly suited for the "political forum" where Quintilian might find his "statesperson" speaking. Kennedy avers that the kind of publicity that Gentile engaged in—about the manner in which criminal trials are conducted—is exactly the kind of thing that lawyers should be speaking about in public. Kennedy's opinion suggests that it was not only Gentile's *prerogative* but perhaps also his *responsibility to the public* to disseminate the information about alleged government corruption. It was not just the client's specific case that demanded Gentile's action (i.e., to stop negative information from prejudicing potential jurors, protect his client's reputation, and help protect his health); it was also

Gentile's duty to inform the public about this pending legal case and its implications to the criminal justice system. The lawyer's likelihood of being believed by the public because of his expertise, Kennedy suggests, is a benefit and can be seen as part of Gentile's perfection as an orator since the job of the orator is to "move" his audience.

Rehnquist, on the other hand, crafts an entirely different vision of Quintilian's "perfect orator." Rehnquist recognizes the same tension that Kennedy does—the tension between lawyers as officers of the court ensuring fair trials and as public speakers providing the public information about the workings of the criminal justice system. But Rehnquist sees the lawyer as more perfect when he errs on the side of silence and absolute discretion in the face of pending litigation. Rehnquist suggests that in these circumstances, Gentile is "not merely a person and not even merely a lawyer. . . . He is an intimate and trusted and essential part of the machinery of justice." In Rehnquist's view, the lawyer's virtue is less in her positioning as a "statesperson" and more in her positioning as a part of the larger whole in a system of justice. This might be read as Rehnquist's alternative assessment of the lawyer as a "statesperson"—public life is in the lawyer's work in the courts, not in the political forum.

Rehnquist and Kennedy agree that lawyers are powerful and persuasive public speakers. But Rehnquist sees this power as a threat and not a strength. Because lawyers are persuasive and have "special access to information," the public will take them seriously, says Rehnquist. This gives lawyers the power to "undermine or destroy" the "fair administration of justice"—just the opposite of what Quintilian's ideal lawyer would do. In the situation Gentile found himself, his job was to refrain from speaking in public and to wait to speak in court. In Quintilian's terms, the lawyer's "goodness"—his pursuit of the just and honorable—comes from biting his tongue in public, not wagging it.

DISCUSSION QUESTIONS

Discussion Question 1: Looking carefully at Kennedy's and Rehnquist's descriptions of the role the lawyer must play as a public speaker, which version of the lawyer, speaking in public, is closer to Quintilian's "perfect orator"?

As described in the critical analysis, either Kennedy's or Rehnquist's idealization of the lawyer speaking in public might match Quintilian's "perfect orator" characteristics. Compare the language Kennedy and Rehnquist use to describe Gentile, his character, and his behavior. How would you describe the competing themes that the justices deploy to describe the lawyer? What are the implications of each justice's version of the lawyer?

If both justices' versions of the good lawyer do not meet Quintilian's definition of "good people," can we even classify lawyers as orators? What is the implication of that conclusion?

Discussion Question 2: Can lawyers misrepresent and mislead and still be perfect orators? What if a lawyer is "insincere" in Quintilian's terms? What do Kennedy and Rehnquist think about this?

Quintilian makes the argument that a perfect orator can, for good reason, "attempt to conceal the truth from the judge." What are those reasons as Quintilian describes them?

Today, the Model Rules of Professional Conduct, the model rules upon which various ethics rules governing lawyers in practice are based, prohibit lawyers from being dishonest.[9] Would Quintilian's perfect lawyer "bend" these ethics rules if he or she thought the ends were just?

In contrast to his characterization that a "good" person might sometimes mislead, Quintilian says that an ideal orator must always be "sincere." How does he describe "sincerity"? How is it different from lying?

Interestingly, while misrepresentation is condemned by the Model Rules of Professional Conduct, a lawyer's "insincerity" is arguably tolerated. For example, the rules provide that a lawyer who *represents* a client does not need to *approve* of or share the client's political, economic, social or moral perspectives.[10] The rules also suggest that although a lawyer must be truthful with others in negotiations, statements that are commonly known as "puffery"—"estimates of price or value placed on the subject of a transaction"—are acceptable.[11] Are these examples of Quintilian's "evil" quality of insincerity? Or are these also forms of misrepresentation, which Quintilian, paradoxically, might find acceptable given the circumstances?

A close read of the *Gentile* excerpts suggests that the ability of the lawyer to mislead or be insincere comes into play in the justices' thinking. How close does Rehnquist come to characterizing Gentile as misleading in his press conference? Or might he describe Gentile as "insincere"? Looking back at the transcript from Gentile's press conference, do you think there is something devious about Gentile's behavior at the press conference that should be subject to ethical constraints? On the other hand, if he is being misleading (or even insincere), is it to one of the good ends Quintilian describes? Why does it matter?

Discussion Question 3: Do the ways Kennedy and Rehnquist imagine the scene in which the lawyer acts impact their views of the appropriateness of the lawyer's influence on public perception?

Both Kennedy and Rehnquist seem to be concerned with the question of how much influence (and what kind) a lawyer has on public perception. Rehnquist thinks lawyers are dangerous because they are extra skilled in persuasion; Kennedy thinks that what lawyers know—and their ability to persuade—is valuable to the public.

Compare and contrast the ways Kennedy, Rehnquist, and Quintilian describe the *scene* in which the lawyer acts. How do the justices differ in how they draw the scene in which Gentile was acting when he spoke? Does the way each draws the scene impact whether they find Gentile's persuasion appropriate? How might Quintilian respond to Rehnquist on the dangers of the lawyer's persuasive abilities based on an assessment of the scene?

ADDITIONAL READINGS

Bizzell, Patricia, and Bruce Herzberg, eds. *The Rhetorical Tradition: Readings from Classical Times to the Present.* 3rd ed. Boston: Bedford, 2020.

Dauphinais, Kirsten A. "Quintilian's Curriculum." *Nevada Law Journal* 2, no. 3 (2020): 917–33.

Murphy, James J., Richard A. Katula, and Michael Hoppman. "Quintilian's Place in Roman Rhetorical and Educational Theory with a Synopsis of His *Institutio Oratoria*." In *A Synoptic History of Classical Rhetoric,* 4th ed, 182–207. New York: Routledge, 2014.

Quintilianus, Marcus Fabius. *Institutio Oratoria.* Translated and edited by Harold Edgeworth Butler. Cambridge, MA: Harvard University Press, 1920.

———. *On the Teaching of Speaking and Writing: Translation from Books One, Two, and Ten of the* Institutio Oratoria. Edited by James J. Murphy and Cleve Wiese. 2nd ed. Carbondale: Southern Illinois University Press, 2015.

14

Saint Augustine

The Place of Rhetoric in the Law and Religion Interface

Mark A. Hannah

INTRODUCTION

Religious freedom is a hallmark of American democracy. Former President Bill Clinton went so far as to characterize it as the most precious of all American liberties.[1] Expressed at his signing of the Religious Freedom Restoration Act, Clinton's words foreshadowed the increasing influence of religion in political and legal decision-making. Contemporary disagreements over issues such as the rights of business owners to refuse the provision of services to gay, lesbian, bisexual, or transgender individuals, as well as the rights of religious institutions to be exempt from public health mandates, highlight this influence. In religious freedom cases, the plaintiffs claim that a third party seeks to compel them to act against their sincerely held religious beliefs in violation of the First Amendment. They argue they are exempt from the requirement to act even if that exemption overrides competing claims for the rights of others, such as the right to equal protection under law. As these cases demonstrate, religion forges messy entanglements of political, legal, religious, and moral interests that resist easy resolution.

In negotiating these competing interests, the Supreme Court historically upheld a wall of separation between church and state, but in recent years, its decisions have chipped away at the wall's foundation, leading some to ask if the separation still exists.[2] Critics of these decisions point to the outsized political influence of nonprofit organizations and institutes whose explicit aim is to expand religious freedom at the expense of other established rights.[3] Battles over Supreme Court nominees who will decide the fate of religious freedoms further signal concerns about the changing attitudes toward the relationship between law and religion.[4]

The growing tension over religion's place in daily life is traceable to St. Augustine of Hippo's scholarly interest in rhetoric following the fall of the Roman Empire. Widely known for developing a Christian rhetoric, St. Augustine (354–430 CE) was influential in the return of classical norms after the stylistic excess of the Second Sophistic.[5] Trained in rhetoric and law, St. Augustine taught rhetoric in North Africa and Rome (373–84 CE) and later became chair of rhetoric to the imperial court in Milan in 384. As a teacher, St. Augustine was influenced by Christian and Manichaeistic principles.[6] After converting to Christianity in 386, St. Augustine resigned as chair of rhetoric and returned to North Africa to pursue a monastic life. In 391 he was ordained a priest and later became a famous preacher of the Christian faith. Around 396 St. Augustine became Bishop of Hippo, a position he held until his death.

St. Augustine's life involved a fundamental shift from secularity to one of religiosity, a shift motivated in part by his understanding that rhetoric, despite its pagan roots, can be used productively in daily life. St. Augustine lived during a period of pervasive instability due to the uneasy coexistence of surviving pagan influences of the Roman Empire and the teachings of the emerging Christian Church. He thus sought to articulate a pragmatic understanding of rhetoric that recognized rhetoric's potential use not only for corrupt purposes but also for good, which entailed serving Christianity by acquiring sacred, religious knowledge through scriptural understanding rather than serving oneself through acquiring rational, scientific knowledge in the secular world.

St. Augustine developed a comprehensive account of a religious rhetoric in *On Christian Doctrine*, which is widely considered his most important contribution to the history of rhetoric. In that work, St. Augustine articulated a set of rules for helping individuals interpret scriptures (books 1 through 3) as well as guidelines for delivering sermons eloquently, namely in using speech to instruct, delight, and move listeners to action (book 4). Throughout, St. Augustine seeks to redeem rhetoric from its sophistic grip by emphasizing its teaching role in drawing individuals closer to God's truth.

St. Augustine also sought to capture the conditions of public life that shaped the need for his Christian rhetoric. In *The City of God*, St. Augustine defends Christianity as not answerable for the fall of the Roman Empire but instead offering the eternal, sacred knowledge that leads to heavenly peace. In *The City of God*, he sets the grounds for Christianity's promise by describing daily life in a persistently conflicted, inescapable, mixed society comprised of good and evil forces. St. Augustine casts this ever-pressing conflict as occurring in the *saeculum*, a temporal field of experience wherein the Earthly City and Heavenly City are irreducibly entangled.[7] Viewing the saeculum as comprising individuals who occupy themselves with secular knowledge and earthly pleasures, as well as pilgrims who forego such pleasures and pursue sacred, religious knowledge, St. Augustine uses the construct of the saeculum to put the two cities in conversation, describing how Christian and pagan virtues differently motivate participation in the Earthly City, creating the conflict that individuals endure in the pursuit of eternal life.

This chapter provides an excerpt from *The City of God* to prompt reflections about the tension between secular and religious life in contemporary legal practice. The tension between pagan and religious influences in the saeculum is manifest today in the rhetorical choices that lawyers and judges make in arguing and deciding religious freedom cases. The excerpt is followed by portions of an oral argument transcript from a 2018 Supreme Court case, *Masterpiece Cakeshop v. Colorado Civil Rights Commission*,[8] in which a baker's religious beliefs conflicted with a same-sex couple's right to request that he bake them a wedding cake. The transcript illustrates the rhetorical struggle judges engage in when evaluating claims with competing rights grounded differently in faith and reason.

SAINT AUGUSTINE, *THE CITY OF GOD*

Editors' Note: The translation of *The City of God* is that of the Rev. Marcus Dods, M.A. (1834–1909), a Scottish minister and biblical scholar, freely available from Project Gutenberg since 2014. The excerpt is taken from volume 2, and book and chapter numbers are noted. Breaks in text are indicated by ellipses; internal page references and footnotes have been removed. Some formatting of the text has been changed to improve readability. Textual additions and emendations are indicated by brackets.

[Book 14, chapter 28]

[T]wo cities have been formed by two loves: the earthly by the love of self, even to the contempt of God; the heavenly by the love of God, even to the contempt of self. The former, in a word, glories in itself, the latter in the Lord. For the one seeks glory from men; but the greatest glory of the other is God, the witness of conscience. The one lifts up its head in its own glory; the other says to its God, "Thou art my glory, and the lifter up of mine head."[9] In the one, the princes and the nations it subdues are ruled by the love of ruling; in the other, the princes and the subjects serve one another in love, the latter obeying, while the former take thought for all. The one delights in its own strength, represented in the persons of its rulers; the other says to its God, "I will love Thee, O Lord, my strength."[10]

And therefore the wise men of the one city, living according to man, have sought for profit to their own bodies or souls, or both, and those who have known God "glorified Him not as God, neither were thankful, but became vain in their imaginations, and their foolish heart was darkened; professing themselves to be wise,"—that is, glorying in their own wisdom, and being possessed by pride,—"they became fools, and changed the glory of the incorruptible God into an image made like to corruptible man, and to birds, and four-footed beasts, and creeping things." For they were either leaders or followers of the people in adoring images, "and worshipped and served the creature more than the Creator, who is blessed for ever."[11] But in the other city there is no human wisdom, but only godliness, which offers due worship to the true God, and looks for its reward in the society of the saints, of holy angels as well as holy men, "that God may be all in all." . . .[12]

[Book 15, chapter 4]

But the earthly city, which shall not be everlasting (for it will no longer be a city when it has been committed to the extreme penalty), has its good in this world, and rejoices in [sharing] it with such joy as such things can afford. But as this is not a good which can discharge its devotees of all distresses, this city is often divided against itself by litigations, wars, quarrels, and such victories as are either life-destroying or short-lived. For each part of it that arms against another part of it seeks to triumph over the nations through itself in bondage to vice. If, when it has conquered, it is inflated with pride, its victory is life-destroying; but if it turns its thoughts upon the common casualties of our mortal condition, and is rather anxious concerning the disasters that may befall it than elated with the successes already achieved, this victory, though of a higher kind, is still only short-lived; for it cannot abidingly rule over those whom it has victoriously subjugated. Now, when victory remains with the party which had the juster cause, who hesitates to congratulate the victor, and style it a desirable peace? These things, then, are good things, and without doubt the gifts of God. But if they neglect the better things of the heavenly city, which are secured by eternal victory and peace never-ending, and so inordinately covet these present good things that they believe them to be the only desirable things, or love them better than those things which are believed to be better,—if this be so, then it is necessary that misery follow and ever increase. . . .

[Book 15, chapter 5]

. . . For the possession of goodness is by no means diminished by being shared with a partner either permanent or temporarily assumed; on the contrary, the possession of goodness is increased in proportion to the concord and charity of each of those who share it. In short, he who is unwilling to share this possession cannot have it; and he who is most willing to admit others to a share of it will have the greatest abundance to himself. . . .

[Book 18, chapter 2]

The society of mortals spread abroad through the earth everywhere, and in the most diverse places, although bound together by a certain fellowship of our common nature, is yet for the most part divided against itself, and the strongest oppress the others, because all follow after their own interests and lusts, while what is longed for either suffices for none, or not for all. . . .

[Book 18, chapter 51]

. . . The heretics themselves also, since they are thought to have the Christian name and sacraments, Scriptures, and profession, cause great grief in the hearts of the pious, both because many who wish to be Christians are compelled by their dissensions to hesitate, and many evil-speakers also find in them matter for blaspheming the Christian name, because they too are at any rate *called* Christians. By these and similar depraved manners and errors of men, those who will live piously in Christ suffer persecution, even when no one molests or vexes their body; for they suffer this persecution, not in their bodies, but in their hearts. . . .

[Book 18, chapter 54]

. . . [W]hat is the mortal course of the two cities, the heavenly and the earthly, which are mingled together from the beginning down to the end[?] Of these, the earthly one has made to herself of whom she would, either from any other quarter, or even from among men, false gods whom she might serve by sacrifice; but she which is heavenly, and is a pilgrim on the earth, does not make false gods, but is herself made by the true God, of whom she herself must be the true sacrifice. Yet both alike either enjoy temporal good things, [and] are afflicted with temporal evils, but with diverse faith, diverse love, until they must be separated by the last judgment, and each must receive her own end, of which there is no end. . . .

[Book 19, chapter 17]

But the families which do not live by faith seek their peace in the earthly advantages of this life; while the families which live by faith look for those eternal blessings which are promised, and use as pilgrims such advantages of time and of earth as do not fascinate and divert them from God, but rather aid them to endure with greater ease, and to keep down the number of those burdens of the corruptible body which weigh upon the soul. Thus the things necessary for this mortal life are used by both kinds of men and families alike, but each has its own peculiar and widely different aim in using them. . . . The earthly city, which does not live by faith, seeks an earthly peace, and the end it proposes, in the well-ordered concord of civic obedience and rule, is the combination of men's wills to attain the things which are helpful to this life. The heavenly city, or rather the part of it which sojourns on earth and lives by faith, makes use of this peace only because it must, until this mortal condition which necessitates it shall pass away. Consequently, so long as it lives like a captive and a stranger in the earthly city, though it has already received the promise of redemption, and the gift of the Spirit as the earnest of it, it [does not hesitate] to obey the laws of the earthly city, whereby the things necessary for the maintenance of this mortal life are administered; and thus, as this life is common to both cities, so there is a harmony between them in regard to what belongs to it. . . .

[Book 19, chapter 27]

. . . In this, then, [justice is only present in each man when] he submit[s] himself to God, his body to his soul, and his vices, even when they rebel, to his reason, which either defeats or at least resists them; [justice is only present when it is from God himself that the person] . . . he begs[s] from God grace to do his duty, and the pardon of his sins, and that he render[s] to God thanks for all the blessings he receives.

MASTERPIECE CAKESHOP V. COLORADO CIVIL RIGHTS COMMISSION 584 U.S. ___, 138 S. CT. 1719 (2018)

Hannah Note: *Masterpiece Cakeshop* involved a struggle between equal rights for same-sex couples and First Amendment freedoms under the US Constitution. A bakery owner had refused to create a wedding cake for a same-sex couple, and the Colorado Civil Rights Commission found the baker in violation of Colorado's Anti-Discrimination Act. On appeal to the Supreme Court, the baker argued that Colorado's law violated (1) his freedom of speech by compelling him to speak against his religious beliefs, and (2) his religious freedom by forcing him to participate in a union he sincerely and conscientiously opposed.[13] The court did not reach the freedom of speech issue, that is, whether the cake qualified as artistic expression and thus protected speech but ruled in favor of the baker. Justice Kennedy, writing for the majority, held the commission's hostility toward the baker's religious beliefs throughout its proceedings violated his religious freedom and its order was invalid.[14]

The transcript excerpts included here depict the rhetorical challenges that lawyers and judges face when crafting and evaluating legal arguments in religious freedom cases. Though the colloquy—the saeculum in the judicial system—focuses largely on the issue of whether baking a cake is a speech act, the excerpts also illustrate the argumentative pull and tug that ensues when judges attempt to balance and resolve, via line drawing, the conflicting values between free speech, religious freedom, and public accommodations claims.[15] In these exchanges, readers witness the justices perform key acts of rhetorical argument such as framing of legal issues, working with competing interpretive frames, balancing social and political issues, and using persuasive strategies like humor and appeals to credibility.

Editors' Note: Excerpted text is from the justices' colloquy with Solicitor General Noel J. Francisco, who supported the bakery and bakery owner. Em dashes indicate interruptions. Ellipses indicate pauses in questioning and responses.[16]

GENERAL FRANCISCO: Mr. Chief Justice, and may it . . . may it please the court:

This case raises an important issue for a small group of individuals; namely, whether the state may compel business owners, including professional artists, to engage in speech in connection with an expressive event like a marriage celebration to which they're deeply opposed.

In those narrow circumstances, we believe the Free Speech Clause provides breathing space—

JUSTICE GINSBURG: How narrow is it? Consider Justice Kagan's question.[17] I mean, we've gotten the answer that the florist is in the same place as the cakemaker, so is the person who designs the invitations and the menus. I don't see a line that can be drawn that would exclude the makeup artist or the hairstylist.[18]

GENERAL FRANCISCO: Well, Your Honor, that's, of course the question that the Court . . . Court has to answer at the threshold of every Free Speech Case. Is the thing that's being regulated something we call protected speech? I think the problem for my friends on the other side is that they think the question doesn't matter. So they would compel an African American sculptor to sculpt a cross for a Klan service—

JUSTICE KENNEDY: But the problem for you is that so many of these examples . . . and a photographer can be included . . . do involve speech. It means that there's basically an ability to boycott marriages.

GENERAL FRANCISCO: Well, Your Honor, I think what it boils down to is that in a narrow category of services that do cross the threshold into protected speech . . . and I do think it's a relatively narrow category . . . you do have a protection. For example, I don't think you could force the African American sculptor to sculpt a cross for the Klan service just because he'd do it for other religious—

JUSTICE SOTOMAYOR: Well—

JUSTICE KENNEDY: If you prevail could the baker put a sign in his window, we do not bake cakes for gay weddings?

GENERAL FRANCISCO: Your Honor, I think that he could say he does not make custom-made wedding cakes for gay weddings, but most cakes—

JUSTICE KENNEDY: And you would not—

GENERAL FRANCISCO: . . . would not cross that threshold.

JUSTICE KENNEDY: . . . think that affront to the gay community?

GENERAL FRANCISCO: Well, Your Honor, I . . . I agree that there are dignity interests at stake here, and I would not minimize the dignity interests to Mr. Craig and Mr. Mullins one bit, but there are dignity interests on the other side too.

JUSTICE SOTOMAYOR: Counsel, sometimes it's not just dignity. A couple of the briefs . . . one of the amici briefs pointed out that most military bases are in isolated areas far from cities and that they're in areas where the general population, service population, is of one religion or close to one religious belief. So where there might be two cake bakers. They name a couple of military bases like that. Or two florists or one photographer. Very small number of resources.

GENERAL FRANCISCO: Right.

JUSTICE SOTOMAYOR: And in those situations, they posit, and I don't think probably wrongly, that it may come to pass where the two cake bakers will claim the same abstention here. So how do we protect the military men and women who are of the same sex who want to get married in that town because that's where all their friends are, because the base is there?

GENERAL FRANCISCO: Right.

JUSTICE SOTOMAYOR: All right? How do we protect those people?

GENERAL FRANCISCO: And, Your Honor, I think that is precisely a situation where the state would be able to satisfy heightened scrutiny because their interests in providing access to goods and services would be narrowly tailored.

JUSTICE SOTOMAYOR: So . . . but isn't that . . . isn't that the same for everybody? Meaning, look, we live in a society with competing beliefs, and all of our cases have always said where LGBT people have been . . . you know, they've been humiliated, disrespected, treated uncivilly. The briefs are filled with situations that—

GENERAL FRANCISCO: Right.

JUSTICE SOTOMAYOR: . . . the gay couple who was left on the side of the highway on a rainy night, people who have been denied medical treatment or whose children have been denied medical treatment because the doctor didn't believe in same-sex parenthood, et cetera.

GENERAL FRANCISCO: Mm-hmm.

JUSTICE SOTOMAYOR: We've always said in our public accommodations law we can't change your private beliefs, we can't compel you to like these people, we can't compel you to bring them into your home, but if you want to be part of a community, or our civic community, there's certain behavior, conduct—

GENERAL FRANCISCO: Right.

JUSTICE SOTOMAYOR: . . . you can't engage in. And that includes not selling products that you sell to everyone else to people simply because of their either race, religion, national origin, gender, and in this case sexual orientation.

So we can't legislate civility and rudeness, but we can and have permitted it as a compelling state interest legislating behavior.

GENERAL FRANCISCO: And—

JUSTICE SOTOMAYOR: So why is not selling or selling to one group as opposed to another not behavior?

GENERAL FRANCISCO: And, Your Honor, if I could respond, I think it's because here we have speech involved, and this case is essentially the flip side of the Hurley case.

In Hurley, we couldn't force a parade to include a particular speaker. Here, we don't think you can—

JUSTICE SOTOMAYOR: That was a private parade.

GENERAL FRANCISCO: And here, Your Honor, we don't think you can force a speaker to join the parade. Because when you force a speaker to both engage in speech and contribute that speech to an expressive event that they disagree with, you fundamentally transform the nature of their message from one that they want to say to one that they don't want to say.

JUSTICE GINSBURG: How about it it's a—

JUSTICE KAGAN: So, General, you started by—

JUSTICE GINSBURG: . . . if it's a question of race? There's a certain irony in here because one of the things that anti-discrimination in public accommodations is supposed to do is to protect religion, minority religions. So you . . . you have already said that you put . . . might put race in a different category, right?

GENERAL FRANCISCO: Yes, Your Honor.

JUSTICE GINSBURG: How about gender?

GENERAL FRANCISCO: Well, Your Honor, I think that race is particularly unique because when it comes to racial discrimination—

JUSTICE GINSBURG: Well, I asked you what about—

GENERAL FRANCISCO: Sure, I think . . . I think—

JUSTICE GINSBURG: I have your answer on race. How about gender? How about national origin—

GENERAL FRANCISCO: Right

JUSTICE GINSBURG: . . . and religion?

GENERAL FRANCISCO: I think pretty much everything but race would fall in the same category, but as this Court made clear in the Bob Jones case, the IRS could withdraw tax-exempt status from a school that discriminated on the basis of interracial marriage, but I'm not at all sure that it would reach the same result if it were dealing with a Catholic school that limited married student housing to opposite-sex couples only.

I think when you get to this case, if you agree with our test [on how to decide the case before the Court] . . . and I know that I have a little bit of an uphill battle in convincing some of you of that. If you agree with our test, I think the heightened scrutiny standard is particularly easy because they're the same interests at stake as were at stake in Hurley.

And if I could—

JUSTICE KAGAN: General, it . . . it seems as though there are kind of three axes on which people are asking you what's the line? How do we draw the line? So one axis is what we started with, like what about the chef and the florist—

GENERAL FRANCISCO: Speech, non-speech.

JUSTICE KAGAN: . . . and . . . and, you know, everybody else that participates in a wedding? A second axis is, well, why is this only about a gay couple? Why isn't it about race? Why isn't it about gender? Why isn't it about people of different religions? So that's a second axis.

And there's a third axis, which is why is it just about weddings? You say ceremonies, events. What else counts? Is it the funeral? Is it the Bar Mitzvah or the communion? Is it the anniversary celebration? Is it the birthday celebration?

So there are all three of these that suggest like, whoa, this doesn't seem like such a small thing. And so let me give you one hypothetical and then you can answer more broadly.

GENERAL FRANCISCO: Thank you.

JUSTICE KAGAN: Which, you know . . . so I'll just pick one of these. It's like how about a . . . a . . . a . . . a couple, a same-sex couple goes to a great restaurant with a great chef for an anniversary celebration, and the great chef says I don't do this for same-sex couples? How about that?

GENERAL FRANCISCO: So, Your Honor, if I could answer that question starting out with another example that illustrates the point in a reply to your example—

JUSTICE KAGAN: Well, I'd like my example, please.

(Laughter.)

GENERAL FRANCISCO: Sure. So in your example I would first say, one, there's no speech involved and, two, there's—

JUSTICE KAGAN: No, there is.

GENERAL FRANCISCO: . . . no expressive event.

JUSTICE KAGAN: The chef is expressing something about how he feels—

GENERAL FRANCISCO: Right.

JUSTICE KAGAN: . . . about same-sex couples and same-sex marriages. He doesn't want to celebrate a same . . . the anniversary of a same-sex marriage.

GENERAL FRANCISCO: And that's where—

JUSTICE KAGAN: Just like—

GENERAL FRANCISCO: Sure.

JUSTICE KAGAN: . . . the baker doesn't want to celebrate a same-sex marriage.

GENERAL FRANCISCO: And that's where I would go to something that I think that my friends on the other side have to deal with, is often is the case in the First Amendment law you are dealing with something that everybody clearly agrees is speech. And what makes this case difficult is because we're kind of on that line. Is it speech or is it not speech?

We think it is on the speech side of the line. But take, for example, the sculptor who does not want to sculpt the cross.

JUSTICE KAGAN: Well, I . . . Mr. . . . General, really, I mean, could we just . . . I guess I would like an answer to my hypothetical.

GENERAL FRANCISCO: Sure. So the answer to your hypothetical is, as this Court has repeatedly said, not everything that expresses a message is speech. I think then it comes to—

JUSTICE KAGAN: So the baker is speech, but the great chef who is like everything is perfect on the plate and it's a work of art, it is a masterpiece?

GENERAL FRANCISCO: Well, Your Honor, you have to confront that issue in every First Amendment case, if you're—

JUSTICE KAGAN: General, my colleagues I think go to more elite restaurants than I do, but my—

(Laughter.)

GENERAL FRANCISCO: Same here, Your Honor.

JUSTICE ALITO: I think that if—

JUSTICE KAGAN: Well, Ollie's Barbecue.

JUSTICE ALITO: If . . . if in my . . . if in my dreams I could go to a Michelin, I don't know, one-tenth star, I don't know, two-star restaurant, and there was a menu of wonderful dishes created by the chef with . . . with great creativity, and I said I really don't want any of these. Here is the recipe. I want you to make this for me. Do you think he would that?

GENERAL FRANCISCO: Probably not, Your Honor, but I think the critical questions always—

JUSTICE ALITO: He's serving up . . . he creates something when he makes . . . when he devises those dishes and when somebody comes in and asks to buy one, he is just mechanically producing another example of the thing that he created earlier.

GENERAL FRANCISCO: Yes. Justice . . . Mr. Chief Justice, may I answer?

CHIEF JUSTICE ROBERTS: Why don't you take an extra five minutes and I'll accord the same to your friends.

GENERAL FRANCISCO: Well, thank you. And so what happens, though, in every free-speech case you have got to make that initial cut. Does it cross the line into protected speech? And if it does, and I understand—

JUSTICE KAGAN: Okay. How about the same cake, if you don't . . . if you want to, as I understand it, you want to treat the chef differently than the baker, but let's say the same cake, and a couple comes in, a same-sex couple, and says it's our first-year anniversary, and we would like a special cake for it.

Can he then say no? No cake?

GENERAL FRANCISCO: Well, Your Honor, if it is the exact same cake and it crosses that threshold into speech, I would say—

JUSTICE KAGAN: It's a great cake. What do you mean is it the exact same cake?

GENERAL FRANCISCO: No, what I'm saying is if it's the same type of highly-sculpted stylized cake that Mr. Phillips makes, such that in our view it crosses the line into speech, then you can't force him to create that any more than you can force the sculptor—

JUSTICE GORSUCH: So General, what . . . what is the line? How would you have this Court draw the line?

GENERAL FRANCISCO: Sure. There are a couple of—

JUSTICE GORSUCH: You make a lot of specifics—

GENERAL FRANCISCO: Yeah.

JUSTICE GORSUCH: . . . but I'd . . . I'd appreciate a more abstract general rule that the government suggests.

GENERAL FRANCISCO: I think there are a couple of ways to draw that line, and this is something that the Court has to struggle with in a lot of cases. I think the first way to draw that line is you analogize it to something that everyone regards as traditional art and everyone agrees is protected speech.

JUSTICE GORSUCH: Like the Jackson Pollock?

GENERAL FRANCISCO: Exactly. And here you have a cake that is essentially synonymous with a traditional sculpture except for the medium used. But I also think that the Second Circuit's decision in the Mastrovincenzo case provides a good and workable standard when you've got something that is part art and part utilitarian.

And what the Second Circuit asks is it predominantly art or predominantly utilitarian? And here people pay very high prices for these highly sculpted cakes, not because they taste good, but because of their artistic qualities.

I think the more important point—

JUSTICE GORSUCH: In fact, I have yet to have a . . . a wedding cake that I would say tastes great.

(Laughter.)

GENERAL FRANCISCO: And, Your Honor, my wedding cake, the top of it is still sitting in our freezer, and I'm sure it no longer tastes great.

But I think the point is when you cross that threshold into free speech, the question is can you compel somebody to create and contribute speech to an expressive event—

JUSTICE GORSUCH: Is it a purpose test—

GENERAL FRANCISCO: . . . that they—

JUSTICE KAGAN: How about this—

JUSTICE GORSUCH: . . . or is it . . . would you say it's a predominant purpose or a predominant effect? How would you characterize that?

GENERAL FRANCISCO: So if you're talking about the line between speech and non-speech—

JUSTICE GORSUCH: Yes.

GENERAL FRANCISCO: . . . with the item that is part utilitarian and part art—

JUSTICE GORSUCH: Yes, yes.

GENERAL FRANCISCO: I would say is it predominantly expressive or predominantly utilitarian?

JUSTICE GORSUCH: In its purpose or its effects on others?

GENERAL FRANCISCO: I think both. And I think one of the key factors that the Second Circuit looks to, it looks to a bunch of different factors, but one factor is price. Are people paying for the utilitarian side of it or are they paying for the artistic side of it?

JUSTICE SOTOMAYOR: What—

JUSTICE GINSBURG: I'm not going to—

JUSTICE KAGAN: What if somebody comes in, it's a baker who's an atheist and really can't stand any religion, and somebody comes in and says I want one of your very, very special, special cakes for a First Communion or for a Bar Mitzvah. And the baker says no, I don't . . . I don't . . . I don't do that. I don't want my cakes to be used in the context of a religious ceremony.

GENERAL FRANCISCO: Well, and, again, I think if you apply these tests, you first have to decide whether—

JUSTICE KAGAN: I just want the answer.

GENERAL FRANCISCO: Well, what I'm saying is that when you apply these tests you first have got to decide if the cake rises to the level of speech.

JUSTICE KAGAN: It's a special, special cake.

GENERAL FRANCISCO: Well, you know, if so, and it rises to the level of speech, then I think he has a claim just like that same baker could refuse to sculpt that cake—

JUSTICE BREYER: Would I . . . could I ask you your answer to what I think is the same question going on in different forums.

Forget the doctrine for a minute. There's a category of people called artisans. An artisan is a kind of artist. They are in many fields. They are also people who are discriminated against. And we're in a country of minorities, there are many different groups that have been discriminated against.

For many years Congress has passed laws saying, at least to the artisans: You cannot discriminate on the basis of . . . race, religion, dah, dah, dah.

GENERAL FRANCISCO: Mm-hmm

JUSTICE BREYER: Sexual orientation. If we were to write an opinion for you, what would we have done to that principle? And, of course, the concern is that we would have caused chaos with that principle across the board because there is no way of confining an opinion on your side in a way that doesn't do that. So tell me how?

GENERAL FRANCISCO: Well, Your Honor, I think that the way you do it is because none of these Courts' cases has ever involved requiring somebody to create speech and contribute that speech to an expressive event to which they are deeply opposed.

And if I could go back to my example, when you force the African-American sculptor to sculpt that cross for a Klan service, you are transforming his message.

He may want his cross to send the message of peace and harmony. By forcing him to combine it with that expressive event, you force him to send a message of hate and division.

JUSTICE SOTOMAYOR: I . . . I . . . I am very confused—

JUSTICE KENNEDY: What would the government—what would the government's position be if you prevail in this case, the baker prevails in this case, and then bakers all over the country received urgent requests: Please do not bake cakes for gay weddings. And more and more bakers begin to comply.

Would the government feel vindicated in its position that it now submits to us?

GENERAL FRANCISCO: Your Honor, I think in that case, the case for strict scrutiny would be much stronger, because you'd be able to show that your . . . that the application of the law is narrowly tailored to the government's interests in ensuring access.

Here, of course, you have these products that are widely available from many different sources. And I would submit, just to finish up, that if you were to disagree with our basic principle, putting aside the line about whether a cake falls on speech or non-speech side of the line, you really are envisioning a situation in which you could force, for example, a gay opera singer to perform at the Westboro Baptist Church just because that opera singer would be willing to perform at the National Cathedral.

And the problem is when you force somebody not only to speak, but to contribute that speech to an expressive event to which they are deeply opposed, you force them to use their speech to send a message that they fundamentally disagree with.

And that is at the core of what the First Amendment protects our citizenry against.

CHIEF JUSTICE ROBERTS: Thank you, General.

GENERAL FRANCISCO: Thank you, Mr. Chief Justice.

CRITICAL ASSESSMENT

The bakery owner's refusal to create a cake for the same-sex couple surfaces the tension between the Earthly and Heavenly Cities described by St. Augustine. In Augustinian terms, the baker, a pilgrim seeking eternal life in the Heavenly City, is entangled with a couple whose union he perceives as an evil force in the Earthly City. What does *The City of God* suggest would be the right response?

As the oral argument excerpt suggests, the court focused largely on what constitutes protected speech in this context as a way of resolving the scope of the bakery owner's religious freedom. Presumably, if the bakery owner's cake were protected speech, he could not be compelled to speak in violation of his religious beliefs. The court's narrow holding, namely, that the commission's order was invalid because of its demonstrated hostility toward the bakery owner's religious beliefs, did little to resolve the question of conflicting, guaranteed rights and freedoms but magnifies the creep of religion into contemporary law. Religious freedom claims are on the uptick in state and federal courts, and increasingly, religious freedom advocates find a favorable judiciary,[19] leading some legal commentators to lament the crumbling of the wall of separation of church and state. In light of this persistent creep, regardless of which side of the lament an individual might fall, religious discourse and faith-based reasoning are rhetorical resources that are here to stay, and lawyers and judges should understand how they operate. The following questions initiate relevant considerations.

DISCUSSION QUESTIONS

Discussion Question 1: What does the colloquy in *Masterpiece Cakeshop* suggest about the relationship between rhetoric and religious values (i.e., reason and faith)?

St. Augustine's work was motivated by his sincere belief that rhetoric can be used productively in daily life, and he used the tense, uneasy relationship between the Earthly and Heavenly Cities to demonstrate rhetoric's potentially corrupt and just uses. Though St. Augustine demonstrates a clear preference for the virtues and ideals of the Heavenly City, *The City of God* provides insight into the values, prejudices, biases, and aspirations that motivate religious decision-making. For example, St. Augustine describes how the religious may encounter and internalize concepts like justice, sharing, accommodation, compliance with law, and victory, and the persecution they may feel if any of these are denied. He makes clear that faith, not law or reason, is the primary lens through which these matters are understood in the saeculum.

The distinction between faith and reason is relevant to the contemporary practice of law, prompting readers to consider the rhetorical force of religious values in framing legal issues. Though originalists might argue that religion has no place in legal decision-making, recent decisions make clear that religious values are persuading judges at the highest levels of our judicial system. The consequence is rising skepticism about rhetoric's role in shaping legal arguments that draw on traditional legal norms.

In the majority opinion, Justice Kennedy drew attention to "the rights and dignity of gay persons who are, or wish to be, married but who face discrimination when they seek goods or services."[20] Though a central feature of Christian thought, dignity is not a legally cognizable category for decision-making. How does St. Augustine inform your understanding of an issue like dignity and its potential as an argumentative frame in the case? How would you distinguish between dignity as an Earthly concept versus a Heavenly one? As a judge, how would you have accounted for a value like dignity in deciding *Masterpiece Cakeshop*? As an advocate for the gay couple, are there other values with secular and spiritual implications that you could marshal successfully in a free exercise case? Should we have a court that grounds its reasoning in both the secular and spiritual worlds?

Discussion Question 2: What role should politics and religious values play in legal decision-making?

Intimately connected with concerns about the relationship between rhetoric and religious values are concerns about the force of politics in religion cases. A review of recent decisions and law review articles about religion and law reveals authors' proclivity to pepper their writings with political language—progressives, liberals, conservatives, the political Right, political leanings of Supreme Court nominees.[21] The tenor of the justices' questions in *Masterpiece Cakeshop* reveals the close connection between politics and law. For example, Justice Sotomayor explicitly states that we live in a society of competing beliefs, and to be part of a community, we cannot engage in certain behaviors, or using St. Augustine's logic, exempt ourselves from legal compliance.[22] Justice Sotomayor's argument reflects her progressive political philosophy. As an advocate, how would you account for Justice Sotomayor's political leanings? Should those interests count toward the decision? Are there other examples in the excerpts where you see politics at play? How would you respond in those examples?

Discussion Topic 3: What does the colloquy in *Masterpiece Cakeshop* suggest about the status of knowledge in religious freedom cases?

At its core, legal argument is a problem of knowledge. The rhetorical situations in which religious issues circulate are fraught with social and interpersonal dynamics that constrain opportunities for developing the knowledge necessary for effective problem-solving. Religious knowledge, that is, the sacred, is beyond the pale of argumentation. Advocates and judges should not pretend otherwise, and in instances of imperfect knowledge, they ought to develop an understanding of how rhetorical knowledge is developed and applied on a case-by-case basis.[23] Rhetorical knowledge is the relational, practical result of two or more parties working together framing issues and making judgments that do not achieve authoritative certitude.[24]

As St. Augustine wrote, citizens of the Earthly and Heavenly Cities rely on different authorities to direct their lives—faith for the pilgrims and man's laws and reason for all other citizens. The baker in *Masterpiece Cakeshop* is a pilgrim relying on faith to make day-to-day decisions and achieve eternal life, whereas the same-sex couple, who dwell in the Earthly City and must obey its laws, rely on the presumed rationality of Colorado's antidiscrimination laws to achieve justice in the face of a discriminatory act. Each had a strong belief in religion and law's certitudes, yet in the colloquy, the grounds for those beliefs were refigured. As the justices framed and reframed the issues to tease out the significance of the baker's claims, the legal bases for the issues shifted between free speech, free exercise, and public accommodations claims.[25] In light of the colloquy, what counts as knowledge in the practice of law? Would you describe it as dynamic or static? What rhetorical and religious knowledge was produced in *Masterpiece Cakeshop*? Does St. Augustine's description of the saeculum offer you a new framework and vocabulary for describing the tensions between rhetorical and religious knowledge in the law and religion interface?

ADDITIONAL READINGS

Berg, Thomas C. "Religious Freedom and Nondiscrimination." *Loyola University Chicago Law Journal* 50 (2018): 181–209.

Griffin, Leslie. "The Relevance of Religion to a Lawyer's Work: Legal Ethics." *Fordham Law Review* 66 (1997): 1253–81.

Kendrick, Leslie, and Micah Schwartzman. "The Etiquette of Animus." *Harvard Law Review* 132 (2018): 133–70.

Laycock, Douglas. "The Broader Implications of *Masterpiece Cakeshop*." *Brigham Young University Law Review* no. 1 (2019): 167–204.

Mootz, Francis J. *Rhetorical Knowledge in Legal Practice and Critical Legal Theory*. Tuscaloosa: University of Alabama Press, 2006.

Movsesian, Mark L. "Masterpiece Cakeshop and the Future of Religious Freedom." *Harvard Journal of Law and Public Policy* 42 (2019): 711–50.

Rivera, Joseph. *Political Theology and Pluralism: Renewing Public Dialogue*. New York: Springer, 2018.

Saint Augustine. *On Christian Teaching*. Translated by R. P. H. Green. New York: Oxford University Press, 1997.

———. *The City of God*. Translated by Rev. Marcus Dods, M.A. Project Gutenberg.

Tell, Dave. "Augustinian Political Theory and Religious Discourse in Public Life." *Journal of Communication and Religion* 30, no. 2 (2007): 213–35.

Afterword

Brian N. Larson

The chapters in this book have presented, and encourage, a critical reading of several contemporary American legal texts, all from the last hundred years or so, and most from the last thirty. They invite readers to use the rhetorical theories described or embodied in another set of texts, all but two of which are more than fifteen hundred years old. This afterword describes how that focus for this volume arose from a reading group. This resort to texts principally from the ancient Western rhetorical tradition is not intended to exclude other rhetorical traditions. Rather, our interest was in restoring an understanding of the roots of contemporary law practice in a particular line of ancient texts. We recognize that scholars have reached different conclusions about the utility of the ancient Western rhetorical tradition. Finally, we suggest that there are questions all scholars and students of law and rhetoric should ask about any text, of whatever time or tradition, when considering its use as a lens or frame for understanding contemporary legal practice.

This book arose out of discussions of a reading group with members from law schools around the country that began in 2017. The group was curious about whether ancient Western rhetorical texts, which we referred to as "classical rhetoric," had continuing relevance to modern legal scholars' understanding of contemporary legal rhetoric and theory. We observed that most law scholarship that referred to this ancient tradition focused on Aristotle, with rare mentions of Plato and Cicero, and much of it relied on citations to secondary sources rather than to the original texts. This was concerning, because we also knew that in the Mediterranean West, the disciplines of law and rhetoric were born together around the fifth century BCE, and they were closely intertwined as they grew and developed from that period through the Roman Empire of the fourth century CE. Yet, at some point, the disciplines disconnected. What caused this disconnect? Due in part to scientific advances of the nineteenth century and subsequent changes in university and legal education during the last hundred and fifty years, the influence of these ancient rhetorical texts has become invisible to law students and most legal scholars (see chapter 2). Our group sought to explore the possibility of a reconnection, to better understand what the largely lost texts of ancient rhetoric—lost, at least, from much of contemporary legal education—might contribute to our contemporary work on the law. We designed that project to explore these resources.

One fruit of the reading group's work was a symposium published in the spring 2020 issue of the *Nevada Law Journal* that made scholarly contributions to contemporary legal theory using these ancient texts.[1] The articles in that symposium engaged in various ways with some of the texts excerpted in this volume. Professor Laura Webb, for example, adopts some of Plato's critique of rhetoric (see chapter 8) as a foil for analyzing the ways that law students are socialized to the practice of law and its determinacy (or under- or indeterminacy).[2] Professor Clarke Rountree, on the other hand, performs a philological examination of the word "kairos" across ancient Greek texts, uses it to challenge Lloyd Bitzer's conception of the rhetorical situation as something preexisting in which the rhetor intervenes, and shows instead how to analyze rhetorical situations in the law as something that rhetors often *create*.[3] Professors Susan Provenzano and Brian Larson combine the rational stases of Cicero and the *Rhetorica ad Herennium* with contemporary argumentation theory to formulate a model of contemporary civil procedure that sees the lawsuit as a sustained argument between the parties.[4]

The editors of this book could see the fertile ground that the scholars in the symposium volume were cultivating, so we invited scholars[5] to pair excerpts of ancient texts with contemporary ones with the goal of exploring how the ancient texts might generate a deeper understanding of the ways in which the discourses of contemporary law operate. The aim of this book was to show the ways in which the ancient Western tradition influences, reveals, and challenges the practices of contemporary American law.

Of course, in a different context, these ancient texts are anything but invisible influences. Some criticism of their impact has focused on their canonicity in rhetorical studies, the fact that they may crowd out other rhetorical traditions, and concerns that they arose from a cultural context that excluded women from speaking and condoned slavery (see chapters 1 and 2). This book, however, was not meant to provide a definitive answer to readers on the question of whether and how the themes, ideas, and perspectives of classical rhetoric have continuing application to contemporary law. If the ancient Western rhetorical texts are useful to contemporary thinking, this must be demonstrated rather than assumed. The authors do not claim that any of the ancient texts excerpted here are *necessary* to the analysis of contemporary legal rhetoric. And in no case can we imagine any of these texts serving as a *sufficient* lens for understanding contemporary legal rhetoric. But we invite readers of every chapter to ask whether the attitudes, ideas, and practices of ancient Greek and Roman authors align with the methods of contemporary judges and advocates, if they offer us any insight into those practices, or if they give us the means of challenging and critiquing those practices. This book strives to foster a group discussion and to respect the intellectual independence of the reader. As the style of the chapters makes clear, the goal of the book is to offer one view of the value of an ancient rhetorical text and, even more importantly, to create spaces for the readers to interrogate the possible value for themselves.

Contemporary rhetorical and legal scholars can choose whether to make use of ancient Western rhetorical texts in analyzing contemporary legal rhetoric according to the needs of their projects. There are many studies where scholars embrace, borrow from, distance themselves from, or ignore the classics. For example, Martin Camper's *Arguing over Texts: The Rhetoric of Interpretation* illustrates an embrace. He fuses classical rhetorical texts with contemporary theory to adapt the interpretive or legal stases of classical rhetoric (see chapter 12) to function as "a standard, field-independent method for conducting fine-grained rhetorical analysis of interpretive arguments" about texts.[6] Camper uses two legal examples in his chapter on definition as a stasis. Contrast Camper's embrace of ancient theory with Lolita Buckner Inniss's work, which indirectly borrows the ancient Greeks' concept of *phronesis*. Inniss explores a judicial opinion in *In re African-American Slave Descendants*.[7] That case "concerned the efforts of a group of modern-day descendants of enslaved African-Americans to obtain redress for the harms that slavery caused not only to their ancestors, but also to themselves."[8] Inniss uses as a frame the *critical legal rhetoric* developed by Marouf Hasian in the 1990s, which itself depended on *phronesis*.[9]

Other contemporary scholars distance themselves from the Western tradition (at least as it is received in the West today). Rasha Diab challenges the erasure of Arab and Islamic rhetoric in Western rhetorical scholarship, in particular how Arab and Islamic scholars' work has been seen principally as a reception of or response to Aristotle. In her 2016 award-winning volume, *Shades of Ṣulḥ: The Rhetorics of Arab-Islamic Reconciliation*, she describes and provides examples of the "culturally inflected peacemaking practice called ṣulḥ," which has its origin in traditional rhetorical practices in the Islamic world.[10] Nevertheless, Diab adapts concepts from Aristotle's work—particularly epideictic and, to a lesser extent, *phronesis*—in her analysis of *ṣulḥ* in Anwar al-Sādāt's 1977 speech to the Israeli Knesset.

Finally, many examples explore contemporary law with no apparent attention at all to classical rhetoric. For example, Mary Lay Schuster and Amy D. Propen explore the rhetorical work of guardians at litem and victim advocates and victim-impact statements.[11] In *Victim Advocacy in the Courtroom: Persuasive Practices in Domestic Violence and Child Protection Cases*, they fuse contemporary rhetorical genre theory, citing scholars such as Carolyn Miller and Clay Spinuzzi, with contemporary theorists of cultural studies Michel Foucault and Michel de Certeau. They make only a single passing reference to Aristotle and none to other ancient Western rhetorical figures. There can thus be fine rhetorical analyses that do not expressly draw on the ancient texts; this does not, however, render the ancient texts superfluous.[12]

These scholars took different stances toward the ancient Western rhetorical tradition, and still others are possible. Readers of this volume must similarly assess the utility of the ancient texts excerpted here based on the particular circumstances of their rhetorical projects, testing them for relevance, utility, and bias. We invite readers to continue that testing—to read ancient and non-Western rhetorical texts and ask, "What can I learn from this that tells me something meaningful about contemporary legal rhetoric?" Scholars and students considering such works should ask questions such as these:

- Is this text widely known, either among scholars or among some broader human community?
- Is it, or was it, influential in its historical or cultural context?
- Does it relate sufficiently to contemporary legal discourse to say something about that discourse?
- Does it offer insights into how legal language and argument operate?
- Does it help scholars see something about the law that is more difficult to reveal without its help?
- What voices are or were absent from it? Are there characteristics of its author or their milieu that may limit its perspectives?
- Can it offer something emancipatory, helpful, insightful, or revelatory even if the text or its author(s) exhibited biases and limitations or that were inherent in their cultural contexts and norms? Others are asking this question regarding the ancient Western tradition, with a range of conclusions. (See chapter 1.)

Of course, this book is only a starting point for discussions about ancient rhetoric's utility as a framework for deeper understanding of law and legal practice. It is a collection of examples of how we might put other ancient Western texts to the test of telling us something insightful and informative about contemporary law. We hope, too, that it is a model for a broader project of using rhetorical ideas from other traditions, drawn from other times and places, to test them as provocative resources for understanding contemporary legal practice.

Notes

Chapter 1

1. Brian L. Porto, *Rhetoric, Persuasion, and Modern Legal Writing: The Pen Is Mightier* (Lanham, MD: Lexington Press, 2020), 93–114.

2. Ed Cray, *Chief Justice: A Biography of Earl Warren* (New York: Simon and Schuster, 1997), 273.

3. Cheryl Glenn, "The Language of Rhetorical Feminism, Anchored in Hope," *Open Linguistics* 6, no. 1 (2020): 335.

4. A strong articulation of this critique is offered by rhetoric scholar Karma Chávez, who asserts that the intellectual history of rhetoric is "dominated by a perspective that belongs unambiguously to Western, white, heterosexual, physically and mentally able, educated, cisgender, citizen men in Europe and the United States." Karma R. Chávez, "Beyond Inclusion: Rethinking Rhetoric's Historical Narrative," *Quarterly Journal of Speech* 101, no. 1 (2015): 162. As a result, she asserts, the classical Western rhetorical tradition maintains a power structure that centers and privileges the discourses of whites and renders other people, perspectives, and discourses invisible. Chávez contends that classical texts are written on behalf of and by the Western "citizen," which by definition does not include "non-citizen, non-Western perspectives" (163). Chávez further describes three examples of "ruptures" in the Western canon that offer visions of rhetoric alternative to the classic tradition: a rhetoric of difference in border rhetorics of Chicanas, slave narratives as alternative rhetorics and epistemologies, and invitational rhetoric as an ethical alternative to traditional persuasion (166–70).

5. This is a cornerstone of the hermeneutical and rhetorical philosophy of Hans-Georg Gadamer. See his "The Hermeneutical Significance of Temporal Distance," in *Truth and Method*, trans. Joel Weinsheimer and Donald G. Marshall (New York: Crossroad, 2nd rev. ed. 1989), 291–300.

6. Erica Strandjord uses the same distinction between classical texts that provoke understanding and their use in the passive defense of a canon, explained in terms of contemporary rhetorical theory. Erica Claire Strandjord, "Making, Not Curating, the Rhetorical Tradition: Ways through and beyond the Canon," Rhetoric Review 35, no. 4 (2016): 281–93. Stanford encourages us not to confuse the "rhetorical tradition" we inhabit with the "Western rhetorical canon" (281). The former refers to "a human interest in and commitment to persuasion and meaning-making while still allowing

room for specificity when we discuss [the literature of] particular communities and peoples" (282).

7. Marouf Hasian Jr.'s critical legal rhetoric theory is an example of a contemporary rhetorical theory that places value in classical rhetorical concepts as part of its basic theoretical assumptions. Hasian's theory asserts that law is a constitutive rhetoric that is the site of interaction between both elite and vernacular voices. His theory challenges the opposing views that law is either foundational and nonrhetorical or completely illegitimate. One of the theory's basic assumptions is that the law should be seen not as a "deductive, logical system of inquiry" but as a subject related to the "Greek notion of phronesis, or practical wisdom." Marouf Hasian Jr., *Legal Memories and Amnesias in America's Rhetorical Culture* (Boulder, CO: Westview, 2000), 4.

8. Feminist rhetorical scholars Sonja Foss and Cindy Griffin emphasize that "theories that have come to us from our discipline's origins in classical Greece and Rome or from theorists on whose work significant aspects of our discipline have been built" should be questioned and challenged. Sonja K. Foss and Cindy L. Griffin, "A Feminist Perspective on Rhetorical Theory: Toward a Clarification of Boundaries," *Western Journal of Communication* 56 (Fall 1992): 330–31.

Chapter 2

1. As you will read, "rhetoric" can also refer to all types of speech as well as speech that is false, manipulative, or misleading.

2. Dialectic is the exchange of ideas between people holding different points of view to establish truth through reasoned argument. Plato's dialogues demonstrate this method.

3. Like many others, Plato's Socrates attributes this statement to Protagoras. Plato, *The Theaetetus of Plato*, ed. Miles Burnyeat, trans. Margaret Jane Levett (Indianapolis: Hackett, 1990), 284.

4. Aristophanes, "The Clouds," *Aristophanes I: Clouds, Wasps, Birds*, trans. Peter Meineck (Indianapolis: Hackett, 1998).

5. Some estimates place the number of male citizens in Athens during this era at around thirty thousand, with as many as ten thousand metics and eighty thousand enslaved people. Carolyn R. Miller, "The Polis as Rhetorical Community," *Rhetorica* 11, no. 3 (1993): 211–40. Several important figures in Athenian rhetoric were metics born elsewhere, including Aristotle (in Stagira, northern Greece) and Gorgias (in Leontini, Sicily).

6. Plato, "Menexenus," in *The Collected Dialogues of Plato*, ed. Edith Hamilton and Huntington Cairns, trans. Benjamin Jowett (New Jersey: Princeton University Press, 1961), 186–99.

7. For this reference and a broader discussion of Aspasia's role, see Cheryl Glenn, "Sex, Lies, and Manuscript: Refiguring Aspasia in the History of Rhetoric," *College Composition and Communication* 45, no. 2 (1994): 180–99.

8. Plato, "Symposium," in *The Collected Dialogues of Plato*, ed. Edith Hamilton and Huntington Cairns, trans. Michael Joyce (Princeton University Press, 1961), 526–74.

9. Katherine Fredlund, "Antinarcissistic Rhetoric: Reinforcing Social Inequities through Gender Performance," *Rhetoric Review* 33, no. 1 (2014): 21–37.

10. Mogens Herman Hansen, *The Athenian Democracy in the Age of Demosthenes: Structure, Principles, and Ideology* (Oxford: Blackwell, 1991), 181–90.

11. Hansen, *Athenian Democracy*, 181–90. See also Robert Johnson Bonner, *Lawyers and Litigants in Ancient Athens: The Genesis of the Legal Profession* (Chicago: University of Chicago Press, 1927).

12. Catarina Dutilh Novaes, *The Dialogical Roots of Deduction: Historical, Cognitive, and Philosophical Perspectives on Reasoning* (Cambridge, UK: Cambridge University Press, 2021).

13. Aristotle, *On Rhetoric: A Theory of Civic Discourse*, trans. George A. Kennedy, 2nd ed. (Oxford: Oxford University Press, 2007), 1.2.1.

14. "*Logos* has many meanings through the long history of the Greek language; it is anything that is 'said,' but that can be a word, a sentence, part of a speech or a written work, or a whole speech. . . . Thus it can also mean 'argument' and 'reason,' and that can be further extended to mean 'order' as perceived in the world or as given to it by some divine creator. . . . *[L]ogos* was consistently regarded as a positive factor in human life, and teachers of rhetoric often celebrated it." George A. Kennedy, *A New History of Classical Rhetoric* (Princeton, NJ: Princeton University Press, 1994), 11–12. See also chap. 5 in this volume.

15. Aristotle, *On Rhetoric*, 3.13.4.

16. Aristotle, *On Rhetoric*, 3.1.2 and 3.2.1.

17. The difference between these approaches is not as stark as it might seem. For a nuanced treatment of *ethos* in ancient Greece and Rome, see Janja Žmavc, "The Ethos of Classical Rhetoric: From Epieikeia to Auctoritas," in *Topical Themes in Argumentation Theory: Twenty Exploratory Studies*, ed. Frans H. van Eemeren and Bart Garssen (Dordrecht: Springer Netherlands, 2012), 181–91.

18. In this work, however, he refers to a *stasis* or *status* as a "*constitutio*." Cicero, *De Inventione, De Optimo Genere Oratorum, Topica*, trans. H. M. Hubbell (Cambridge, MA: Harvard University Press, 1949), 20–21.

19. Cicero, *De Inventione*, 3.

20. [Cicero], *Rhetorica Ad Herennium*, trans. Harry Caplan, repr. (Cambridge, MA: Harvard University Press, 1954).

21. The summary that follows owes much to O. F. Robinson, *The Sources of Roman Law: Problems and Methods for Ancient Historians, Approaching the Ancient World* (New York: Routledge, 1997), 80–93.

22. Quintilian, *Institutio Oratoria*, trans. H. E. Butler (Cambridge, MA: Harvard University Press, 1920), 355.

23. For a discussion of the purposes and nature of panegyric and epideictic rhetoric in this period—and a review of five recent texts on the subject—see Catherine Ware, "Panegyric and the Discourse of Praise in Late Antiquity," *Journal of Roman Studies* 109 (2019): 291–304.

24. Augustine, *De Doctrina Christiana*, ed. and trans. R. P. H. Green (Oxford: Clarendon Press, [ca. 426CE] 1995), IV.59.

25. James J. Murphy, "Western Rhetoric in the Middle Ages," *Latin Rhetoric and Education in the Middle Ages and Renaissance* (Abingdon, UK: Ashgate, 2005), 11–12.

26. Murphy, "Western Rhetoric in the Middle Ages." See also James. J. Murphy, "The Scholastic Condemnation of Rhetoric in the Commentary of Giles of Rome on the *Rhetoric* of Aristotle," in *Latin Rhetoric and Education in the Middle Ages and Renaissance* (Abingdon, UK: Ashgate, 2005), chap. 5.

27. John Locke, *An Essay Concerning Human Understanding*, 25th ed. (London: Thomas Tegg, [1690] 1836), 3.10.34.

28. We omit from our treatment the elocutionary movement's focus on delivery, as it had little impact on judicial rhetoric.

29. Sublimity referred to the profound emotional effect of the writing on the reader. See, e.g., Hugh Blair, "Lecture IV, the Sublime in Writing," in *Lectures on Rhetoric and Belle Lettres*, 3rd ed., vol. 1 (London: A. Strahan, 1787), 72–77.

30. "Questions Answers and Difficulties Met for Students of the Law," *Law Student's Helper* 2, no. 3 (1894): 116.

Chapter 4

1. Chaïm Perelman and Lucie Olbrechts-Tyteca, *Traité de l'argumentation: La nouvelle rhetorique*, 2 vols. (Paris: Presses Universitaires de France, 1958); Chaïm Perelman and Lucie Olbrechts-Tyteca, *The New Rhetoric: A Treatise on Argumentation*, trans. John Wilkinson and Purcell Weaver (Notre Dame, IN: University of Notre Dame Press, 1969).

2. Chaïm Perelman, *Justice* (1945; repr. New York: Random House, 1967).

3. The excerpt's sections draw from the following page ranges: (1) The Rule of Justice, pp. 218–220; (2) Confused Notions, pp. 13–132; (3) Argumentation, pp. 1–3, 514; (4) Epideictic Discourse, pp. 48–51; (5) The Universal Audience, pp. 31–53.

4. See Norberto Bobbio, "Scienza del diritto e analisi del linguaggio," *Rivista Trimestrale di Diritto e Procedura Civile* 4, no. 2 (1950): 342–67 and Hans Kelsen, *Reine Rechtslehre: Einleitung in die rechtswissenschaftliche Problematik* (Leipzig: F. Deuticke, 1934).

5. Sheryl Gay Stolberg, "Justice Anthony Kennedy's Tolerance Is Seen in His Sacramento Roots," *New York Times*, June 21, 2015.

Chapter 5

1. Plato, *Phaedrus* 276a.

2. Michael Gagarin, "Probability and Persuasion: Plato and Early Greek Rhetoric," in *Persuasion: Greek Rhetoric in Action*, ed. Ian Worthington (London, UK: Routledge, 1994): 46–68 (discussing many of the works of fifth-century Sophists and orators, all of which show clearly that probability arguments were considered less conclusive than direct evidence or truth but were seen as necessary in the absence of truth).

3. The excerpts from the four speeches of Antiphon's *First Tetralogy* (no. 2 in the corpus of Antiphon's speeches) are taken from Michael Gagarin and Douglas M. MacDowell, trans. *Antiphon and Andocides* (Austin: University of Texas Press, 1998), with slight modifications. Most of the introductions and final remarks are omitted from all

four speeches, as they say nothing about probability. One of the anonymous peer reviewers who evaluated this manuscript before it was accepted for publication notes that "even the best forensic evidence is circumstantial evidence—it is never direct evidence." True, the difference may be only a matter of degree, but the distinction between the two types is routinely accepted.

Chapter 6

1. For example, see William M. Sullivan et al., *Educating Lawyers: Preparation for the Profession of Law* (San Francisco: Jossey-Bass, 2007), 56–59.

2. The excerpts are from pp. 30–35 of the Brief for Mother, Appellant, and pp. 37–41 of the Brief for Father, Appellee.

3. Meaning "from the new." When interpreting the law, an appellate court considers the legal questions in a case anew rather than deferring to a lower court.

4. Ferdinand de Saussure, *The Course in General Linguistics*, trans. Wade Baskin (New York: Philosophical Library, 1959).

5. Claude Lévi-Strauss, *Mythologiques*, vol. 4, *The Naked Man*, trans. John and Doreen Weightman (Chicago: University of Chicago Press, 1971), 537–60.

6. Kimberlé Crenshaw, "Mapping the Margins: Intersectionality, Identity Politics, and Violence Against Women of Color," *Stanford Law Review* 43, no. 6 (1991): 1241–99.

7. Krista Ratcliffe, *Rhetorical Listening: Identification, Gender, Whiteness* (Carbondale: Southern Illinois University Press, 2005).

Chapter 7

1. Marcus Fabius Quintilianus, *The Orator's Education Books 1–2*, ed. and trans. by Donald A. Russell (Cambridge, MA: Harvard University Press, 2001).

2. The Persians are typically understood as an Iranian ethnic group today, and in ancient history were a people that lived across much of modern-day Iran, Turkey, and the Caucuses.

3. Glenn W. Most, "Athens as the School of Greece," in *Classical Pasts: The Classical Traditions of Greece and Rom*, ed. James I. Porter (Princeton: Princeton University Press, 2006), 383–84. Most explains that Isocrates was much concerned with praising Athens and Athenians because he could not argue that Athens should be a leader in the region because of its military dominance. The military was weak at that time. So, Isocrates had to argue that Athens was a sort of cultural and civilized force throughout the ancient world, in a speech that was epidictic (384).

4. Stephen Usher argues that the speech contains many elements of forensic rhetoric. Usher, *Greek Orators III: Isocrates: Panegyricus and To Nicoles* (Oxford: Oxford University Press, 1990). Yet, H. Ll. Hudson-Williams finds much more of the epideictic tradition in Isocrates's speech. Hudson-Williams, "Isocrates and Recitation," *Classical Quarterly* 43, no. 1 (1949): 65–69.

5. Isocrates, "To Philip," in *Isocrates with an English Translation in Three Volumes*, ed. George Norlin, trans. Larue Van Hook (New York: W. Heinemann, 1980), 5–130.

6. USA PATRIOT ACT, 115 Stat. 272 (2001).

7. *Hamdi v. Rumsfeld*, 542 US 507 (2004).
8. *Rasul v. Bush*, 542 US 466 (2004).
9. *Hamdan v. Rumsfeld*, 548 US 557 (2006)
10. *Al-Aulaqi v. Panetta*, 35 F. Supp. 3d 56 (D.D.C. 2014).
11. *Shelby County v. Holder*, 570 US 529 (2013).

Chapter 8

1. The so-called Sophists were a group of philosopher-teachers who traveled among the ancient Greek city-states teaching rhetoric. Famous sophists, such as Gorgias, Antiphon, and Isocrates, were talented teachers and performers yet criticized in part because they challenged assumptions about the certainty of truth in civic contexts. For more information on the Sophists, see chapters 5, 6, and 7 in this book.

2. By sophistry, Socrates refers here to the manipulative rhetoric he accused the Sophists of teaching.

3. Socrates plays here with the name "Polus," which means colt or a young male horse.

4. Anaxagoras was a Greek philosopher whose theory of the universe Plato criticized.

5. The case generated five separate opinions: Justice Kennedy wrote the majority opinion, Justices Roberts and Scalia filed concurring opinions, and Justices Stevens and Thomas filed opinions concurring and dissenting in part. Only the majority opinion is excerpted here. Section 441b, the statute at issue in the case, prohibited corporations from spending general funds to engage in "electioneering communications" within thirty days of an election or expressly advocate for or against specific candidates in certain elections. The plaintiff-appellant, Citizens United, is a politically conservative, nonprofit corporation "dedicated to restoring our government to citizens' control."

6. "General treasury funds" refers to the assets of an organization used to defray costs as a normal part of doing business. "Independent expenditures" refers to money spent to advocate expressly for or against a specific candidate and not at the request of the candidate, the candidate's authorized political committee (including political action committees), or a political party. "Electioneering communications" are broadcast, cable, or satellite communications that refer to a clearly identified candidate for federal office made within thirty days of a primary or sixty days of a general election. 2 U.S.C. § 441b, transferred to 52 U.S.C. § 30101(17) and 2 U.S.C. § 434(f)(3), transferred to 52 U.S.C. § 30104(f)(3).

7. Although the law cannot discriminate against speakers based on their viewpoint, the court has held that even political speech can be subject to reasonable time, place, and manner restrictions.

8. Notice the court's presumed differentiation between logic (reason) and the arguments addressed in this section.

9. 435 U.S. 765 (1978).

10. In this popular 1939 movie, James Stewart played a newly appointed and naive US Senator caught in the web of a corrupt political system.

11. *Citizens United*, 558 U.S. at 349.

12. *Citizens United*, 558 U.S. at 355.

13. *Citizens United*, 558 U.S.
14. *Citizens United*, 558 U.S., at 354.
15. Due to space constraints, Stevens's dissent is not excerpted here but available at the Oyez website, 393–479.
16. *Citizens United*, 558 U.S. at 393.
17. *Citizens United*, 558 U.S. (emphasis added).
18. *Citizens United*, 558 U.S. at 394.
19. *Citizens United*, 558 U.S. at 396.
20. *Citizens United*, 558 U.S. at 396–408.
21. *Citizens United*, 558 U.S. at 419.
22. *Citizens United*, 558 U.S. at 418.
23. *Citizens United*, 558 U.S. at 420.
24. *Citizens United*, 558 U.S. at 420–21.
25. *Citizens United*, 558 U.S. at 425–26.
26. *Citizens United*, 558 U.S. at 446.
27. *Citizens United*, 558 U.S. at 465.
28. *Citizens United*, 558 U.S. at 349–50.
29. *Citizens United*, 558 U.S. at 441.
30. *Citizens United*, 558 U.S. at 396.

Chapter 9

1. Aristotle, *Rhetoric*, trans. W. Rhys Roberts (New York: Modern Library, 1954).
2. "The syllabus is prepared by the Supreme Court's clerk and is not part of the official opinion. As its title suggests, it provides a helpful summary."
3. John Stuart Mill, *On Liberty* (Indianapolis: Hackett, 1978 [1859]), 27–28.
4. Charles S. Peirce, *Collected Papers of Charles Sanders Peirce*, ed. Charles Hartshorne and Paul Weiss (Cambridge, MA: Harvard University Press, 1931), 2:635.

Chapter 11

1. *Washington v. Glucksberg*, 521 U.S., 702, 719 (1997); also at 720–21.
2. An amicus curiae brief, as discussed further in a subsequent note, is written by someone who is interested in the case but is not a party to it. Amicus briefs are often found in cases that have broad policy implications, such as civil rights cases. In *Obergefell*, the arguments made in Virginia's amicus brief were also advanced by other advocates, including the petitioners themselves. Because this brief concisely demonstrates a modern use of tradition in legal argument, it provides a useful illustration for our discussion.
3. Located in Thessaly, in close proximity to Macedon, the Thessalians and the Dolopians submitted to Philip without resistance and collaborated with him in his expansionist plans.
4. Located in the Peloponnese, the Arcadians, the Messenians and the Argives acquiesced to Philip's expansion.
5. Pella was the capital of the ancient kingdom of Macedon.
6. Mysia was a region in the northwest of ancient Asia Minor. The phrase "Mysian

plunder" became the proverbial example of cowardly nonresistance and applied to those who had been wronged by many but had not pursued the wrongdoers.

7. Demosthenes responds to Aeschines's criticism of his policy toward the Euboeans and the Byzantines (3.86–105, 256) by demonstrating that the Athenians, in a spirit of high-mindedness, intervene on behalf of former enemies in order to defend Greek freedom.

8. Demosthenes refers to events taking place during the third and last phase of the Peloponnesian War (commonly called as the Decelean War) and shortly after its end (404/403 BCE), when Sparta was at the height of its power. The list of places offered here represents a circle of Spartan power enclosing Athens that, nevertheless, did not prevent Athens to join former enemies in the battles of Haliartus (395 BCE) and Corinth (394 BCE) against Sparta.

9. 371 BCE.

10. Trierarchs undertook the responsibility and significant expense of maintaining a publicly owned warship (trireme) for one year. By mentioning in passing that he volunteered for this role, Demosthenes indirectly boasts about his patriotism and selflessness, both of which were demonstrated in practice.

11. Aeschines and his friends.

12. Often written by interest groups for cases in which the outcome has broad societal implications, amicus briefs can provide "additional information or perspectives to assist courts in deciding issues of public importance." Helen A. Anderson, "Frenemies of the Court: The Many Faces of Amicus Curiae," *University of Richmond Law Review* 49, no. 2 (2015): 361. US Supreme Court Rules note that an amicus brief "may be of considerable help to the Court" when it provides "relevant matter not already brought to [the court's] attention by the parties." Sup. Ct. R. 37. In practice, the court may choose to incorporate language from such briefs into its opinions or rely on arguments advanced there. See generally Paul M. Collins Jr., Pamela C. Corley, and Jesse Hamner, "The Influence of Amicus Curiae Briefs on U.S. Supreme Court Opinion Content," *Law and Society Review* 49, no. 4 (2015): 917–44.

13. See chapter 4 of this volume for additional discussion of the *Bowers* and *Lawrence* decisions. The framing of the right at issue in those contrasting cases (whether it is the right "to engage in sodomy" or the right to engage in consensual intimate conduct in the privacy of one's own home) highlights a rhetorical move similar to that made here: defining the relevant question, right, or tradition in a way that leads a reader to the speaker's desired conclusion.

14. Readers might consider how this reference to textualism compares or contrasts to the use of textualism you have seen in other chapters in this volume.

15. Adamidis discusses this question. Vasileios Adamidis, "Populist Rhetorical Strategies in the Courts of Classical Athens," *Athens Journal of History* 7, no. 1 (January 2021): 21–40.

Chapter 12

1. *Hively v. Ivy Tech Community College of Indiana*, 853 F.3d 339, 352 (7th Cir. 2017) (en banc) (Posner, J., concurring).

2. For the ancients, the interpretive stases applied equally to private-ordering documents, such as wills and contracts, and to public legislative enactments. See Martin Camper, *Arguing over Texts: The Rhetoric of Interpretation* (Oxford: Oxford University Press, 2018).

3. This trust relationship, first articulated by the Supreme Court in *Cherokee Nation v. Georgia*, 30 U.S. 1 (1831) and now a deeply engrained legal principle, imposes a fiduciary duty on the United States to protect tribal rights and resources and to respect tribal expectations resulting from the centuries-long course of dealing. See "Bureau of Indian Affairs Frequently Asked Questions," Bureau of Indian Affairs (website), U.S. Department of the Interior.

Chapter 13

1. James J. Murphy, introduction to Quintilian. *On the Teaching of Speaking and Writing: Translation from Books One, Two, and Ten of the* Institutio Oratoria, ed. James J. Murphy and Cleve Wiese. 2nd ed. (Carbondale: Southern Illinois University Press, 2015), xvii.

2. James J. Murphy, Richard A. Katula and Michael Hoppman, "Quintilian's Place in Roman Rhetorical and Educational Theory with a Synopsis of His *Institutio Oratoria*," chap. 6 in *A Synoptic History of Classical Rhetoric*, 4th ed. (New York: Routledge, 2014).

3. Quintilian, *Institutio Oratoria*, trans. and ed. by Harold Edgeworth Butler (Cambridge, MA: Harvard University Press, 1920): 1.Pr.9. *Vir bonus* translates in English to "good man."

4. Murphy, Katula, and Hoppman, *Synoptic History of Classical Rhetoric*, 184.

5. The court said that the rule "misled [Gentile] into thinking that he could give his press conference without fear of discipline." *Gentile v. State Bar of Nevada*, 501 U.S. 1030, 1048 (1991). Specifically, the court said that the rule's safe harbor provision allowing a lawyer to give a press conference and state the "general nature of the . . . defense" "without elaboration" would have required Gentile to "guess at [the] contours" of the safe harbor. *Gentile v. State Bar of Nevada*, 501 U.S. 1030, at 1048–49.

6. This language persists in lawyer ethics rules today. For example, the American Bar Association's *Model Rules of Professional Conduct*, upon which individual states base their state ethics rules for lawyers, includes Rule 3.6(a), which states that a "lawyer who is participating or has participated in the investigation or litigation of a matter shall not make an extrajudicial statement that the lawyer knows or reasonably should know will be disseminated by means of a public communication and will have a substantial likelihood of materially prejudicing an adjudicative proceeding in the matter." *Model Rules of Professional Conduct*, r. 3.6(a) (Chicago: American Bar Association, 2020).

7. In the published version of the *Gentile* case, Justice Kennedy's opinion appears first and has both a majority view and a dissenting view. Five justices joined the part of Kennedy's opinion that found the Nevada rule unenforceable because it was vague. But only four justices joined the rest of Kennedy's opinion, and thus that part of his opinion represents a dissenting view. Similarly, Rehnquist's opinion, which appears second in the published case, has parts that garnered a majority of the justices' votes and parts

that were joined by only a minority of justices. The excerpts given follow the pattern of the original case: a portion of Kennedy's dissenting opinion appears first followed by Rehnquist's majority opinion and then his dissent.

8. Rhetorical enactment is the idea that a speaker or rhetor embodies an identity or ideology. The rhetor himself becomes the proof of the argument. A. Cheree Carlson, "'You Know It When You See It': The Rhetorical Hierarchy of Race and Gender in *Rhinelander v. Rhinelander*," *Quarterly Journal of Speech* 85, no. 2 (1999): 120.

9. For example, the American Bar Association's *Model Rules of Professional Conduct* Rule 4.1 prohibits "mak[ing] a false statement of material fact or law to a third person." Rule 3.3 prohibits knowingly "mak[ing] a false statement of fact or law to a tribunal or fail[ing] to correct a false statement of material fact or law previously made to a tribunal by the lawyer." Rule 8.4(d) prohibits lawyers from engaging in any "conduct involving dishonesty, fraud, deceit, or misrepresentation."

10. Model Rules of Pro. Conduct r. 1.2(b) cmt. 5.

11. Model Rules of Pro. Conduct r. 4.1 cmt. 2.

Chapter 14

1. Thomas C. Berg, "Religious Freedom and Nondiscrimination," *Loyola University of Chicago Law Journal* 50 (2018): 194.

2. Compare *Abington Sch. Dist. v. Schempp*, 374 U.S. 203 (1963); *Wallace v. Jaffree*, 472 U.S. 38 (1985); *Lee v. Weisman*, 505 U.S. 577 (1992); *Santa Fe Indep. Sch. Dist. v. Doe*, 530 U.S. 290 (2000), with *Espinoza v. Montana Dept. of Revenue*, 591 U.S. __ (2020); *Roman Catholic Diocese of Brooklyn New York v. Andrew M. Cuomo, Governor of New York*, 592 U.S. __ (2020); *Fulton v. City of Philadelphia*, 593 U.S. __ (2021); *Carson v. Makin*, 596 U.S. __ (2022); *Joseph A. Kennedy v. Bremerton School District*, 597 U.S. __ (2022).

3. See generally Erik Eckholm, "Legal Alliance Gains Host of Court Victories for Conservative Christian Movement," *New York Times*, May 12, 2014; Adam Liptak, "How Conservatives Weaponized the First Amendment," *New York Times*, June 30, 2018; Rich Barlow, "Religion versus Other Rights: The Supreme Court Weighs In," *Boston University Today*, July 10, 2020, web.

4. Leslie Kendrick and Micah Schwartzman, "The Etiquette of Animus," *Harvard Law Review* 132 (2018): 162.

5. During the Second Sophistic (50–400 CE), rhetoric transitioned from a practical art tied to civic affairs to a performative art focused on style and delivery apart from civic life. The stylistic excesses of this period undermined rhetoric's concern with thought. See generally George A. Kennedy, *Classical Rhetoric and Its Christian and Secular Tradition from Ancient to Modern Times*, 2nd ed. (Chapel Hill: University of North Carolina Press, 1999), 29–52; James J. Murphy, *Rhetoric in the Middle Ages: A History of Rhetorical Theory from Saint Augustine to the Renaissance* (Oakland: University of California Press, 1974), 33–88.

6. Manichaeism perceives the world as governed by the struggle between equal forces of good and evil, a spiritual world of light and a material world of darkness. See Ludwig Koenen, "Augustine and Manichaeism in Light of the Cologne Mani Codex,"

Illinois Classical Studies 3 (1978): 157; Michel Tardieu, *Manichaeism* (Champaign: University of Illinois Press, 1981). St. Augustine rejected this dualistic cosmology for not casting God as the almighty.

7. The word *saeculum* appears in book 16, chapter 26. Book 16 describes the progress of the Earthly and the Heavenly Cities. Because this part of the text does not focus specifically on the persistent tension between the two cities, it is not included here.

8. 584 U.S. ____, 138 S. Ct. 1719 (2018).

9. Psalms 3:3.

10. Psalms 18:1.

11. Romans 1:21–23.25.

12. 1 Corinthians 15:28.

13. Framing religious freedom cases as freedom of speech claims to get to religious freedom has proved to be a useful litigation strategy, see Kendrick and Schwartzman, *supra* note 4, at 136 (observing that "the Supreme Court has for decades rejected granting special privileges to religion in the form of exemptions under the Free Exercise Clause").

14. *Masterpiece Cakeshop v. Colo. Civ. Rts. Comm'n*, 138 S. Ct. at 1729.

15. Colorado law prohibits places of public accommodation from discriminating based on disability, race, creed, color, sex, sexual orientation, marital status, national origin, or ancestry. A public accommodation is any business providing goods or services to the public. Colo. Rev. Stat. § 24–34–601(2)(a) (2017).

16. As a nonparty, General Francisco was granted permission to argue on behalf of the United States as a "friend of the court" in this case.

17. Early in the colloquy, Justice Kagan asked petitioners how to determine when an artist speaks through their creative work, attempting to draw the line between business owners who "speak," e.g., bakers and florists, and those who don't, e.g., hairstylists, make-up artists, chefs, and tailors. *Masterpiece Cakeshop, Ltd., et al. v. Colo. Civ. Rts. Comm'n* (No. 16–111), transcript of Oral Argument at 11–14.

18. The baker's claims revolved around which vendors could refuse on religious grounds to provide services for a wedding, such as bakers, photographers, florists, graphic designers, videographers, and wedding venue owners. The baker claimed that his cakes were different from ordinary goods and services; in particular, his sculpting and painting of wedding cakes was artistic expression amounting to protected speech. See, e.g., Douglas Laycock, "The Broader Implications of Masterpiece Cakeshop," *Brigham Young University Law Review* no. 1 (2019): 179–82.

19. For example, in the October Term 2021, the court ruled invalid a tuition assistance program that excluded religious schools, see *Carson*, *supra* note 3, and later permitted an assistant football coach's prayer on a football field after games at a public high school, see *Kennedy*, *supra* note 2.

20. *Masterpiece Cakeshop*, 138 S. Ct. at 1724.

21. See generally, Jack Shafer, "Let's Be Real: The Supreme Court Is Political and Always Has Been," *Politico*, January 28, 2022; Robert Barnes, "With Sweep and Speed, Supreme Court's Conservatives Ignite a New Era," *Washington Post*, July 2, 2022; Nicholas Fandos, "Barrett Sworn in to Supreme Court after a 52-48 Vote," *New York Times*, October 27, 2020.

22. Oral Argument, *supra* note 17, at 29.

23. Francis J. Mootz, III, *Rhetorical Knowledge in Legal Practice and Critical Legal Theory* (Tuscaloosa: University of Alabama Press, 2006), 36.

24. Mootz, *Rhetorical Knowledge*, 109–13.

25. Examples of these shifts include General Francisco's initial attempt to frame the issue as related to speech; Justice Kennedy's identification of dignity interests; Justice Sotomayor's public accommodations' arguments; Justice Ginsburg's follow-up on public accommodations' arguments; Justice Kagan's identification of the three axes of the claim; Justice Alito's interest in line drawing, Justice Gorsuch's interest in rules and tests for line drawing; Justice Breyer's questions regarding discrimination; and General Francisco, at the close of his time, identifying the tension between forced speech and the attendant messages that a person fundamentally disagrees with on religious grounds.

Afterword

1. "Symposium: Classical Rhetoric as a Lens for Contemporary Legal Praxis," *Nevada Law Journal* 20, no. 3 (2020): 845–1208.

2. Laura A. Webb, "Speaking the Truth: Supporting Authentic Advocacy with Professional Identity Formation," *Nevada Law Journal* 20, no. 3 (2020): 1079–136. On determinacy in law, see Timothy Endicott, s.v. "Law and Language," *The Stanford Encyclopedia of Philosophy*, ed. Edward N. Zalta (Spring 2022 Edition); Brian Bix, *Law, Language, and Legal Determinacy* (Oxford: Clarendon Press, 1993); and Lawrence B. Solum, "Indeterminacy, Determinacy, and Underdeterminacy," *Legal Theory Lexicon*, October 17, 2021.

3. Clarke Rountree, "Kairos and American Legal Praxis," *Nevada Law Journal* 20, no. 3 (2020): 855–76. Bitzer's foundational essay was the first essay ever in the journal *Philosophy and Rhetoric*. Lloyd F. Bitzer, "The Rhetorical Situation," *Philosophy and Rhetoric* 1, no. 1 (1968): 1–14. Rountree is not the first scholar to push back on the concept. See, e.g., Richard E. Vatz, "The Myth of the Rhetorical Situation," *Philosophy and Rhetoric* 6, no. 3 (1973): 154–61.

4. Susan E. Provenzano and Brian N. Larson, "Civil Procedure as a Critical Discussion," *Nevada Law Journal* 20, no. 3 (2020): 967–1036. Larson and Provenzano make use of the other category, often called the "legal" stases, in chapter 12 of this book.

5. The group issued a call on mailing lists such as H-Rhetor, WPA (writing program administrators), Legal Writing Institute, and others, inviting scholars to submit their contributions to "a reader intended to highlight intersections between classical rhetorical texts and contemporary legal texts" and offering matchmaking services to connect legal scholars with scholars of rhetoric or the classics to enrich the experiences of both. Chapter 11 resulted from such a connection.

6. Martin Camper, *Arguing Over Texts: The Rhetoric of Interpretation* (Oxford: Oxford University Press, 2018), 8.

7. *In re African-Am. Slave Descendants Litig.*, 375 F. Supp 2d. 721, 726 (N.D. Ill. 2005).

8. Lolita Buckner Inniss, "A Critical Legal Rhetoric Approach to In re African-American Slave Descendants Litigation," *St. John's Journal of Legal Commentary* 24, no. 4 (2010): 650

9. See Marouf Hasian Jr. and Earl Croasmun, "Rhetoric's Revenge: The Prospect of a Critical Legal Rhetoric," *Philosophy and Rhetoric* 29, no. 4 (1996): 384–99; Marouf Hasian Jr., *Legal Memories and Amnesias in America's Rhetorical Culture* (New York: Routledge, 2021).

10. Rasha Diab, *Shades of Ṣulḥ: The Rhetorics of Arab-Islamic Reconciliation* (Pittsburgh: University of Pittsburgh Press, 2016): 3.

11. Mary Lay Schuster and Amy D. Propen, *Victim Advocacy in the Courtroom* (Boston: Northeastern University Press, 2011).

12. Of course, given that Foucault was well familiar with concepts from the ancient Western tradition and sometimes made use of them in his own work, it is difficult to argue that Schuster and Propen's work does not at least *descend* from the Western tradition. For a discussion of Foucault's turn later in his career to the ancient Greek concept of *parrhesia*, see Zacharia Simpson, "The Truths We Tell Ourselves: Foucault on *Parrhesia*," *Foucault Studies* 13 (2012): 99–115.

Bibliography

Legal References

Abington School District v. Schempp, 374 U.S. 203 (1963).

Al-Aulaqi v. Panetta, 35 F. Supp. 3d 56 (D.D.C. 2014).

American Bar Association. *Model Rules of Professional Conduct and Code of Judicial Conduct*. Chicago: American Bar Association, 2020.

Carson v. Makin, 142 S. Ct. 1987 (2022).

Citizens United v. Federal Election Commission, 558 U.S. 310 (2010).

Colo. Rev. Stat. § 24–34–601(2)(a) (2017).

Espinoza v. Montana Department of Revenue, 140 S. Ct. 2246 (2020).

First National Bank of Boston v. Bellotti, 435 U.S. 765 (1978).

Fulton v. City of Philadelphia, 141 S. Ct. 1868 (2021).

Hamdan v. Rumsfeld, 548 U.S. 577 (2006).

Hamdi v. Rumsfeld, 542 U.S. 507 (2004).

Hively v. Ivy Tech Community College of Indiana (7th Cir. 2017).

In re African-American Slave Descendants Litig., 375 F. Supp 2d. 721 (N.D. Ill. 2005).

Kennedy v. Bremerton School District, 139 S. Ct. 634 (2019).

Lee v. Weisman, 505 U.S. 577 (1992).

Masterpiece Cakeshop v. Colorado Civil Rights Commission,, 138 S. Ct. 1729 (2018).

Masterpiece Cakeshop v. Colorado Civil Rights Commission, No. 16–111 (n.d.). Transcript of Oral Argument at 11–14.

"Questions Answers and Difficulties Met for Students of the Law." *Law Student's Helper* 2, no. 3 (1894): 116–17.

Rasul v. Bush, 542 U.S. 466 (2004).

Roman Catholic Diocese of Brooklyn New York v. Andrew M. Cuomo, Governor of New York, 141 S. Ct. 63 (2020).

Santa Fe Independent School District v. Doe, 530 U.S. 290 (2000).

Shelby County v. Holder, 570 U.S. 529 (2013).

Trump v. Hawaii, 138 S. Ct. 2392 (2018).

Uniting and Strengthening America by Providing Appropriate Tools Required to Intercept and Obstruct Terrorism (USA PATRIOT ACT) Act of 2001, Pub. L. no. 107–56, 115 Stat. 272 (2001).

Wallace v. Jaffree, 472 U.S. 38 (1985).
Washington v. Glucksberg, 521 U.S. 702 (1997).

Other References Cited

Adamidis, Vasileios. "Populist Rhetorical Strategies in the Courts of Classical Athens." *Athens Journal of History* 7, no. 1 (January 2021): 21–40.

Allen, Danielle S. *Why Plato Wrote*. Blackwell-Bristol Lectures on Greece, Rome and the Classical Tradition. Chichester, UK: Wiley-Blackwell, 2010.

Anderson, Helen A. "Frenemies of the Court: The Many Faces of Amicus Curiae." *University of Richmond Law Review* 49, no. 2 (2015): 361–416.

Anonymous. "Dissoi Logoi or Dialexeis." In *The Older Sophists*, edited and translated by Rosamond Kent Sprague, 279–93. Columbia: University of South Carolina Press, 1972.

Aristophanes. "The Clouds." In *Aristophanes I: Clouds, Wasps, Birds*, translated by Peter Meineck. Indianapolis: Hackett, 1998.

Aristotle. "Introduction." In *On Rhetoric: A Theory of Civic Discourse*, translated by George A. Kennedy, 2nd ed., 1–26. Oxford University Press, 2007.

———. *On Rhetoric: A Theory of Civic Discourse*. Translated by George A. Kennedy. New York: Oxford University Press, 1991.

———. *Rhetoric*. Translated by W. Rhys Roberts. New York: Modern Library, 1954.

Augustine. *The City of God: Volume II*. Edited and translated by Rev. Marcus Dods, MA. Delhi: Lector House, 2019.

———. *De Doctrina Christiana*. Edited and translated by R. P. H. Green. Oxford: Clarendon Press, 1996.

Bacon, Francis. "The First Book of Francis Bacon of the Proficience and Advancement of Learning, Divine and Human." In *Selected Writings of Francis Bacon*, edited by Hugh G. Dick, 157–220. New York: Modern Library, 1955.

Balkin, Jack M. "A Night in the Topics: The Reason of Legal Rhetoric and the Rhetoric of Legal Reason." In *Law's Stories: Narrative and Rhetoric in the Law*, edited by Peter Brooks and Paul Gerwitz, 211–24. New Haven, CT: Yale University Press, 1996.

Balkin, Jack M., and Sanford Levinson. "Constitutional Grammar." *Texas Law Review* 72, no. 7 (1994): 1771–803.

Barlow, Rich. "Religion versus Other Rights: The Supreme Court Weighs In." *Boston University Today*, July 10, 2020. Web.

Barnes, Robert. "With Sweep and Speed, Supreme Court's Conservatives Ignite a New Era." *Washington Post*, July 2, 2022.

Barnett, Randy, and Josh Blackmun. "Citizens United v. Federal Election Comm'n." In *An Introduction to Constitutional Law: 100 Supreme Court Cases Everyone Should Know*. Accessed August 29, 2022. Web.

Berg, Thomas C. "Religious Freedom and Nondiscrimination." *Loyola University of Chicago Law Journal* 50, no. 1 (2018): 181–209.

Berger, Linda L. "What Is the Sound of a Corporation Speaking? 'Just Another Voice,'

According to the Supreme Court." *Administrative and Regulatory Law News* 35, no. 3 (2010): 8–9, 15.

Bergin, Thomas G. "On the Study Methods of Our Time. Giambattista Vico, Elio Gianturco." *Journal of Modern History* 40, no. 4 (1968): 691–92.

Beydoun, Khaled A. *American Islamophobia: Understanding the Roots and Rise of Fear*. Oakland: University of California Press, 2018.

Bitzer, Lloyd F. "The Rhetorical Situation." *Philosophy and Rhetoric* 1, no. 1 (1968): 1–14.

Bizzell, Patricia, Bruce Herzberg, and Robin Reames, eds. *The Rhetorical Tradition: Readings from Classical Times to the Present*. 3rd ed. Boston: Bedford, 2020.

Blair, Hugh. "Lecture IV, the Sublime in Writing." In *Lectures on Rhetoric and Belle Lettres*, 3rd ed., vol. 1, 72–77. London: Printed for W. Strahan, 1787.

Bobbio, Norberto. "Scienza del diritto e analisi del linguaggio." *Rivista Trimestrale di Diritto e Procedura Civile* 4, no. 2 (1950): 342–67.

Bobbitt, Philip. *Constitutional Fate: Theory of the Constitution*. New York: Oxford University Press, 1982.

Bolduc, Michelle K., and David A. Frank. "Chaïm Perelman and Lucie Olbrechts-Tyteca's 'On Temporality as a Characteristic of Argumentation': Commentary and Translation." *Philosophy and Rhetoric* 43, no. 4 (2010): 308–15.

Bonner, Robert Johnson. *Lawyers and Litigants in Ancient Athens: The Genesis of the Legal Profession*. Chicago: University of Chicago Press, 1927.

Calboli Montefusco, Lucia. *La dottrina degli "status" nella retorica greca e romana*. Hildesheim: Olms-Weidmann, 1986.

Camargo, Martin. *Ars Dictaminis, Ars Dictandi*. Typologie des sources du Moyen Âge occidental. Turnhout: Brepols, 1991.

Camper, Martin. *Arguing over Texts: The Rhetoric of Interpretation*. Oxford: Oxford University Press, 2018.

Carlson, A. Cheree. "'You Know It When You See It:' The Rhetorical Hierarchy of Race and Gender in Rhinelander v. Rhinelander." *Quarterly Journal of Speech* 85, no. 2 (1999): 111–28.

Chávez, Karma R. "Beyond Inclusion: Rethinking Rhetoric's Historical Narrative." *Quarterly Journal of Speech* 101, no. 1 (2015): 162–72.

Cicero. *Brutus. Orator*. Translated by G. L. Hendrickson and H. M. Hubbell. Vol. 5 Revised. Cambridge, MA: Harvard University Press, 1962.

———. *[Cicero] Rhetorica Ad Herennium*. Translated by Harry Caplan. Cambridge, MA: Harvard University Press, 1954.

———. *De Inventione, De Optimo Genere Oratorum, Topica*. Translated by H. M. Hubbell. Cambridge, MA: Harvard University Press, 1949.

———. *On the Ideal Orator [De Oratore]*. Translated by James M. May and Jakob Wisse. New York: Oxford University Press, 2001.

Collins, Paul M., Jr., Pamela C. Corley, and Jesse Hamner. "The Influence of Amicus Curiae Briefs on U.S. Supreme Court Opinion Content." *Law and Society Review* 49, no. 4 (2015): 917–44.

Cooper, Lane. *The Collected Dialogues of Plato*. Edited by Edith Hamilton Huntington Cairs. Princeton: Princeton University Press, 1961.

Cray, Ed. *Chief Justice: A Biography of Earl Warren*. New York: Simon and Schuster, 1997.

Crenshaw, Kimberlé. "Mapping the Margins: Intersectionality, Identity Politics, and Violence against Women of Color." *Stanford Law Review* 43, no. 6 (1991): 1241–99.

Crosswhite, James. *Deep Rhetoric: Philosophy, Reason, Violence, Justice, Wisdom*. Chicago: University of Chicago Press, 2013.

Dauphinais, Kirsten A. "Quintilian's Curriculum." *Nevada Law Journal* 20, no. 3 (2020): 917–33.

Demosthenes. "In Defense of Ctesiphon on the Crown." In *Demosthenes, Speeches 18 and 19*, translated by Harvey Yunis, 23–113. Austin: University of Texas Press, 2005.

Descartes, Rene. *Discourse on the Method*. London: SMK Books, 2018.

Diab, Rasha. *Shades of Sulh: The Rhetorics of Arab-Islamic Reconciliation*. Pittsburgh: University of Pittsburgh Press, 2016.

Eckholm, Erik. "Legal Alliance Gains Host of Court Victories for Conservative Christian Movement." *New York Times*, May 12, 2014.

Endicott, Timothy. "Law and Language." In *The Stanford Encylopedia of Philosophy*, edited by Edward N. Zalta. Spring 2022 edition. Web.

Eskridge, William N., Jr. "The New Textualism." *UCLA Law Review* 37 (1990): 621–92.

Eskridge, William N., Jr., and Phillip P. Frickey. "Statutory Interpretation as Practical Reasoning." *Stanford Law Review* 42 (1990): 321–84.

Eskridge, William N., Jr., Phillip P. Frickey, and Elizabeth Garrett. *Cases and Materials on Legislation: Statutes and the Creation of Public Policy*. 5th ed. St. Paul, MN: West Academic Publishing, 2014.

Fandos, Nicholas. "Barrett Sworn in to Supreme Court After a 52–48 Vote." *New York Times*, October 27, 2020.

Forde-Mazrui, Kim. "Tradition as Justification: The Case of Opposite-Sex Marriage." *University of Chicago Law Review* 78, no. 1 (2011): 281–344.

Foss, Sonja K., and Cindy L. Griffin. "A Feminist Perspective on Rhetorical Theory: Toward a Clarification of Boundaries." *Western Journal of Communication* 56, no. 4 (Fall 1992): 330–49.

Foucault, Michel. *Discourse and Truth and Parrēsia*. Chicago: University of Chicago Press, 2019.

Frank, David A. "The New Rhetoric, Judaism, and Post Enlightenment Thought: The Cultural Origins of Perelmanian Philosophy." *Quarterly Journal of Speech* 83, no. 3 (1997): 311–31.

Frank, David A., and Michelle K. Bolduc. "Chaïm Perelman's 'First Philosophies and Regressive Philosophy': Commentary and Translation." *Philosophy and Rhetoric* 36, no. 3 (2003): 177–206.

Fredlund, Katherine. "Antinarcissistic Rhetoric: Reinforcing Social Inequities through Gender Performance." *Rhetoric Review* 33, no. 1 (2014): 21–37.

Frost, Michael H. *Introduction to Classical Legal Rhetoric: A Lost Heritage*. Abingdon, UK: Routledge, 2005.

Gadamer, Hans-Georg. "The Hermeneutical Significance of Temporal Distance." In *Truth and Method*, translated by Joel Weinsheimer and Donald G. Marshall, 2nd rev. ed., 291–300. Bloomsbury Revelations Series. New York: Crossroad, 1989.

Gagarin, Michael. *Antiphon the Athenian: Oratory, Law, and Justice in the Age of the Sophists*. Austin: University of Texas Press, 2002.

———. "Probability and Persuasion: Plato and Early Greek Rhetoric." In *Persuasion: Greek Rhetoric in Action*, edited by Ian Worthington, 46–68. London: Routledge Press, 1994.

Gagarin, Michael, and Douglas M. MacDowell, trans. *Antiphon and Andocides*. Austin: University of Texas Press, 1998.

Gagarin, Michael, and Paul Woodruff. *Early Greek Political Thought from Homer to the Sophists*. Cambridge, UK: Cambridge University Press, 1995.

Garver, Eugene. *Aristotle's Rhetoric: An Art of Character*. Chicago: University of Chicago Press, 1995.

———. *For the Sake of Argument: Practical Reasoning, Character, and the Ethics of Belief.* London: University of Chicago Press, 2004.

Glenn, Cheryl. "The Language of Rhetorical Feminism, Anchored in Hope." *Open Linguistics* 6 (July 2020): 334–43.

———. *Rhetoric Retold: Regendering the Tradition from Antiquity through the Renaissance*. Carbondale: Southern Illinois University Press, 1997.

———. "Sex, Lies, and Manuscript: Refiguring Aspasia in the History of Rhetoric." *College Composition and Communication* 45, no. 2 (1994): 180–99.

Grassi, Ernesto. "The Priority of Common Sense and Imagination: Vico's Philosophical Relevance Today." *Social Research* 43, no. 3 (1976): 553–80.

Guthrie, W. K. C. *The Sophists*. London: Cambridge University Press, 1969.

Habinek, Thomas N. *Ancient Rhetoric and Oratory*. Blackwell Introductions to the Classical World. Oxford: Blackwell, 2005.

Hansen, Hans V., Lilian Bermejo-Luque, James B. Freeman, and Fred J. Kauffeld, eds. *Presumptions and Burdens of Proof: An Anthology of Argumentation and the Law*. Tuscaloosa: University of Alabama Press, 2019.

Hansen, Mogens Herman. *The Athenian Democracy in the Age of Demosthenes: Structure, Principles, and Ideology*. Oxford: Blackwell, 1991.

Harris, Edward. "Demosthenes (2), Athenian Orator." *Oxford Classical Dictionary*, March 2021.

Harris, William F. *The Interpretable Constitution*. Johns Hopkins Series in Constitutional Thought. Baltimore: Johns Hopkins University Press, 1992.

Hasian, Marouf, Jr. *Legal Memories and Amnesias in America's Rhetorical Culture*. New York: Routledge, 2021.

Hasian, Marouf, Jr., and Earl Croasmun. "Rhetoric's Revenge: The Prospect of a Critical Legal Rhetoric." *Philosophy and Rhetoric* 29, no. 4 (1996): 384–99.

Haskins, Ekaterina V. *Logos and Power in Isocrates and Aristotle*. Columbia: University of South Carolina Press, 2010.

Healy, Thomas. *The Great Dissent: How Oliver Wendell Holmes Changed His Mind—and Changed the History of Free Speech in America*. New York: Metropolitan Books, 2013.

Heerwig, Jennifer, and Katherine Shaw. "Through a Glass, Darkly: The Rhetoric and Reality of Campaign Finance Disclosure." *SSRN Electronic Journal* 102, no. 5 (2014): 1443–500.

Hubbell, H. M. and Cicero. "Introduction." In *De Inventione, de Optimo Genere Oratorum, Topica*. Cambridge, MA: Harvard University Press, 1949.

Hudson-Williams, H. Ll. "Isocrates and Recitations." *Classical Quarterly* 43, no. 1–2 (1949): 65–69.

Inniss, Lolita Buckner. "A Critical Legal Rhetoric Approach to In Re African-American Slave Descendants Litigation." *St. John's Journal of Legal Commentary* 24, no. 5 (2010): 649–96.

"'Introduction' to 'Gorgias.'" In *Plato, Plato's Dialogues*, Gutenberg Project, 1871 (2022).

"'Introduction' to 'Gorgias.'" In *The Collected Dialogues of Plato*, xiii–xxv. Princeton, NJ: Princeton University Press, 1961.

Isocrates. "To Philip." In *Isocrates, with an English Translation by George Norlin . . . in Three Volumes*, edited by George Norlin, translated by La Rue Van Hook, 5–130. The Loeb Classical Library. New York: W. Heinemann, 1980.

Kelly, Donald R. "Vico's Road: From Philology to Jurisprudence and Back." In *Giambattista. Vico's Science of Humanity*, edited by Giorgio Tagliacozzo and Donald Philip Verene, 15–29. Baltimore: Johns Hopkins University Press, 1976.

Kelsen, Hans. *Reine Rechtslehre: Einleitung in die Rechtswissenschaftliche problematik*. Leipzig: F. Deuticke, 1934.

Kendrick, Leslie, and Micah Schwartzman. "The Etiquette of Animus." Accessed August 29, 2022. Web.

Kennedy, George A. *Classical Rhetoric and Its Christian and Secular Tradition from Ancient to Modern Times*. 2nd ed. Chapel Hill: University of North Carolina Press, 1999.

———. *A New History of Classical Rhetoric*. Princeton, NJ: Princeton University Press, 1995.

Kerferd, G. B. *The Sophistic Movement*. New York: Cambridge University Press, 1981.

Koenen, Ludwig. "Augustine and Manichaeism in Light of the Cologne Mani Codex." *Illinois Classical Studies* 3 (1978): 154–95.

Langford, Catherine L. *Scalia v. Scalia: Opportunistic Textualism in Constitutional Interpretation*. Rhetoric, Law, and the Humanities. Tuscaloosa: University of Alabama Press, 2017.

Laycock, Douglas. "The Broader Implications of Masterpiece Cakeshop." *Brigham Young University Law Review* no. 1 (2019): 167–204.

Lévi-Strauss, Claude. *Mythologiques*. Vol. 4, *The Naked Man*, translated by John Weightman and Doreen Weightman. Chicago: University of Chicago Press, 1971.

Levy, Leonard W. *Origins of the Bill of Rights*. Contemporary Law Series. New Haven, CT: Yale University Press, 1999.

Lilla, Mark. *G. B. Vico: The Making of an Anti-Modern*. Cambridge, MA: Harvard University Press, 1993.

Liptak, Adam. "How Conservatives Weaponized the First Amendment." *New York Times*, June 30, 2018.

Llewellyn, Karl N. "Remarks on the Theory of Appellate Decision and the Rules or Canons about How Statutes Are to Be Construed." *Vanderbilt Law Review* 3 (1950): 395–406.

Locke, John. *An Essay Concerning Human Understanding*. 25th ed. London: Thomas Tegg, 1825 [1690].

Lunsford, Andrea A. *Reclaiming Rhetorica: Women in The Rhetorical Tradition*. University of Pittsburgh Press, 1995.

MacDowell, D. M. *Demosthenes the Orator*. Oxford: Oxford University Press, 2009.

Malik, Maleiha, ed. *Anti-Muslim Prejudice: Past and Present*. New York: Routledge, 2010.

May, James M., Jakob Wisse, and Cicero. "Introduction." In *On the Ideal Orator [De Oratore]*, 3–48. Oxford: Oxford University Press, 2001.

McKeon, Richard. "Rhetoric and Poetic in the Philosophy of Aristotle." In *Aristotle's Poetics and English Literature; a Collection of Critical Essays*, 201–36. Patterns of Literary Criticism. Chicago: University of Chicago Press, 1965.

McManis, Charles R. "The History of First Century American Legal Education: A Revisionist Perspective." *Washington University Law Review* 59, no. 3 (1981): 597–659.

Mendelson, Michael. *Many Sides: A Protagorean Approach to the Theory, Practice, and Pedagogy of Argument*. Argumentation Library, vol. 5. Boston: Kluwer Academic, 2002.

Mill, John Stuart. *On Liberty*. Edited by Elizabeth Rapaport. Indianapolis: Hackett, 1859 (1978).

Miller, Carolyn R. "The Polis as Rhetorical Community." *Rhetorica* 11, no. 3 (1993): 211–40.

Molinelli, Sebastiano. "Dissoi Logoi: A New Commented Edition." PhD diss., Durham University, 2018.

Mooney, Michael. *Vico in the Tradition of Rhetoric*. New York: Lawrence Erlbaum Associates, 1994.

Mootz, Francis J., III. "Introduction to Recalling Vico's Lament: The Role of Prudence and Rhetoric in Law and Legal Education." *Chicago-Kent Law Review* 83, no. 3 (2008): 1097–105.

———. *Rhetorical Knowledge in Legal Practice and Critical Legal Theory*. Rhetoric, Culture, and Social Critique. Tuscaloosa: University of Alabama Press, 2006.

———. "Vico and Imagination: An Ingenious Approach to Educating Lawyers with Semiotic Sensibility." *International Journal for the Semiotics of Law* 22 (2009): 11–22.

———. "Vico, Llewellyn, and the Task of Legal Education." *Loyola Law Review* 57 (2011): 135–56.

———. "Vico's Ingenious Method and Legal Education." *Chicago-Kent Law Review* 83 (2008): 1261–302.

Most, Glenn W. "Athens as the School of Greece." In *Classical Pasts: The Classical Traditions of Greece and Rome*, edited by James I. Porter, 383–84. Princeton, NJ: Princeton University Press, 2006.

Murphy, James, J. *Demosthenes' "On the Crown": Rhetorical Perspectives*. Landmarks in Rhetoric and Public Address. Carbondale: Southern Illinois University Press, 2016.

———. "Introduction to Quintilian." In *Quintilian on the Teaching of Speaking and Writing: Translations from Books One, Two, and Ten of the Institutio Oratoria*. 2nd ed. Carbondale: Southern Illinois University Press, 2015.

———. *Rhetoric in the Middle Ages: A History of Rhetorical Theory from Saint Augustine to the Renaissance*. Berkeley: University of California Press, 1974.

———. "The Scholastic Condemnation of Rhetoric in the Commentary of Giles of Rome on the Rhetoric of Aristotle." In *Latin Rhetoric and Education in the Middle Ages and Renaissance*, 832–41. Abingdon, UK: Ashgate, 2005.

———. *A Synoptic History of Classical Rhetoric*. 4th ed. New York: Routledge, 2014.

———. "Western Rhetoric in the Middle Ages." In *Latin Rhetoric and Education in the Middle Ages and Renaissance*, 1–26. Abingdon, UK: Ashgate, 2005.

Murphy, James J., Richard A. Katula, and Michael Hoppman. "Quintilian's Place in Roman Rhetorical and Educational Theory with a Synopsis of His Institutio Oratoria." In *A Synoptic History of Classical Rhetoric*, 4th ed. New York: Routledge. 2014.

Nadeau, Ray. "Classical Systems of Stases in Greek: Hermagoras to Hermogenes." *Greek, Roman, and Byzantine Studies* 2, no. 1 (1959): 51–71.

Novaes, Catarina Dutilh. *The Dialogical Roots of Deduction: Historical, Cognitive, and Philosophical Perspectives on Reasoning*. Cambridge, UK: Cambridge University Press, 2021.

Peirce, Charles S. *Collected Papers of Charles Sanders Peirce*. Edited by Charles Hartshorne, Paul Weiss, and Arthur W. Burks. Cambridge, MA: Belknap, 1931.

Perelman, Chaïm. *The Idea of Justice and the Problem of Argument*. New York: Routledge, 1963.

———. *Justice*. 1945; Repr., New York: Random House, 1967.

Perelman, Chaïm, and Harold Berman J. *Justice, Law, and Argument: Essays on Moral and Legal Reasoning*. Synthese Library Studies in Epistemology, Logic, Methodology, and Philosophy of Science, vol. 142. Dordrecht, Holland: D. Reidel, 1980.

Perelman, Chaïm, and Lucie Olbrechts-Tyteca. *The New Rhetoric: A Treatise on Argumentation*. Translated by John Wilkinson and Purcell Weaver. Notre Dame, IN: University of Notre Dame Press, 1969.

———. *Traité de l'argumentation: La nouvelle rhétorique*. 2 vols. Paris: Presses Universitaires de France, 1958.

Pernot, Laurent. *Rhetoric in Antiquity*. Translated by W. E. Higgins. Washington, DC: Catholic University of America Press, 2005.

Plato. "Menexenus." In *The Collected Dialogues of Plato*, edited by Edith Hamilton and Cairns Huntington, translated by Benjamin Jowett, 186–99. Princeton, NJ: Princeton University Press, 1961.

———. "Symposium." In *The Collected Dialogues of Plato*, edited by Edith Hamilton and Cairns Huntington, translated by Michael Joyce, 526–74. Princeton, NJ: Princeton University Press, 1961.

———. *The Theaetetus of Plato*. Edited by Miles Burnyeat, translated by Margaret Jane Levett. Indianapolis: Hackett, 1990.

Porto, Brian L. *Rhetoric, Persuasion, and Modern Legal Writing: The Pen Is Mightier*. Lanham, MD: Lexington Press, 2020.

Poulakos, John. *Sophistical Rhetoric in Classical Greece*. Studies in Rhetoric/Communication. Columbia: University of South Carolina Press, 1995.

Protagoras, Gorgias, Prodicus, Hippias, Antiphon, Thrasymachus, Critias, Euthydemus, Dionysodorus, and Alcidamas. *The Greek Sophists*. Translated by John Dillon and Tania Gergel. Penguin Classics. London: Penguin Books. 2003.

Provenzano, Susan E., and Brian N. Larson. "Civil Procedure as a Critical Discussion." *Nevada Law Journal* 20, no. 3 (2020): 967–1035.

Provenzano, Susan E., Sarah O. Schrup, Carter G. Phillips, and Jeffrey T. Green. *Advanced Appellate Advocacy*. Frederick, MD: Aspen Publishing, 2016.

Quintilian. *Institutio Oratoria*. Translated by Harold Edgeworth Butler. Cambridge, MA: Harvard University Press, 1920.

Quintilianus, Marcus Fabius. *The Orator's Education: Books 1–2*. Edited and translated by Donald A. Russell. Cambridge, MA: Harvard University Press, 2001.

Ratcliffe, Krista. *Rhetorical Listening: Identification, Gender, Whiteness*. Studies in Rhetorics and Feminisms. Carbondale: Southern Illinois University Press, 2005.

Robertson, Christopher, D. Alex Winkelman, Kelly Bergstrand, and Darren Modzelewski. "The Appearance and the Reality of Quid Pro Quo Corruption: An Empirical Investigation." *Journal of Legal Analysis* 8, no. 2 (2016): 375–438.

Robinson, O. F. *The Sources of Roman Law: Problems and Methods for Ancient Historians, Approaching the Ancient World*. New York: Routledge, 1997.

Robinson, T. M., ed. *Contrasting Arguments: An Edition of the Dissoi Logoi*. Greek Texts and Commentaries. New York: Arno Press, 1979.

Robinson, Thomas M. "The Dissoi Logoi and Early Greek Scepticism." In *Scepticism in the History of Philosophy: A Pan-American Dialogue*, edited by Richard H. Popkin, 27–36. International Archives of the History of Ideas / Archives Internationales d'Histoire Des Idées. Dordrecht: Springer Netherlands, 1996.

Rountree, Clarke. "Kairos and American Legal Praxis." *Nevada Law Journal* 20, no. 3 (2020): 855–76.

Saunders, Kurt M. "Law as Rhetoric, Rhetoric as Argument." *Journal of Legal Education* 44, no. 4 (1994): 566–78.

Saussure, Ferdinand de. *Ferdinand de Saussure, The Course in General Linguistics*. Translated by Wade Baskin. New York: Philosophical Library, 1959.

Scallen, Eileen A. "Evidence Law as Pragmatic Legal Rhetoric: Reconnecting Legal Scholarship, Teaching and Ethics." *Quinnipiac Law Review* 21, no. 4 (2003): 813–91.

Schiappa, Edward. "Dissoi Logoi." In *Classical Rhetorics and Rhetoricians: Critical Studies and Sources*, edited by Michelle Ballif and Michael G. Moran, 146–48. Westport, CT: Greenwood, 2005.

———. *Protagoras and Logos: A Study in Greek Philosophy and Rhetoric*. 2nd ed.

Studies in Rhetoric/Communication. Columbia: University of South Carolina Press, 2003.
Schotland, Roy A. "The Post-Citizens United Fantasy-Land." *Cornell Journal of Law and Public Policy* 20, no. 3 (2011): 753–60.
Schuster, Mary Lay, and Amy D. Propen. *Victim Advocacy in the Courtroom: Persuasive Practices in Domestic Violence and Child Protection Cases*. Boston: Northeastern University Press, 2011.
Shafer, Jack. "Let's Be Real: The Supreme Court Is Political and Always Has Been." *Politico*, January 28, 2022.
Simpson, Zacharia. "The Truths We Tell Ourselves: Foucault on Parrhesia." *Foucault Studies* 13 (2012): 99–115.
Sloane, Thomas O. *On the Contrary: The Protocol of Traditional Rhetoric*. Washington, DC: Catholic University of America Press, 1997.
Solum, Lawrence B. "Legal Theory Lexicon 036: Indeterminacy, Determinacy, and Underdeterminacy." *Legal Theory Lexicon*, October 17, 2021.
Stevens, Robert. *Law School: Legal Education in America from the 1850s to the 1980s*. Chapel Hill: University of North Carolina Press, 1987.
Stolberg, Sheryl Gay. "Justice Anthony Kennedy's Tolerance Is Seen in His Sacramento Roots." *New York Times*, June 21, 2015.
Strandjord, Erika Claire. "Making, Not Curating, the Rhetorical Tradition: Ways through and beyond the Canon." *Rhetoric Review* 35, no. 4 (2016): 281–93.
Sullivan, William M., Anne Colby, Judith Welch Wegner, Lloyd Bond, and Lee S. Shulman. *Educating Lawyers: Preparation for the Profession of Law*. Hoboken, NJ: John Wiley and Sons, 2007.
Tardieu, Michel. *Manichaeism*. Champagne: University of Illinois Press, 2008.
Tindale, Christopher W. *Reason's Dark Champions: Constructive Strategies of Sophistic Argument*. Studies in Rhetoric/Communication. Columbia: University of South Carolina Press, 2010.
Too, Yun Lee. *The Rhetoric of Identity in Isocrates: Text, Power, Pedagogy*. Cambridge, UK: Cambridge University Press, 2009.
Toobin, Jeffrey. *The Run of His Life: The People v. O. J. Simpson*. New York: Random House, 1996.
Tribe, Laurence H. "Lawrence V. Texas: The 'Fundamental Right' That Dare Not Speak Its Name." *Harvard Law Review* 117, no. 6 (2004): 1893–955.
Turner, Ronald. "Marriage Equality and Obergefell's Generational (Not Glucksberg's Traditional) Due Process Clause." *Duke Journal of Gender Law and Policy* 23, no. 2 (2015): 145–62.
Usher, S. *Greek Orators III: Isocrates: Panegyricus and to Nicocles*. Oxford: Oxford University Press, 1990.
Vatz, Richard E. "The Myth of the Rhetorical Situation." *Philosophy and Rhetoric* 6, no. 3 (1973): 154–61.
Verene, Donald Phillip. "Vichian Moral Philosophy: Prudence as Jurisprudence." *Chicago-Kent Law Review* 83, no. 3 (2008): 1107–30.
Vickers, Brian. *In Defence of Rhetoric*. New York: Oxford University Press, 1988.

Vico, Giambattista. *The Art of Rhetoric (Institutiones Oratoriae 1711–41)*. Edited by Girogio A. Pinton and Arthur W. Shippee. Amsterdam: Rodopi, 1996.

———. *The New Science*. Edited by Guiseppe F. Mazzotta. Translated by Robert C. Miner and Jason Taylor. New Haven, CT: Yale University Press, 2020.

Ware, Catherine. "Panegyric and the Discourse of Praise in Late Antiquity." *Journal of Roman Studies* 109 (November 2019): 291–304.

Webb, Laura A. "Speaking the Truth: Supporting Authentic Advocacy with Professional Identity Formation." *Nevada Law Journal* 20, no. 3 (2020): 1079–136.

Whately, R. *Elements of Rhetoric: Comprising an Analysis of the Laws of Moral Evidence and of Persuasion, with Rules for Argumentative Composition and Elocution*. Edited by D. Ehninger. Landmarks in Rhetoric and Public Address. Carbondale: Southern Illinois University Press, 2010.

Witteveen, Willem J. "Reading Vico for the School of Law." *Chicago-Kent Law Review* 83, no. 3 (2008): 1197–223.

Worthington, Ian, ed. *A Companion to Greek Rhetoric*. Blackwell Companions to the Ancient World. Oxford: Blackwell, 2007.

Yunis, Harvey, trans. *Demosthenes: On the Crown*. Cambridge Greek and Latin Classics. Cambridge UK: Cambridge University Press, 2001.

———. "The Rhetoric of Law in Fourth-Century Athens." In *The Cambridge Companion to Ancient Greek Law*, edited by David Cohen and Michael Gagarin, 191–208. Cambridge Companions to the Ancient World. Cambridge, UK: Cambridge University Press, 2005.

Žmavc, Janja. "The Ethos of Classical Rhetoric: From Epieikeia to Auctoritas." In *Topical Themes in Argumentation Theory: Twenty Exploratory Studies*, edited by Frans H. van Eemeren and Bart Garssen, 181–91. Argumentation Library. Dordrecht: Springer Netherlands, 2012.

Contributors

Vasileios Adamidis is an associate professor of law at Nottingham Trent University, UK. He has written in the field of legal history and rhetoric, especially in the context of Athenian democracy, identifying intersections between ancient and modern concepts and practices.

Elizabeth C. Britt is a professor of English at Northeastern University. She researches the cultural work of rhetoric at the intersection of institutions, expert knowledge, and common sense, primarily through studying US law. Most recently, she has written about domestic violence advocacy and legal education as rhetorical education.

Kirsten K. Davis is a professor of law and faculty director of online legal education strategies at Stetson University College of Law in Gulfport, Florida. She is the founder of Stetson's Institute for the Advancement of Legal Communication. She has a PhD in human communication from Arizona State University. She has written about law and rhetoric, including subjects related to identity and legal language as well as legal ethics and communication.

David A. Frank is an emeritus professor of rhetoric in the Robert D. Clark Honors College at the University of Oregon. He has written on Chaïm Perelman and Lucie Olbrechts-Tyteca's New Rhetoric Project, argumentation theory, and the rhetorics of the long civil rights movement and the Israeli-Palestinian relationship.

Michael Gagarin is James R. Dougherty Jr. Centennial Professor of Classics Emeritus at the University of Texas in Austin. He has written widely on ancient Greek law and rhetoric and on the Sophists. He has taught Greek law at all levels, including to students at the University of Texas Law School.

Eugene Garver is regents professor of philosophy (emeritus) at the College of St. Benedict's, St. John's University. He has written books on Machiavelli, Aristotle, legal reasoning, and most recently on Spinoza's *Ethics.*

Mark A. Hannah, JD, PhD, is an associate professor of English at Arizona State University. He has written about the relationship between law and rhetoric, applications of rhetoric in the professions, and rhetorics of multidisciplinary communication.

Catherine L. Langford is an associate professor in communication studies at Texas Tech University. A rhetorical scholar interested in public address, her research focuses on legal rhetoric, political rhetoric, and the rhetoric of public memory. She is the author of *Scalia v. Scalia: Opportunistic Textualism in Constitutional Interpretation* and editor of *Rhetoric and Public Affairs.*

Brian N. Larson is an associate professor of law at Texas A&M University School of Law. He has written about argumentation and rhetoric in law, and particularly about arguments by analogy.

Craig A. Meyer is an associate professor of English and director of the writing program at Jackson State University. His research and publications are in rhetoric, disability theory, composition pedagogy, and popular culture.

Francis J. Mootz III is a professor of law at the University of the Pacific, McGeorge School of Law. His scholarly focus has been on the intersections of hermeneutics, rhetoric, and law, particularly as viewed through the philosophies of Hans-Georg Gadamer, Chaïm Perelman, and Karl Llewellyn.

Susan E. Provenzano is an assistant professor at Georgia State University College of Law. She has written on legal philosophy and argumentation. With Brian Larson, she has written about contemporary stases in the law.

Nick J. Sciullo is an associate professor of communications at Texas A&M University-Kingsville. He writes on race, law, argumentation, and cultural studies. His writing on law has appeared in a number of law reviews and in other publications.

Kristen K. Tiscione is a professor of law and legal practice at Georgetown University Law Center. Her scholarly focus includes classical and contemporary rhetoric and how they inform the practice of law and the discipline of legal writing.

Laura A. Webb is a professor of law and legal practice at University of Richmond School of Law in Richmond, Virginia. She has written about legal education and the intersection of classical rhetoric and contemporary law.

Names and Subjects Index

Legal Materials Index